The Concerned Other

How to Change Problematic Drug and Alcohol Users Through Their Family Members

A Complete Manual

Phil Harris

RHP

Russell House Publishing

First published in 2010 by:
Russell House Publishing Ltd.
4 St. George's House
Uplyme Road
Lyme Regis
Dorset DT7 3LS

Tel: 01297-443948
Fax: 01297-442722
e-mail: help@russellhouse.co.uk

www.russellhouse.co.uk

British Library Cataloguing-in-publication Data:
A catalogue record for this book is available from the British Library.

ISBN: 978-1-905541-48-5

Typeset by TW Typesetting, Plymouth, Devon
Printed by Bell & Bain, Glasgow

Contents

Part One: The Context

Part Two: The Programme

Introduction

The Concerned Other presents a reversal for practitioners accustomed to working with problem drug and alcohol users. Practitioners are adept at working with the public face of addiction. They are tasked with addressing the social breakdown that accompanies problematic use that includes areas such as preventing health problems, addressing unemployment and reducing offending. Historically these areas have been singled out for various political reasons. Whilst these priorities change over time, organisations remain funded to alleviate the pressing social concerns of the day for the benefit of the public good. As problematic drug and alcohol use spans so many domains of social breakdown, it has been ideally placed to address wide ranging public concerns. In order to effect change, the substance misuse practitioner must engage the problem user in a meaningful relationship. They must understand the problem user's experience, motives and hopes if they are to direct them towards change. It requires that they see the world from their client's point of view. This point of view tends to include a life history characterised by social disadvantage and interrupted by pressures greater than the individual can bear. Addiction becomes understandable as a kind of solace for those disenfranchised from their own lives by forces beyond their control. They see the problem user as dwelling in an unforgiving environment that is more cause than consequence of their spiralling usage. Such life histories elicit a sympathetic response from professionals. Many practitioners are attracted to the field because of their desire to overcome social injustice. The problem user is the personification of the abstract forces of social inequity. Through the client's presentation and the practitioner's own personal motivations they forge a working relationship that allows change to unfold. In effect, the professional must take the problem user's side in these struggles.

The private life of addictions

However, when the practitioner then encounters the concerned other they bring with them a very different perspective. The concerned other is the mother wracked with anxiety for her once loving son; the father who cannot articulate his defeat for a lost daughter; or the wife who cannot reconcile her love for her husband with the immense pain his drinking has heaped upon their family. The concerned other brings stories of ordinary families ripped apart by extraordinary events. They demonstrate the incredible pressures necessary to tear apart the bonds of kinship and unconditional love. In this way, the concerned other reveals the private life of addictions. Not the public agenda, not the abstract social and political pressures but the raw pain that unravels behind closed doors on quiet streets. In this world view, the problem user is not locked into a world of hostile circumstance, they are the hostile circumstance. The striking feature in working with concerned others is not just the pain that they have endured but the fact they still stand by the loved one. They demonstrate that the only thing more powerful than addiction is love.

The plight of concerned others

Despite major expansion of services for problem drug and alcohol users, the professional field has all but neglected the plight of the wider family members (Orford et al., 2005). Instead, a patchwork of mutual support groups and self-help approaches have populated the chasm between services and families. Underfunded and unevaluated, concerned others have developed services for themselves often in spite of those professional services that have systematically failed to accommodate their needs. However, recent policy developments are challenging the current status quo. A broader trend has emerged in social policy regarding the role of carers and concerned others nationally. For example, the Government publication *Carers at the Heart of 21st Century Families and Communities* (DoH, 2008) has set out a clear framework for the development of family services across the social welfare field. The *Carers (Equal Opportunities) Act* (DoH, 2004) also places a duty on local authorities to inform those involved in the significant care of a loved one of grants for respite care or to support them in their role as carers. Whilst these grants are unlikely to be applicable to most concerned others of problem users, these policies recognise the broader role of significant others in welfare settings. Likewise, the Government's green paper *Independence, Well-being and Choice* (DoH, 2005) has asserted that carers are integral to the development of all social provision.

The role and needs of concerned others

The substance misuse field has also seen greater interest in the role and needs of concerned others. The updated *Drug Strategy* (2002) explicitly recognised the needs of concerned others and pledged that, 'They will receive improved services and support.' Though this achieved little in terms of expanding the range of provision for concerned others, the more recent *Drug Strategy* (2008) has placed even greater emphasis on the concerned other and families' needs. This has been accompanied by guidance for commissioning appropriate services for concerned others. More specifically, *The Hidden Harm Agenda* (ACMD, 2003) has broadened the scope of drug and alcohol interventions to include those affected by problematic use. It recognises the impact of problem drug and alcohol use on parenting. The children of problem users are often isolated, unknown to professional services and what support exists does not reach them. The Hidden Harm Agenda places a duty on professionals who come into contact with the children of problematic using parents to give appropriate support and protection. Not only does it specify that the needs of the child are central to all services, it also makes 48 recommendations which cut across all levels of services involved. These children's needs must be prioritised in a social policy that demands greater inter-agency working to ensure help and support is delivered. Whilst these recommendations focus on children of problematic users, it represents a considerable cultural shift in the focus for agencies. They must now begin to broaden their view beyond the presenting individual user and their own internal motivations and instead begin to accommodate the social relationships that are inextricably affected by their use.

The delivery of drug and alcohol services

Within the realm of the concerned others of problem drug and alcohol use, specific policy change is also affecting the delivery of drug and alcohol services. The National Treatment Agency (NTA) currently holds the remit to ensure robust commissioning of drug services for adults in England. The four key priorities of the NTA are to:

- engage service users in treatment

- retain clients in treatment for at least 12 weeks

- ensure positive outcomes

- support community re-integration

The NTA explicitly recognises the role of families in assisting in this process. 'Carer and family support services are the most effective way to support and enable family members to make changes in their own engagement with treatment behaviour, which can then provide a trigger to the user choosing to.' (NTA, 2006: 6). The NTA have issued a commissioning framework for local partnerships to purchase services specifically for concerned others. This has placed the needs of family members on the national treatment agenda for the first time. Not only does this appreciate the significant contribution that concerned others can play in the treatment of problematic use, it also recognises that concerned others have their own specific needs outside of their loved one's use.

The limitations in the delivery of services

Despite these recommendations and the inclusion of quality standards in working with family members in *Drug and Alcohol National Occupational Standards*, this policy initiative falls short. Whilst the recognition of the support needs of concerned others is an important advancement in providing services for this neglected group, the NTA fails to ascertain *how* this can be achieved. The NTA does suggest that treatment interventions for concerned others should include care plans, harm reduction and structured counselling for family members. But far from addressing the separate and distinct needs of concerned others, these policy proposals simply transpose treatment designed for problem users on to concerned others. It would appear that there is a paucity of ideas on how concerned others' needs can be addressed at both an organisational level and a Governmental one.

The NTA does recommend the expansion of established self-help groups for concerned others. However, these services have often evolved piecemeal, tend to offer generalised support and are not underpinned by effective models of practice. Whilst community based self-help can provide a very important support network for concerned others, there has been no evaluation of their effectiveness. These concerned other groups may be vulnerable to the same problems that can occur in any unfacilitated groups. This can include issues of quality control of the advice and information given; it can be easy for these groups to become dominated by one person or cliques and there may be no accountability in a group that is neither constituted nor accountable to any governing body. These services may also fail those concerned others who want more than consolation for their predicament. Most concerned others seek help initially because they want to restore their loved one. As many group members may have resigned themselves to the belief that this is not possible, this pessimism can soon be transmitted to others. Thus, there are dangers in the current policy recommendations which may institutionalise the limitations of current approaches as the new national standard in the light of no evidenced alternatives.

What can be done?

There is another way of looking at this problem. The assumptions of the services, the limits of national recommendations and the pessimism of concerned others demonstrates a profound gap in the field. It is not that nothing can be done, but it demonstrates a lack of understanding and skills in what can be done. The paucity of skills, tools and approaches places anyone who wishes to help families affected by substance abuse in an unenviable dilemma. On the one hand they are expected to address the specific needs of concerned others. At the same time they are offered little to no guidance on how those needs can be met. Instead, they must rely upon the implementation of treatment models that often militate against the concerned other's very wishes, that is, for the loved one to stop using. As a result, the only option left is for the practitioner to become the broker caught between the concerned other's worry and the problem user's indifference. This can leave the worker exhausted, frustrated and feeling impotent to affect any meaningful change in the loved one or the concerned other.

Helping concerned others to change their loved ones

This manual is a response to these problems and dilemmas. It offers a clear programme of interventions that addresses the specific and distinct needs of the concerned other. This is not limited to their needs, but covers how they can effect change in their loved ones use as well. Not only does it provide the practitioner with important skills, it also offers direction to those who are in the optimum position to effect change in the problem user's life: the concerned others themselves. However, in order to facilitate this skill set, the practitioner needs to re-orientate themselves to a new framework of understanding of addiction, treatment and change. In light of dominant assumptions of the treatment field it would not be possible to merely present the programme. It demands that the practitioner grasps the core issues, themes and contexts that provide the conceptual framework for skills which exist outside the prevailing culture of practice. Many believe that it is simply not possible for the concerned other to change their loved one. This programme suggests that the pressures and demands that emerge in these relationships between the problem user and the loved one is actually intrinsic to the change process. It demonstrates that addictions and pressures to change are synonymous processes.

The manual

In order to reframe our understanding of these issues, the manual is divided into two parts. The first part explores the thematic issues of working with the concerned others whilst the second describes the specific skills component of the Parents and Carers Training Programme (PACT).

Part One of this manual begins by offering a clear definition of problematic substance use. This is important for many reasons. Firstly, many treatment approaches have defined addiction in light of their own concerns and preoccupations. This has led to confusion in the field as vague explanations compete with each other. Therefore establishing a clear and pragmatic understanding of problem use becomes essential in order to orientate any treatment. To do so, it is essential that we replace therapeutic speculation with a clear and evidence-based understanding of the problem that we wish to address. This is particularly important as the practitioner working with the concerned other must make an assessment of problem use in the third person. Without this, there is a danger of creating greater confusion.

The working definitions of problematic use are then extended into the impact on family life. Drugs and alcohol do not have a uniform impact on families or on family members. It is important to recognise how different substances impact on families in very different ways and how family members are likely to be affected. Whilst there is no definitive model that can account for every family experience, research has identified coping strategies that families typically employ and the process that they move through in the battle or surrender to the loved one's use. Critical attention is then given to the fault line where problem use and the family intersect. This interface can best be characterised by the concept of coercion. This section identifies that coercion is not the arbitrary imposition of external pressures but is in fact an integral component of addiction itself. It recognises that coercion is a central driver in the change process. As such, it is not whether the individual should be pressured to change as this is inevitable. The central concern is how to orchestrate these pressures to have the maximum affect on change and the most minimal impact on the relationship between the concerned other and their loved one.

Before examining the core themes of the treatment programme, Part One also explores the existing approaches to helping concerned others that are currently prevalent in popular culture. These ideas and concepts are derived from historical approaches in the self-help movement and from more recent ideas in psychotherapy. Familiarity with these concepts is important for two reasons. Firstly, the assumptions from these approaches may inadvertently influence the practitioner who is delivering the skills programme. As such, it was felt necessary to make a clear statement of where the skills described in this programme sit in relation to these older approaches and concepts. Secondly, many concerned others may have been exposed to historical concepts through the internet, television and self-help groups. They may present with self-diagnosis of their own problems which have little clinical evidence to support them and may exacerbate their anxiety further. Therefore the practitioner must be familiar with these ideas in order to address them should they present. Further to this, Part One evaluates more recent developments in evidence-based approaches to supporting concerned others. These models have demonstrated that interventions can be effective, especially in facilitating changes in problematic use through the concerned other. This will serve as a backdrop to the principles used in the development of the PACT programme described in the treatment manual which is presented in Part Two.

Part Two of this manual describes the complete PACT programme by use of guidance notes and worksheets. This builds from the thematic review of Part One and is divided into five sections. The first section describes the generic assessment and induction into the PACT programme (sub-sections 2.1–2.8). The subsequent sections then describe how each of the four principle goals of the PACT programme can be achieved. This includes:

- How to get the loved one into treatment (sub-sections 2.9–2.23).

- How to reduce the pressures on the concerned other (sub-sections 2.24–2.27).

- How to improve the quality of life of the concerned other (sub-sections 2.28–2.31).

- How to support the loved one in treatment (sub-sections 2.32–2.36).

Each sub-section provides guidance notes, clinical assessment tools and worksheets that will enable the practitioner to work through the sub-sections that the concerned other has highlighted as important to them.

Using the Manual

The sections do not have to be conducted in sequence but can be organised as a menu approach. The initial comprehensive assessment allows the concerned other to identify which of these areas is a priority for them. For example, some concerned others may present for help whilst their loved one is already in treatment. The treatment entry section will obviously not be relevant for them. Alternatively, lapses and setbacks in the loved one's use has a major impact on the positive gains in the concerned other's well-being. In light of these setbacks the practitioner should focus on the tools for dealing with the relapses regardless of the current progress in other areas of the programme. Furthermore, even where a complete section is relevant, not all the work sheets will be needed. As many worksheets were included as possible in order to offer the practitioner a wide variety of tools. The practitioner should use their discretion in cases where worksheets do not relate to the concerned other's immediate situation. We have found that talking through worksheets which are not pertinent can be helpful to touch base or test for a response from the concerned other. On closer examination the worksheet may spark an issue in the concerned other that was not at the forefront of their minds at the outset.

The interventions in this programme rely upon several worksheets. Typically this includes a first sheet which is designed to assess the specific details of the particular area of interest. Once completed, follow-up sheets are designed to provide guidance on any intervention to address the issues raised. Practitioners should check how many worksheets are involved in each intervention and be clear about each worksheet function as explained in the guidance notes. This is important because we do not want simply to raise people's anxiety but provide interventions that change the current situation. Furthermore, certain worksheets have a universal application. For example, Problem Solving (Spivack et al., 1976) and Functional Analysis can be used to address a variety of problems or behaviours, respectively. It is important to check the detail on these variations as some slight changes have been made to provide a better fit for any specific problem. Other worksheets are designed for specific elements such as identifying Rewards for the Loved One.

Assessment tools and worksheets should not be seen as the totality of the intervention. The worksheets are designed to guide the intervention but must be used in a supportive and sensitive atmosphere. When the concerned other reviews the areas dictated by these tools it can instil powerful emotional responses as they evaluate the magnitude of the problems. The practitioner must be able to strike a balance between allowing the concerned other to ventilate their feelings – an experience that they value highly as an outlet for stress – whilst retaining a focus on the tasks that will change their situations. Should a concerned other repeatedly return to an emotional issue despite the practitioner's gentle direction back to a task, it tends to signal a need for acknowledgement. There is usually an important facet of the client situation which they wish to express but the practitioner has missed. Where the concerned other appears stuck on an emotional topic, the practitioner should ask themselves what does the concerned other want me to recognise in the situation? Stepping back in this way often allows the practitioner to consider the concerned other's situation and identify the central issue. Explicit acknowledgement of the concerned other's feelings will often discharge the emotion and allow further 'task-orientated' progress to continue. Where the client does routinely engage in deeper ventilation of feeling, they should be encouraged to enter into any mutual self-support groups that may facilitate this wider expression of feeling.

Using worksheets should not replace rapport or empathy. The worksheets should be understood as providing a framework for empathetic understanding of the concerned other's situation. Initially they can be used as aide memoires for practitioners. PACT is a very comprehensive programme that is rich in detail. It is not necessary for a practitioner to remember every single detail of the programme. The worksheets are there to provide direction and trigger recall in the practitioner without the need for them to focus on memorising the entire programme. The worksheets ensure that the salient facets of the concerned other's experience are explored systematically. As behavioural therapy demands very specific details in order to work, the worksheets can ensure that no detail is neglected. Again, as a rich programme the worksheets can offer the concerned other the very same framework and assist them outside of the sessions to recall, refine and practice their responses.

Despite the skills aspect of the programme, the practitioner should pay specific attention to the quality of the alliance between themselves and their client (Safran and Muran, 1999). It must be remembered that the programme must be broadcast by the practitioner and as such they are integral components of the intervention. Personal qualities of the practitioner should include warmth, empathy, positive regard and the ability to keep the client to tasks with sensitivity. A sincere desire to help is also rated highly by clients in general. This strong bond will foster greater engagement from the concerned other. But we must also consider wider aspects of the working alliance. It is important that we share the concerned other's goals. This is why the negotiation of the menu approach is important to ensure that we are focusing on what the concerned other feels is a priority for them. The tasks of the intervention must also make sense to the client. Hence a good grounding in the research behind the programme is helpful in explaining the approach and placing the individual tasks in context. Again, extensive background detail is provided in this section for practitioners to understand what concerned others 'actually' do rather than 'ought' to do. Many traditional approaches do not appreciate this difference. Concerned others ought to end an abusive relationship; they ought to confront the loved one about their use; they ought to pursue their own goals in life regardless of their obligations of wider relationships. But in everyday life they do not. Asking a concerned other to do something that they do not believe in is wholly pointless. They simply will not do it and it will create barriers between them and the practitioner. It is the duty of the practitioner above all else to respect that this is a collaborative process driven by the priorities, hopes and belief of the concerned other. Without this respect the effect of the programme will not only be diminished but negated.

The practitioner must be able to relate the programme to the lived experience of the concerned other. The more relevant the programme appears to the concerned other, the more effective it will be. Therefore exercises within this programme can be revised or changed. As such, this manual may be used as a resource book or alternatively, it may assist in the development or refinement of working with concerned others. It is recommended that where practitioners do feel that changes would improve the delivery of the programme, this should be done in conjunction with outcome measurement tools. The Outcome Rating Scale and Session Rating Scales are excellent, validated outcomes tools which can provide invaluable feedback to the practitioner regarding the effectiveness of any such changes (Miller et al., 2004; Miller et al., 2005). They are also very simple to use and have been extremely helpful in the delivery of our programme. It is recommended that where changes are made, this should be informed and measured by the use of these tools. (The Outcome Rating Scale and Session Rating Scale are available from www.talkingcure.com.)

Working with Individuals and Groups

The programme described in this manual is intended for one-to-one sessions with concerned others. However, they can be ammended for group sessions. A group work companion is currently under development. Please check the Russell House website for details.

Who this Book is for

Drug and alcohol workers: Commissioning now demands provision for specific services for concerned others. This means that proven approaches are an important component of the delivery of treatment services. This manual will provide complete guidance on working with the concerned other and an off-the-shelf programme that can be used in both one-to-one work and in group settings.

Youth workers: Increasingly youth workers are being tasked to effect change in young people, especially amongst the most socially excluded youth who are also most likely to be involved in drug and alcohol use as well as crime. At the same time, young people are not aware of the consequences of their actions and are more likely to resist change. Social exclusion may also render young people resistant to formal treatment and structured support. This programme will enable youth workers to work effectively with parents to introduce simple but effective measures that can curtail youth involvement in drugs and alcohol and improve the family relationships without recourse to complex therapeutic models.

Criminal justice workers: The most difficult challenge in criminal justice work is transition from prison to the community. Here the greatest number of clients are lost, failing to make contact with community services and undermining treatment gains achieved in custodial settings. This programme can address this gap. The programme can be delivered to the families of offenders in order to equip them with the skills to address and amend substance misuse in their loved ones and facilitate faster treatment entry in the community. In this way it is possible to embed treatment processes in the informal social network of the offender, which can provide a critical safety net to escalating use.

Social workers: Social workers are often the last line of defence for families experiencing problematic use. The pressures that families face are immense and can include parenting problem drug users, the partners of problem users who engage in domestic violence, and supporting grandparents in their role of the primary care-takers of the problem user's children. This programme will offer a range of skills to assist the social worker in their role as a helper in the most complex of family situations.

Housing workers and officers: With the increasing rise of measures such as Anti-Social Behaviour Orders, housing workers now face increasing pressure to support families whose tenancy is threatened by a loved one's use. The family face the terrible dilemma of supporting their loved one and risking losing a tenancy or expelling the loved one in order to preserve their housing situation. This manual offers a structured response to equip families to take control over their own situations and address the problem behaviours before the consequences undermine their own secure accommodation

Family workers: The programme will increase the range of family workers' skills base by extending their repertoire to help address the more specialist and often most intractable area of substance misuse. The programme offers a package of skills which can transcend systemic approaches that demand all family members be present. This programme can offer a clear entry point that facilitates the wider engagement of problematic family members.

Counsellors: Private or generic counsellors can often find it difficult to assist the client who presents with another as the problem. Increasing insight and self-awareness can help clients deal with the pressure that this brings but does not always address the source of their anxiety. This skills programme will empower family members with the skills to address the problems with other people's use, and allow greater focus on their own needs.

Families: Although written with a professional audience in mind, and drawing upon a wide array of clinical research, this programme could also be used as a self-help manual, guiding families through the core issues and developing their own skills where professional help is not available to support them. Research shows that families can mobilize their own resources through focused self-help manuals and make lasting and enduring change. The programme tries to avoid technical jargon where possible. However, the ideas described in this book can be considered as new rather than complex. Case examples are included to facilitate learning for both families and for professionals in order to illuminate the purpose of assessment tools and strategies.

Carers and those who work with them: Residential care workers and foster carers are tasked with supporting young people who are at the highest risk of developing substance misuse problems. This can occur with little support from substance misuse agencies, and problems with drug and alcohol use may not have been identified prior to placement. This can place carers in an impossible position in trying to address problems that they know little about or are not confident in addressing. As young people are unlikely to experience physical dependence on substances but are prone to a wide range of social complications that arise from their use, this book will assist carers, and those who work with them, by offering a clear framework for assessing and understanding problematic use and a set of skills to address it whilst maintaining a positive relationship with the young person.

About the Author

Phil Harris is an independent writer who has worked in direct access drug services for over sixteen years. He has designed and delivered internationally recognised treatment programmes and accredited training courses throughout the UK and Europe. Having worked as a drugs treatment advisor to DSTs, Criminal Justice Services and Youth Services, he has also managed several organisations and implemented innovative, practical and effective approaches to addressing people's problems with misuse of drugs and alcohol. He continues to practice in the south west of England.

How this Manual came About

In my early days as a substance misuse worker I always felt that more could and should be done to support those affected by their loved one's use. Working with the wider family posed many challenges to both my thinking and practice, often exposing the limits of my comprehension and ability. Despite this, whenever my raw intervention could assist the family and their loved one to find common ground there were significant gains for all, myself included. It inspired me to research the area more deeply and formulate some basic strategies that could be useful in practice with those affected by others. Therefore, several years later, when I was approached to develop a specific service for concerned others it was a fantastic opportunity to implement these ideas in an integrated approach. This led to the development of the Parents and Carers Training (PACT) based in Newport, South Wales. The results from an early feasibility trial demonstrated very promising results and the programme was soon expanded.

The success of the PACT programme drew wider interest from families and practitioners across the UK. These individuals reported that very little specialised support was available for concerned others in their own communities. It was apparent that it was not the lack of will to help but a lack of ideas, tools and skills that could help concerned others specifically. Whilst there has been an increasing body of literature on treatment approaches and research on concerned others, there has been no practical guidance on how to apply skills in practice. It was this interest and pressing need for effective skills-based manuals that led to the decision to publish the PACT programme in full and share these ideas more widely. This book will offer practitioners a clear skills set that can support concerned others directly to effect meaningful change. Writing this manual provided an opportunity to reflect on over three years of experience and revise the programme in light of our learning. It is also an ambition of this book to ensure that our findings and ideas might translate into increasing the provision of high quality and effective services for those who suffer intolerably from those that they also love the most. It is also hoped that it will encourage other practitioners working in this area to publish similar manuals.

> **If you are interested in further training in the PACT approach, please contact:**
> **The Training Exchange, Felix Road, Easton Business Park, Easton, Bristol.**
> **www.trainingexchange.co.uk**

Acknowledgements

This book is not of its own creation. Many of the ideas and approaches have been inspired by the work of individuals such as Azrin, Meyers and Barbor. In the development of the PACT programme it was clear that many of the existing research approaches could be synthesised into a wider treatment programme. These clinical researchers pioneered evidence-based approaches to working with family members. I owe them a huge intellectual debt and would advise all readers interested in family-based intervention to vigorously pursue their writing and research.

PACT would also not have happened without the direct involvement of a number of people. Special thanks must go to Ruth Hallett for supporting the initial feasibility trial of the PACT programme. It was her initial impetus that made all the rest happen. Additional thanks must also go to Heidi Anderson, Katherine Jenkins and David Jerimiah for their continued support in South Wales over the last few years. May they experience apricity all their days. Special thanks must also go to Gwent Alcohol Project for their willingness to house the project and provide the day-to-day management. The Welsh Assembly's continued financial support, for which we are very grateful, must also be acknowledged.

As this manual was written I was grateful to a number of individuals in England who were willing to road test it. I am indebted to Paul Wostenholm, Marc Borja and Kane Murphy at Oxford SMART for their encouragement, experience and humour that has been so invaluable in keeping me focused on completing this book. Their feedback was really helpful in adapting the programme to the page. Thanks must also go Leanne Reynolds, formerly of the Zone in Dudley, whose feedback has been invaluable in focusing key aspects of the programme and inspired me to make some big decisions on the final draft. My esteemed colleague Esther Harris deserves special mention for her utter belief in the programme and passionate championing of these ideas.

I am painfully aware that any treatment programme is only as good as the people delivering it. This means that the greatest debt is owed to those workers who have trained, piloted and delivered the programme with such diligence, sensitivity and understanding over the last few years. The Gwent PACT team have done a fantastic job. I will not demean their efforts with a gratuitous offer of money. But offer my thanks and recognition for the hope they have given to so many families. Their feedback has helped the programme enormously. However, one person has been pivotal in the implementation of the PACT programme. The appointment of Karon Edkins as the PACT worker on the initial feasibility study was an inspired choice. The expansion of the programme has been down to Karon's passion, belief and continued effort. She has been the central driving force behind a service that I am immensely proud to be associated with. Whilst I know she will not accept the compliment easily, it has to be said that the success of the programme described in the book is ultimately down to her.

Use of the Worksheets from *The Concerned Other*

The complete programme in *The Concerned Other* includes 66 pages of worksheets. Neither RHP nor Phil Harris either encourage or authorise any use of the worksheets without the guidance and supporting material in the rest of the manual being readily to hand for reference whenever needed.

Copying permission for the worksheets:

RHP and Phil Harris give permission for use of the worksheets on those pages in this manual marked with the footer: '© Phil Harris *The Concerned Other* **www.russellhouse.co.uk**'

(a) When working with clients:

Individuals and **organisations** working directly with clients are permitted to make copies of the worksheets, provided the guidance and supporting material in the rest of the manual is readily at hand to support the worksheets at all times. This means that copies of the worksheets must not be distributed to staff who do not have constant access to the manual. So, in a large organisation, with several people working at several locations, a copy of the manual should be at each location.

(b) When working with trainees or students:

Trainers providing training on the programme in this manual may supply copies of the worksheets to their trainees for ease of reference during training, but should ensure that the trainees have access to the manual whenever they subsequently use the worksheets. Providing training around the worksheets without providing the complete manual – whether to individuals or organisations – is inadequate and neither expressly authorised nor encouraged by either RHP or Phil Harris.

Sale of the worksheets

Under no circumstances should anyone sell copied or digitised material from this manual without the express permission of RHP and Phil Harris.

Discount purchases

RHP can offer significant discounts to anyone wishing to buy 3 or more copies of this manual at any one time. Please contact jan@russellhouse.co.uk for further details, including our terms and conditions.

Other photocopying permission

Anyone wishing to copy all or part of the handouts in any context other than set out here should first seek permission via Russell House Publishing.

Anyone wishing to copy any other part of this book in any context, beyond normal fair trading guidelines. should first seek permission in the usual way:

- either via Russell House Publishing
- or via the Copyright Licensing Agency (see page ii).

Electronic Supply of the Worksheets

A PDF of the 66 pages of this manual on which the worksheets appear, is available free, by email from RHP, to purchasers of the book who complete and return the licence request at the end of the book. The worksheets are those pages in this manual marked with the footer: '© Phil Harris *The Concerned Other* **www.russellhouse.co.uk**'

Please note that anyone who is reading this in a copy of the book from which the tear-out coupon has been removed would need to buy a new copy of the book in order to be able to apply for the electronic materials.

The following terms and conditions for use of the electronic materials apply in all cases:

Terms and conditions for use of worksheets from *The Concerned Other: How to change problematic drug and alcohol users through their family members*

1. Buying a copy of *The Concerned Other: How to change problematic drug and alcohol users through their family members* and completing the form at the back of this book gives the individual who signs the form permission to use the materials in the PDF that will be sent from RHP for their own use only.

2. The hard copies that they then print from the PDF are subject to the same permissions and restrictions that are set out in the 'copying permission' section on page xix of this book.

3. Under no circumstances should they forward or copy the electronic materials to anyone else.

4. If the person who signs this form wants a licence to be granted for wider use of the electronic materials within their organisation, network or client base, they must make a request directly to RHP fully detailing the proposed use. All requests will be reviewed on their own merits.

   - If the request is made when submitting this form to RHP, the request should be made in writing and should accompany this form.

   - If the request is made later, it should be made in an email sent to help@russellhouse.co.uk and should not only fully detail the proposed use, but also give the details of the person whose name and contact details were on the original application form.

RHP and the author expect this honour system to be followed respectfully, by individuals and organisations whom we in turn respect. RHP will act to protect authors' copyright if they become aware of it being infringed.

Part One: The Context

Every treatment model can obscure as much as it reveals. By their nature, treatment approaches draw the practitioner's focus towards selective aspects of the client's life deemed central to change. What falls outside of these assumptions is cast into shadow. Herein resides the central issue that has curtailed the development of approaches that assist the *concerned others* of problem drug and alcohol users. The concerned other's first impulse is to help the problem using loved one and restore their previous relationship. Where this goal feels unobtainable to them through their own natural resources they seek out professional support. Here they encounter the central assumptions of the treatment field. These assumptions are sourced in counselling theory, liberal idealism and established practices. What unites these disparate values is the concept of individualism. Counselling is preoccupied with the 'self,' liberalism with the importance of 'individual choice' and established practices in the addiction field assume that 'authentic change' is an internal event that occurs solely within the individual. Even our most elegant and well-researched models of addiction are limited in understanding the problem as residing 'in' the individual. Whether it is the complexities of biological explanations or that sophistication of psychological models, the assumption remains that the problem is located solely in the user. Problematic use becomes written in the very fabric of the person's brain or mind. The solution is placed beyond reach of everyone other than problem users themselves who are unwilling or unable to implement it.

A treatment field that is so dominated by such beliefs cannot accommodate the aspirations of the concerned other who wants their loved one back. The preoccupation with individualism on so many levels excludes the possibility that a family member could have any influence on their loved one's consumption of such powerful substances. It is almost impossible to imagine that a family member could compete with the hardwired biological necessity for drugs or alcohol, or arrest the desire in the user's mind. The message from the treatment field is clear and consistent: The problem user must not only want to change, but they must want to do so for their 'self.' This is widely believed to be the only legitimate mandate for change to take place. Even the very act of a family member making an appointment for a problem using loved one at a treatment service can be interpreted as symptomatic of a lack of motivation to change in that person.

As a result of the predominance of these assumptions in the treatment field, it is not surprising that concerned others report very poor experiences of professional services in their moment of desperation. They describe three broad responses when seeking help for a loved one. The first strategy advises them that nothing can be done until the problem user decides to change. This appears as an invitation to watch their loved one suffer, even to the point of death. The second option advises them to throw their loved one out. However, families wish to protect loved ones from punishing consequences, not inflict it themselves. Thirdly, the concerned other can be encouraged to see themselves as the real problem that requires treatment. Their illness is affirmed by the very act of seeking help. This is a somewhat insidious formulation of a professional's suspicion that the concerned other is really to blame for the loved one's use. Such a position easily exploits the guilt that so many concerned others already feel. As a result of these impasses, the concerned other's courage to seek help for a loved one is soon reduced to despair. The only salvation left for many who are so exhausted by their own efforts is to simply resign themselves to the belief that nothing can be done. This resignation protects them from the torment that hope can bring. All-consuming pessimism becomes more tolerable than false expectation.

However, it may not be the case that nothing can be done. It could be that our current understanding of the nature of drug and alcohol problems simply cannot accommodate the possibility that concerned others can influence their loved one's problem use. This is an important distinction. To work effectively with concerned others demands a major reorientation in the practitioner in the first instance. It demands that we challenge our most cherished assumptions. To understand how we might assist we must ask questions of our beliefs and be prepared to test them in the light of the evidence. This demands a deep revision of your understanding of the core principles of addiction, change and treatment.

This revision must begin by establishing a clear understanding of the nature of addiction first. This will call on a wider perspective which understands the nature of drug and alcohol problems as not residing in the individual, but as a relational problem that is sensitive to environmental changes. We will then extend this understanding into the family experience and the impact that drug and alcohol use has on the wider family. The collision between an individual's addiction and their family's concern creates unique pressures and stresses that can increase or decrease consumption. Understanding these conflicts offers insight into the leverage for change that already exists within the family. Specific attention will be given to the relationships between addiction and coercion and how these forces are inseparable in the family experience.

We shall then review how historical approaches have attempted to assist concerned others with varying degrees of subtly and success. These pioneering models have created a vast array of myths regarding family involvement. Concepts such as co-dependence, tough love and the need for confrontation are highly speculative and have little scientific evidence to support them. Many concerned others encounter these ideas in the mass media or in self-help material and may believe that they ought to respond in accordance with these ideals. A clear conceptual understanding is necessary in order to address any fears or confusion in the concerned other. Further to this, it is important to make a clear distinction of ideas and frameworks which are incompatible with the spirit of this treatment manual. We will then review emerging models of family intervention that have consistently demonstrated the impact that concerned others can have on a loved one's problem use. This will serve as a backdrop to a thematic review of the treatment programme describe in this manual. It will detail how the Parent and Carer Training Programme (PACT) has synthesised elements of these models. This will include a detailed overview followed by a thematic review of each of the individual components of the programme. Part Two will then provide detailed guidance notes and worksheets of the Parents and Carers Training programme itself. It begins with a section dealing with the comprehensive assessment of the concerned other, outcome measurements and induction methods. This is then followed by sections relating to a specific goal of the programme such as treatment entry, reducing the pressures on the concerned other, improving their quality of life and how to support the loved one in treatment. The final section deals with ending the programme: 'carefrontation' as a last resort and how to end the working relationship between the concerned other on treatment completion. Final summary sheets provide the framework to measure the outcome of the programme for the concerned other.

Social Context

1.1 What is Problematic Use?

Clarity regarding the nature, extent and severity of drug and alcohol problems is difficult to establish. This understanding has been further clouded by a plethora of conflicting definitions. This uncertainty has invited wide speculation from many different disciplines. Each has tended to cast addiction in the image of their own concerns. Thus addiction is seen as a progressive disease in the Twelve Step Movement, it is a bio-genetic problem in the neurological model, a coping deficit in psychological models and the product of inner conflicts in psychotherapy. Some of these models have very little scientific evidence to support them whilst others focus their research into such a narrow area of concern they exclude more than they reveal. The result is that there is little agreement amongst professionals regarding the nature of addiction and a great deal of confusion in the public regarding the problem.

When working with concerned others it is essential that the practitioner has an objective framework within which to assess problematic use. This is important for several reasons. Firstly, it should always be remembered that not all drug and alcohol use is problematic. Under reaction and overreaction can be equally dangerous within a family. Without a clear framework in which to calibrate problematic use we may confuse the severity of the problem with the magnitude of concern shown by the family. Secondly, the practitioner will have to assess the severity of the problem in the third person. As such they need to establish specific information to construct a clear understanding of the loved one's use. This will assist in planning appropriate interventions for when the loved one subsequently enters treatment. This will include whether a physical detoxification is necessary as well as offer an indication of the appropriate intensity of treatment. Thirdly, an objective grasp of the problems that can be explained clearly can clarify uncertainty in the concerned other and foster greater confidence in the practitioner.

The confusion regarding defining addictions led the World Health Organisation to approach alcohol experts to establish what the medical aspects of alcoholism were. This work was undertaken by Edwards and Gross (1976) and they made an important distinction in recognising that the medical aspects of alcohol dependence could be separated from social problems with alcohol. Based on medical observations of problem drinkers, they suggested that the medical aspect of alcohol problems revealed a cluster of repeat symptoms. This led them to formulate a diagnosis of alcoholism as a syndrome. A syndrome describes a repeat clustering of symptoms that appear with sufficient regularly to make a diagnosis but where not all elements need to appear in every case (see Table 1).

Defining the features of dependence at its later stages is important in diagnosis. These include progressively severe withdrawal symptoms from alcohol that include night sweats, tremors and delirium. The severest levels of dependency were indicated by those individuals who reported

Table 1. The alcohol dependence syndrome

Key elements	Descriptors
Narrowing of repertoire	The problem individual begins to drink the same regardless of social context. With advanced drinking, consumption follows a strict daily timetable.
Salience of drinking	Priority is given to maintaining alcohol intake over time, relationships and finances.
Increased tolerance	The drinker can tolerate and still operate under the influence of large doses of alcohol that would incapacitate an ordinary drinker. Will also develop cross-tolerance to other depressant drugs.
Withdrawal symptoms	The client will experience severe and multiple symptoms, usually on waking, that include tremor, nausea, sweating and mood disturbance.
Relief or avoidance of withdrawal symptoms by further drinking	Drinking occurs earlier in the day as dependence progresses to alleviate the onset of withdrawal. Usually the periods of abstinence are limited to 3-4 hours. Drinking is triggered by mild withdrawal in anticipation of worsening symptoms. Often early drinking becomes ritualised with the client knowing the exact amount to consume to avoid rather than alleviate withdrawal.
Subjective awareness of compulsion to drink	The individual can ruminate on alcohol when they do not have access to it or during a period of withdrawal.
Reinstatement after abstinence.	A rapid return to pre-treatment drinking levels after attempts to stop.

that they now only drank to avoid withdrawal. Edwards and Cross (1976) supposed that these symptoms of physical dependence would be proportional to each other. For example, someone with an abnormally high tolerance would also experience profound withdrawal symptoms. These withdrawal symptoms would become increasingly chronic demanding that people drank in order to alleviate them. Where alcohol was not present, the threat of imminent withdrawal would elicit compulsive thinking about the need for alcohol. This would mean that the problem drinker would begin to organise their life around drinking in order to maintain a regular dose of alcohol to stop the onset of withdrawal. This pattern of use would take precedence over other activities and responsibilities.

Edwards and Gross (1976) also suggest that alcoholism could be understood in degrees of severity rather than as an 'either-or' condition that you had or did not have. The World Health Organisation has classified sub-groups of problem drinking on a spectrum. *Hazardous drinking* describes a pattern of use that increases the risk of harmful consequences for the user. However, some would limit the consequences to physical or mental health (as in harmful use). Some would also include social consequences. *Harmful drinking* is a pattern of drinking that is already causing damage to health. The damage can be physical or mental. *Moderate dependency* describes drinking which is characterised by increased tolerance and withdrawal and impaired control over drinking. This may have elicited concern from others but the individual has not reached the stage of drinking to abolish or alleviate profound withdrawal symptoms. *Severe dependence* describes chronic alcohol use accompanied by long standing problems. This includes the experience of abnormal tolerance and profound withdrawal symptoms that may include delirium, tremors and fits. Continued heavy drinking at the highest level can result in the experience of sickness that is so severe that it prevents any more consumption. For long-term drinkers at the highest end of the drinking continuum, they may experience gross and incapacitating intoxication. This is when abnormally high tolerance collapses leading to chronic inebriation, even on low doses of alcohol. This only occurs in the most chronic of cases and little is understood about the physiological cause of this phenomena. However, what is clear is that whilst a period of abstinence may restore the individual's tolerance levels, they are likely to re-experience gross intoxication very quickly once alcohol consumption is resumed.

Subsequent research has supported the existence of the Alcohol Dependence Syndrome, providing a swathe of scientific validity to these insights (see Stockwell et al., 1979; 1983; Chick, 1980; Meehan et al., 1985; Feingold and Rounsaville, 1995; Heather et al., 1983; Rankin et al., 1982; Grant et al., 1992; Cottler, 1993). The overwhelming conclusion from an extensive body of independent research is that the syndrome is a clinical reality (Edwards et al., 1977). It is important to note that the syndrome does not in itself describe the origins of alcoholism. Instead it isolates the symptoms that present as core facets of the current problem. Also, subsequent research has shown that not all elements are as strong predictors as others. Narrowing of repertoire, subjective compulsion and reinstatement have proved more problematic in validating (see Cottler et al., 1995). The most robust indicators of dependence are the presence of tolerance and withdrawal and therefore these two symptoms must be present for a diagnosis to be made. The American DSM (R-IV) does permit a diagnosis to be made without the presence of tolerance and withdrawal. However this diagnostic criterion captures both heavy drinkers as well as those with alcohol dependence and does not discriminate well between the two (Schuckit et al., 1998; Hasin, 2000). This would mean it could not separate those who need a medically assisted detoxification programme from those who do not. As Edwards et al., (2003) state '. . . but for clinical purposes it is probably best to restrict the diagnosis of alcohol dependence to patients who have experienced withdrawal symptoms to at least some degree'. Therefore, it is advised that all practitioners operate using the guidance for the World Health Organisation's International Classification of Disease (ICD-10) in diagnosis and treatment of physical dependence.

The syndrome of physical dependence has also been applied to that of illicit drug use. However there is not a neat correlation across all substances. The syndrome is more usefully applied to substances that cause physical tolerance to increase and induce profound physical withdrawal states that are so severe or dangerous that they demand *medical* attention. Therefore the dependence syndrome applies more directly to the use of depressant drugs such as alcohol, benzodiazepines and opiates. This is important because severe withdrawal from alcohol and benzodiazepines can cause fitting and even death in severe cases. Withdrawal from heroin is not life threatening and its symptoms have been exaggerated (Gossop, 2001). However, it is a very uncomfortable process that can be alleviated through substitute prescribing.

Drugs classified outside of the depressant group can be more complex. Not all drugs produce tolerance and withdrawal in the same way that depressants do. For example, people can become increasingly tolerant to cocaine but do not experience profound *physical* withdrawals to the drug that demand medical attention. Alternatively antidepressant drugs, such as Prozac and Seroxat, do not appear to increase tolerance but can have profound withdrawal effects. The fact that a drug is listed as not being dependency promoting does not mean it does not produce withdrawal but rather it does not produce increased tolerance *and* withdrawal. Practitioners should always check the tolerance and withdrawal potential of the substance being abused by the loved one when they do not know the risk potential. Establishing whether physical dependence is present in the using loved one is important because it will need to be accounted for should they enter treatment. Some consideration will also need to be given as to whether the user is currently exposed to potential or actual harm from their use, even if physical dependence is not present.

1.2 Social Consequences of Use

The development of the Dependence Syndrome does not account for all problems associated with use. The syndrome isolated the medical complications resulting from use. Alongside physical dependence run the social consequences of using. The social consequences of use refer to the user's inability to sustain social commitments in the areas of family, employment, peer relationships and social responsibilities. These consequences may be primary such as domestic violence, loss of a driving licence, divorce or unemployment or homelessness. They can also be secondary, such as a history of alcohol problems interfering with job applications. They can again range in magnitude from failure to do what was expected as a result of a hangover, to major problems such as the complete breakdown of the user's social attachments (Clark and Hilton, 1991; Edwards et al., 1994). This breakdown can be catastrophic leading to the experience of almost total social exclusion. The individual experiencing such profound and global deterioration in social function is likely to become immersed in heavy drug or alcohol using sub-cultures that sustain and even normalise high use.

This social breakdown can be understood as addiction. The working definition of addiction as opposed to dependence is that addiction is the complete erosion of all relationships in pursuit of a single source of satisfaction (Harris, 1997). As such, addiction need not be limited to substances such as drug and alcohol. Any behaviour which interferes with the individual's wider social function will produce a similar outcome, be it gambling, sex, work or a relationship. These individuals would not require a medical detoxification on stopping these behaviours, but the overall effect on their life and immediate family is profound.

This definition does cross over with the concept of salience: as described by the Dependence Syndrome use becomes a priority in the individuals life. Generally, as physical dependence increases, the more likely it is to impede social function. But it is possible for people to experience profound physical dependence without social complications or to experience social complications without physical dependence. As a result many drug and alcohol users may not recognise that they have a problem because of the criteria in which they assess their own use. For example, the crack user whose life is devastated through their bingeing may not feel that they have a problem because they do not have to use it every day like a heroin user might. Alternative the physically dependent drinker who struggles to function in the morning without an 'eye opener,' sweats through to an early lunch where they drink heavily and then returns home early to drink all evening but otherwise manages their responsibilities, may not feel that they are an 'alcoholic'. Even though they have signs of dependency, as their life does not conform to the stereotype of the street drinker, they fail to recognise this use as problematic.

This can be compounded by the fact that people have a tendency to normalise their own drug or alcohol use as typical. Even heavy drinkers believe their drinking is normal as everyone they know may drink a similar amount. The problem drinker and drug user will also always be aware of people that use more heavily or chaotically than they do. Such comparisons can allow them to diminish the impact of their own consumption in comparison.

1.3 Family Hardships

The social complication of drug or alcohol use will affect every aspect of the user's life. However, within this broad range, the majority of the collateral damage befalls the user's family. The number of families affected by problem use is vast. Paolino and McCrady (1977) suggested that for every problem alcohol user, five other people are adversely affected. In the UK, Orford (2001) estimated that with two to three million adults experiencing physical dependence on alcohol alone, the total numbers of those adversely affected could range from four to six million people. At the same time research demonstrates that in any given year, between 90–95 per cent of problem drug / alcohol users do not seek help (Kessler et al., 1994; Price et al., 1991; Reiger et al., 1993; Sobell et al., 1996). A huge population of family members remain isolated and struggling to managing the unbearable burden of a loved one's addiction.

Problematic drug and alcohol use has a profound effect on all members in the family unit. Velleman et al., (1993) identified a range of short and long term consequences. In the short term, families affected by another's problem use are more likely to experience social isolation, fatigue, anxiety, guilt, fear and even suicidal thoughts. In the long term, they are likely to experience physical health problems, depression and anxiety attacks as well as an increase in their own drug, alcohol and tobacco intake. These psychological pressures were further compounded by social pressures such as debt and financial hardships. Consumption does not simply compromise the family's relationship with the problem user, but also places increasing strain on the family's relationships with each other. Households with a problem user tend to become characterised by increased conflict in their wider interactions with each other.

The specific impact on families may also vary according to which substance is being abused. Problematic drug and alcohol consumption can affect families in different ways. In general, the families of illicit drug users are more likely to be subject to stealing to fund a habit; be pressurised into giving the user money for drugs; or experience the disappearance of their loved one for extended periods of time. Alcohol is more likely to lead to increased rates of domestic violence. This is particularly true in the experience of episodic (binge) drinking patterns than in consistent drinking patterns. The unpredictably of a binge drinker's behaviour is often more exhausting than that caused by the daily drinker. Family members await the return of their loved one, unsure whether they will be happy, sensate or aggressive. The constant peaks and troughs of crises can rapidly diminish the emotional reserves of the entire family. Alcohol features in one third (360,000 cases) of domestic violence cases reported in the UK every year (DoH, 2004). Domestic violence against the mother also correlates with them adopting a more punitive parenting style with their children, allowing aggression to trickle down through the family unit. Children in problem alcohol households have been found to be more vulnerable to all form of abuse, including physical, emotional and sexual. In contrast, problems with prescribed drugs are more likely to be met with ambivalence by the wider family. As they are prescribed by a medical authority, families may accept the usage without question or lack the confidence to challenge professionals.

The types of stresses concerned others experience also depends upon their relationship with the problem user. Spouses are much more likely to experience domestic violence, threats and to be pressurised for money. Parents of problem users report higher incidences of manipulation and deceit. Their shock was often greater when problem use finally emerged. Problematic consumption also disperses an uneven burden of responsibility on family members. In most research studies, 'contact with family' often equates to contact with the mother or wife of problem users, who is more likely to sustain the relationship and seek out help. The needs and response of the father's of problem users is not well understood. Grandparents may have to take on the role of primary care taker for the problem user's children if they are unwilling or unable to do so themselves. Over 200,000 grandparents care for their grandchildren in the UK with substance misuse being the principle reason for this (Adfam, 2006). Child rearing late into their lives with often very disturbed children is incredibly demanding and little support is available to them, increasing the financial strain many are already under.

Estimates of the numbers of children affected by parental substance misuse vary. Brisby et al. (1997) extrapolated the numbers of children likely to experience harm in the UK. This is based on 13.5 million parents with a harmful drinking pattern occurring at a rate of seven per cent of the population. This gives an estimate of 800,000 children in England and Wales; 85,000 children in Scotland; and 35,000 in Northern Ireland living in a family where a parent has an alcohol problem. They recognised that not all of these children would experience profound problems but they would be at increased risk of abuse and harm. Orford (2001) suggested that over one million children would be living in homes profoundly affected by serious alcohol problems. The UK Government recognises that 1.3 million children in the UK are affected by parental alcohol abuse and they account for fifty per cent of all child protection cases (AHRSE, 2004). Problematic drug and alcohol use remains the principle reason why children are taken into care. Hidden Harm (ACMD, 2003) suggests that there are between 250,000–350,000 children of problem drug users in the UK. As distribution of drug and alcohol problems can vary considerably from region to region, these families will not be distributed evenly, geographically.

In terms of the stability of these family units, research shows that only 37 per cent of fathers and 64 per cent of mothers with drug problems remained living with their children (ACMD, 2003). Children of problem using parents demonstrate increased social withdrawal, increased responsibilities for caring for siblings and their parents, as well as increased risk of psychological disturbance. There has been anecdotal evidence that the impact of parental use differs on boys and girls. Boys may be more prone to acting out behaviour whilst girls may have a tendency to internalise their problems and experience greater mental illness and withdrawal. If the problem parent is the mother, the elder daughter may be 'promoted' into the vacant mother's role with increased family responsibilities.

Dore and Alexander (1996) identified that low self-esteem, guilt, shame and isolation were common emotional reactions in children who often felt that their parents' use was their fault. The children of problem drug users, particularly heroin users, are three times more likely to suffer abuse and four times more likely to suffer neglect (Kelleher et al., 1994). Whilst neglect and abuse was connected to the stability of parental use, the risk to the children does not necessarily decrease because the parents were in treatment. One study of methadone using parents found that 83 per cent of their children suffered untreated medical or nutritional problems (Shulman et al., 2000). High adjunct use on top of substitute prescriptions mean that parents being in regular contact with services does not necessarily equate with stability for these children.

The effect of problem drug use on siblings is under-researched. The over focus on the problem user will invariably displace attention from their siblings as parents become increasingly absorbed in battling with one of their children's acute problems. Whilst it does not appear that siblings suffer the same degree of psychological distress, it does appear to breed greater animosity and resentment. Furthermore, whilst parental use does have an impact on subsequent use in the children of drug users, a continual finding in research consistently reveals that older brothers and peers have a greater impact on inducting siblings into subsequent use (see Brook et al., 1989; Duncan et al., 1996; Vakalia, 2001; Boyd and Guthrie, 1996).

The long-term impact of parental use on the child's development is less clear. Research has often assumed that the impact of problematic parental use will inevitably lead to problems in future life adjustment. Some research has found evidence for increased rates of substance misuse problems in the children of problem drinkers (Mohr, 2000; Gogineni, 1995). Godsall

(1995) found that being raised in a family characterised by conflict caused deeper self-esteem issues than high substance use itself. However, children of problem users do show a broad spectrum of responses in adult life. Many studies have found little evidence of long term impact in the children of problem users, who show similar levels of adjustment as their peers or even better (Curran and Chassin, 1996; Gordon, 1995; Cavell et al., 2002; Hill et al., 1992). Resilience may be rooted in several factors. Laybourn et al. (1997) suggested that birth order was a significant factor, with older siblings protecting younger ones by absorbing the aggression or violence in their stead. Kroll and Taylor (2003) summarised individual factors promoting resilience including attachment, high self-esteem, good problem-solving, good mental health, lack of trauma and an ability to draw upon adults as resources. Perceived support from other adults may be more important than actual support.

1.4 Family Coping

Research by Hurcom et al. (2000) has demonstrated that there are no typical family responses to problem use. With this caveat, studies have elucidated critical themes that provide some insight into the family reaction to use. Marshal (2001) identified that concealment was a commonly employed strategy in order to maintain the family unit. Here, the problem use was hidden in order to protect wider family members or abate the fear of the situation becoming even more aggravated through other's over reaction to use. This research also found that concerned others attempted to cope with the situation in isolation for long periods of time before seeking help. In general, families experiencing problem drug use are far more likely to seek out professional help compared to families with a member experiencing difficulties with alcohol. Families are more likely to attempt to resolve alcohol problems themselves. Seeking professional help can be experienced as a profound failure to help their loved one and was often accompanied by feelings of guilt and shame. The caveat to this was in elderly populations. Problematic alcohol use is often tolerated within this group because of the age of the drinker and cultural mores which would suggest that people might be more entitled to some fun at their venerable age. This negates the fact that drinking in these elderly populations is usually characterised by depression, isolation and fear. Increased falls, blackouts and malnutrition do little to enhance this generation's life.

Where the family do respond, some research has suggested that family tend to adopt three broad primary strategies: engagement, tolerance and withdrawal (see Orford et al., 1998; Hurcom et al., 2000). Engagement strategies can be characterised by action. Family members deploy strategies such as *attack* through threat or assault; *manipulation* in employing covert interventions such as shaming or playing on the drinkers guilt; and *constructive helping* which entails seeking out information, advice or meeting with professionals to explore potential strategies and treatment options. Tolerance is a more passive response. This includes *spoiling* the problem user by taking care of them when hung over or sick. Promises of treats can be used to try to entice a change in behaviour. It can also include *inaction*, that is to merely tolerate the current situation. Withdrawal can be characterised by *circumvention*. Here the concerned other begins to retract from the problem other emotionally, physically and socially even whilst sharing the same accommodation. Essentially they begin to lead separate lives, with the concerned other investing their energies into *constructive management* of the home, their own career and the family. This often leaves the problem user isolated and alone, even whilst still residing physically within the family unit. In general terms, women are more likely to remain with problem using spouses whilst the men are more likely to separate from problem using partners.

1.5 Family Contact with the Problem User

Despite the pressures and stresses generated by problem use, families maintain a high level of contact with their loved one. Typically, problem alcohol users, with a later age of onset of consumption, are more likely to be married and entwined within a family life – albeit one under increasing conflict or isolation. This strain is often locked in a reciprocal relationship with use. For example, O'Farrell (1995) found that marital discord can increase drinking or re-instigate it after periods of abstinence. Maisto et al. (1988) found a similar relationship in that marital conflict was often the cause of relapse and the stimulus to stop drinking as well. It appears that alcohol and marital problems are in a reciprocal relationship, each exerting a powerful influence on the other.

Whilst problem drug users are perceived to be more excluded from family life, research suggests a high proportion of opiate and poly-drug users maintain regular contact with their families. Perzel and Lamon (1979) found that 48 per cent of heroin users and 42 per cent of poly drug users lived with their parents, whereas only seven per cent of their non-using peers did. Furthermore, even if the problem user does not live at home, the parental address is often given as the best contact point in case of any emergency. Stanton (1982) found that of 696 opiate users aged between 20–35, 86 per cent of them met with one parent at least weekly. Perzel and Lamon's (1979) study found that 64 per cent of the heroin users and 51 per cent of the poly-drug users spoke to their parents on the phone daily, compared to only 9 per cent of non-using individuals. Comparison studies with cocaine users demonstrated that the frequency of contact with parents was even higher than in opiate using populations. Douglas (1987) found that in matched opiate, cocaine and non drug users, opiate users had twice the face-to-face contact with parents and cocaine users had three times the amount of parental contact than their non-using peers. These high frequency patterns of contact occur across all cultures where problematic use is prevalent (see Stanton, 1982). Furthermore, these results appear consistent whether the problem user was a treatment seeker or not (Rounsaville and Kleber, 1985). For example, Kidorf et al. (1997) found that 85 per cent of opiate using clients could identify a drug free concerned other who was willing to become involved in their treatment when it became a condition of prescribing methadone.

This is in direct contradiction to the impression many practitioners have of problem users. Problem drinkers and especially drug users are thought to be wholly alienated from their families. Further to this, they often report that their families are the source of their troubles. The hostility they report from family may be caused by the family challenging their using behaviour rather than causing it. The user then purports that their problems stem from this conflict. This problem may be acerbated by the manner in which problem users present explanations for their use and their current situation (see Harris, 2007). Users may be prone to *triangulation*. Schwartzman and Bokos (1979) noted the occurrence of triangulation as a competitive process that is better to known to practitioners when exhibited between agencies. For example, the client may present at drug service B, complaining about how drug service A failed to meet their needs. This is met with agreement because the practitioner also dislikes the rival agency A. The client then returns to agency A complaining about agency B which is greeted by a receptive practitioner here as well. Similar dynamics can be enacted between the family and the treatment service. Because the family are pressuring the problem user to change, the problem user can also triangulate this relationship. Hence the loved one complains to the agency that their parents, partners or family are the source of their problems. This may give the impression of alienation. The problem user may then reverse this and tell their concerned others how inept their treatment service is and this is hampering their attempt at change.

This can create a divisive situation which sets families and agencies against each other. For example, Campbell's (1992) analysis of counsellors' notes found that 90 per cent of this material was negative about their client's family. Whilst Balaban and Melchionda (1979) found workers frequently got into conflict with family members over the client, forcing the client to drop out as the only way to appease the worker-family tensions. Certainly problem users tend to attribute their problems to those around them first, before recognising that their consumption is the common denominator in the tensions that they experience (De Leon, 1996). As such, practitioners working with problem users may be vulnerable to inadvertently forestalling the client's evolving awareness of their problems by siding with the client against the family.

Triangulation can profoundly undermine treatment. Therefore, in the development of our services we have found significant advantage in housing services for concerned others within existing treatment services rather than as separate organisations. Referral rates, treatment response and comprehensive care planning has been significantly enhanced in comparison to concerned other services that are freestanding and consequently greater friction is encountered between treatment providers. Annexing concerned other services to treatment providers reduces the possibility of polarisation between the services and the family and eliminates organisational championing of the concerned other or the problem user.

There will be occasions when it is inappropriate to work with concerned others or family members who have been the source of physical, sexual or emotional abuse. However, it is very unlikely that these families will be volunteering themselves to assist the problem user in constructive change. In the majority of cases, families are a source of support. The expression of this support may have been ineffective, unhelpful or emotionally exhausting but is important none-the-less. In her extensive study of families of problem users, Barnard (2007: 153) observed '. . . for better or worse the problem drug user is part of their family and it is the family that is likely to play a crucial role in shaping the destiny of that drug user. Indeed the family is frequently a good deal more significant and influential than any drug or social welfare agency will ever be.' It may be a professional conceit to believe that a professional working relationship may amount to more than that of kinship. It is important that the worker adopt a position of equanimity with concerned others and the problem user, anticipating hurts and blames on both sides.

What we can conclude from these studies is that family life remains important to most problem users, offering a reference point for chaotic and difficult lives. This also emphasises the fact that the majority of families find it difficult to separate entirely from their loved one as they are often advised to do by professional or self-help movements. If the problem user and their family do become wholly estranged, this loss is felt powerfully by both parties. It is often a major landmark in the recovery process when the problem user initiates contact with their families after years of separation. This first contact is usually accompanied by powerful emotions of fear, guilt and relief. In direct contrast, many concerned others want to play a proactive role in supporting and helping their loved ones, even in dire circumstances. As such, the family represents an extraordinarily powerful force in treatment and are often the critical factor in initiating change and treatment engagement.

1.6 Family Pressure and Treatment Entry

Substance misuse and contact with the family do not reside peacefully together. Whilst the problem user often has greater contact with their families than non-using peers, these relationships are characterised by stresses, conflict and entreaties for the problem user to change. The concept of coercing people to change their behaviour sits uncomfortably amongst the humanistic values of the addiction treatment field. There is a powerful assumption that authentic change emanates solely from individual choice. It is widely assumed that the problematic user must want to change for it to be truly enduring. This axiom has an extremely wide currency in both the treatment and related professional fields. However, the research on what motivates people to change problematic use demonstrates that there is no evidence to support this assumption. Reviewing research on why people change, we see that external pressures are an intrinsic component of motivation. For example, Marlowe et al. (2001: 105) study of 415 substance misusers' motivation to enter treatment concluded that: 'Virtually all participants reported a combination of both negative and positive pressures to enter treatment, and both externally mediated and non-externally mediated pressures.' This suggests that we cannot make clear distinction between problem users that are pressured to change by external pressures and those that volunteer for treatment. Instead we need to appreciate that substance misusers are motivated to change by both internal psychological reasons *and* external pressures. Marlowe et al. (2001) found that these external pressures could be described by five sub-groups: social and financial pressures; solely financial; legal; medical; and the largest sub-group (35 per cent) was family pressure. Simpson and Sells (1990) found that in a 12-year follow-up of opioid users, 75 per cent of problem users cited family as the principle reason for entering treatment. In contrast, Hartjen et al. (1976) found that only 5 per cent of clients who presented for treatment had freely elected to do so without any external pressure. Furthermore, Loneck et al. (c.f. Landau, 2004) found that drug and alcohol users who self-referred in this way had lowest treatment completion rates compared to those who were legally mandated or had received a family based intervention.

What is also striking in the research literature is who gets coerced. Polcin and Weisner (1999) study of 987 problem alcohol users presenting for treatment found that ultimatums to change came from family members first, and then legal mandates second, even amongst individuals who were not in relationships. It appears then that coercion emanates from informal social relationships first, and where these fail or are indifferent, formal social structures such as the law begin to exert pressure. However, what is most striking in the clinical research is that the number of ultimatums to change do not correspond with the actual severity of physical dependence. 'These findings suggest that for clients entering treatment, severity of alcohol problems *per se* is not what results in family, friends, or representatives from community institutions to become concerned and pressure them into treatment. Rather, it is the type of alcohol related problem that makes a difference.' (Polcin and Weisner, 1999). This is the common finding in studies conducted in other non-familial settings (see Lawental et al., 1996; Weisner, 1992; Weisner et al., 1995; Kaskutas et al., 1997).

It is assumed that people are coerced into treatment simply because they chose substances which are deemed socially unacceptable. As such, we might treat coercion as a civil liberties issue in the first instance. However, research suggests that it is not what substances people consume or how much they consume which instigates pressure to change. It is the social consequences of the individual's use that attracts the concern of others. Dependence that does not impinge upon others attracts little concern. It is when drug or alcohol use affects the relationships around the user that triggers pressures for change. For example, the gentle middle-aged male that drinks himself to sleep in front of the television every night but is otherwise a 'happy drunk' will attract little attention. In contrast, the woman who after few drinks on a Saturday night out on the town becomes abusive and aggressive will be pressured to change her use if it affects or embarrasses those closest to her. This is despite the fact that she might consume a fraction of the alcohol that the perpetual armchair drinker is imbibing. This also explains why those individuals who experience problems with prescribed drugs such as antidepressants, tranquillisers or SSRIs, receive little attention from their loved ones. Besides being sanctioned by a medical authority, behaviours associated with these drugs do not infringe upon others lives in such dramatic manner. Prescribed medications are more likely to present as issues of physical dependency than social complications.

If we make a distinction between the physical dependency and social consequences we can understand why coercion is an integral part of the change process. When drug and alcohol consumption begins to threaten the substance user's social relationships, the concerned others in their life do not ignore these tensions. As their relationships come under increasing pressure, others in the problem user's life will respond with attempts to restore the previous status quo of the relationship. These pressures can take the form of gentle social pressure to well-intended but drastic responses born out of sheer desperation to rescue their loved one from terrible self-inflicted harm. Therefore, when consumption interferes with relationships, coercion will always occur.

As such, coercion is not an incidental product of use or a civil liberties issue: it is the other side of addiction itself. Coercion and addiction are two sides of the same coin. The problem user experiences this as their relationships breaking down leaving them increasing isolated. The concerned other experiences this as a desperate attempt to protect the loved one and their relationship until they cannot tolerate the situation any more. In this way, addiction and coercion are harnessed as equal but opposing forces sourced in the same event. Concerned others appear motivated to intervene by the harm that the user inflicts on themselves and others. The greater the harm, the greater the coercion will become. These continued external pressures therefore constitute an inevitable response to problem use and remain proportionate to the consequence of use. As a result, family pressures remain one of the most important catalysts in changing patterns of addiction. This tension is double edged. If these informal pressures to change prove indifferent, ineffective or too exhausting to sustain, they can break into tolerance, withdrawal and finally termination. Severing the relationship entirely is the last sanction. This leaves the problem user estranged and isolated amplifying use as a source of comfort.

Where the family fail, the coercion will continue whilst the drug or alcohol use affects others. This may move through friendship groups, employment and, where it affects the general public, the law will coerce people. Again, it is important to emphasise that this is driven not by the physical dependence but by the behaviour of the individual. From a societal point view, most people are somewhat indifferent to individual's use of drugs and alcohol as long as it does not have a detrimental effect on their life. This has led to the disparity of funding to address drug problems such as heroin use which is related to acquisitive crime committed on the wider public versus alcohol. Alcohol is more likely to led to assaultive crime in the users own informal network and so does not attract public concern to the same degree.

This analysis strongly suggests that far from being helpless to address a loved one's use, families are an inevitable and essential component in the change process. The consistency of this external pressure is important. Internal motivation that occurs solely in the individual can fluctuate dramatically. We can commit to change in one moment and lose sight of the importance of these changes the next. Our well intended aspirations may soon be undermined by sub-goals and doubts. It is the phenomena of the New Year's Resolution: we resolve to make a change and do this purely for ourselves but this is absolutely no guarantee that our efforts will still be sustained one week later. Likewise, those who self-present for treatment of their own volition are not guaranteed success. Conversely, external pressures remain consistent. This may sustain a more continuous effort over longer periods of time. Both these factors are essential to positive outcomes in addiction treatment. This suggests that it is not a question of whether problem users should be coerced as this will occur within the natural course of addictions. The issue becomes how the practitioner can orchestrate these pressures to change in a manner which is effective and acceptable to the concerned other and the loved one. Historically, early models of intervention have attempted to utilise these pressures but without such sensitively to the parties involved.

Therapeutic Context

1.7 Self-help: Al Anon and Ala Teen

Reviewing the history of interventions for concerned others may appear as a detour from the practitioner's current concern of acquiring skills to help those presently struggling with a loved one's use. However this is important for a number of reasons. Firstly, historical approaches have often deployed highly intrusive methods to foster change. This has created divided opinions across the professional field of substance misuse. At one end of the professional spectrum, these models have been readily adopted as they once represented the only strategies available to assist concerned others. In the centre ground, the assumptions of these approaches have seeped into the professional consciousness without clear definition. At the other end of the spectrum, the highly intrusive nature of these approaches can be regarded with deep concern, being considered tantamount to a form of abuse. As such, it is important to evaluate their efficacy; elucidate the concepts which underpin them; and understand how recent developments have eliminated the more draconian elements to address this broad swathe of professional response. It is also important to clarify the assumptions inherent in these models that have established themselves in the field of supporting the concerned others. Many of these assumptions are incompatible with the delivery of the PACT making a clear demarcation between approaches is important.

The concept of supporting the family members of problematic users dates back to the 1930s and the birth of the Alcoholics Anonymous movement. This movement was pioneered by two recovering alcoholics, Bill W. and Dr Bob. They fused recent medical thinking that conceptualised alcoholism as an allergy that affected certain individuals with the spiritual values of protestant temperance movements such as the Oxford Group. This fusion led to the creation of the self-help fellowship of recovering alcoholics, Alcoholics Anonymous. The emphasis on anonymity was two-fold. Firstly, it respected the privacy of its members but secondly, its traditions explicitly forbid that any individual could use the organisation for their own financial advantage. The movement was also known as the Twelve Step approach, a name derived from the eponymous twelve exercises which the recovering individuals had to work through in order to achieve sobriety. This is done under the watchful tutelage of a sponsor, themselves a recovering alcoholic, who would ensure that the programme was adhered to. Adherence to this programme would culminate in a vivid spiritual awakening that was so profound it would deliver the individual from alcoholism.

1. We admitted we were powerless over alcohol-that our lives had become unmanageable.

2. Came to believe that a power greater than ourselves could restore us to sanity.

3. Made a decision to turn over our will and our lives over to the care of God as we understood Him.

4. Made a searching and fearless moral inventory of ourselves.

5. Admitted to God, to ourselves, and to another human being the exact nature of our wrongs.

6. Were entirely ready to have God remove all these defects of character.

7. Humbly asked Him to remove our shortcomings.

8. Made a list of all persons we had harmed and became willing to make amends to them all.

9. Made direct amends to such people wherever possible, except when to do so would injure them or others.

10. Continued to take personal inventory and when we were wrong promptly admitted it.

11. Sought through prayer and meditation to improve our conscious contact with God as we understood Him, praying only for knowledge of His will for us and the power to carry that out.

12. Having had a spiritual awakening as a result of these steps, we tried to carry this message to others, and to practice these principles in all our affairs.

Figure 1.   The twelve steps of Al-Anon

The movement initially attracted male drinkers to its ranks. However, as early as 1935 the wives of problem drinkers began to accompany their recovering husbands to local meetings. Whilst these spouses did not participate in the group treatment, they did take on wider roles such as coffee making and planning outings. These supportive duties led to the early formation of sub-groups such as the AA Auxiliaries or AA Family Groups. After a tour of US Alcohol Anonymous groups in 1950, Bill W. noticed the increasing proliferation of these auxiliary groups. He suggested to his wife, Lois Wilson, and colleague, Anne 'B', that they create an umbrella organisation to support their continued development. At the following AA General Service Conference of 1951, Lois Wilson invited AA delegates' wives to lunch at her home with other family members and the project was initiated. In a questionnaire of the same year they stated that their purpose was to unify these family groups. The name Al Anon was decided and they adopted both the Twelve Steps and Twelve Traditions as their guiding principles. The specific needs of children of problem drinkers was the focus of a speech at the Alcoholic Anonymous 1955 conference. This led to the creation of Ala Teen, a specific group for the teenage children of problem drinkers who again subscribed to the traditions of the Twelve Steps. The first group met in Pasadena in 1957.

The Al-Anon family movement gathered pace and implemented its own world conferences. Its popularity began to attract a wider range of family members to its services than just the wives of alcoholics. This included the husbands, partners, friends and even employers of Alcoholics

Anonymous members. Furthermore, concerned others whose loved ones were not seeking treatment for problem use also began to engage in high numbers, at times constituting 50 per cent of the attendance. Here they could meet with others, share their experiences and find support for themselves where little other help existed. Presently, Al-Anon is operating in over 33,000 groups in over 112 countries. The prescribed treatment for those in Al Anon and Ala Teen closely resembles the Twelve Steps of Alcohol Anonymous (see Figure 1). This included the concerned other's need to surrender to a higher power and acknowledgment of the limits of one's control over another. And the pledge to make amends to others wherever it would not cause more hurt to do so.

However, Al-Anon was not specifically constituted to support the concerned others whose loved ones were not in treatment. It was for family members whose loved one was attending Alcoholics Anonymous. To meet this new need the movement drew inspiration from the folk wisdom of the Fellowship. Principally this was the idea that the addict was powerless to control their addiction, and therefore any attempt to intervene and help them would prove futile. It was felt that change would only occur when the user reached 'rock bottom,' a point of complete emotional, physical and spiritual collapse. Any interference in this process through constructive helping was deemed counter-productive as it would only stave off this necessary personal crisis that precipitated change. Instead, the movement advocated loving detachment from the problem user and termination of their relationships until they were ready for change. This 'tough love' philosophy soon spread and established itself as the accepted norm in dealing with another's problem use.

1.8 Co-dependency Movement

During the evolution of the Al-Anon movement in the 1950s the term 'alcoholic wife' or 'co-alcoholic' began to be used widely. This term was used to describe the psychological stresses experienced by the family as a result of living with a loved one's problematic use. It described family members as suffering 'with' alcoholism whilst their loved ones suffered 'from' alcoholism. This recognised the impact of problem use on the wider family life in terms of stress, pressures, hardships and social isolation. However, Al-Anon and Ala-Teen had diverged from the Alcohol Anonymous tradition in that it did not consider that the family themselves were suffering from a 'disease' as their loved ones did. Instead they suffered from the consequences of the alcoholic disease which they themselves would find impossible to control. In this way, issues concerning personal powerless remained true to the Twelve Step tradition and allowed them to maintain close ties to Alcohol Anonymous. 'Co-alcoholism' was re-phrased as 'co-dependency' as treatment services broadened their focus to include a wider range of problem substances such as illicit drugs in the 1960s.

Outside of the Twelve Step tradition, professionals were increasingly interested in the family members of problem users. This largely took a more negative view of the wives of problem drinkers. In the 1950s psychodynamic theorists had suggested that women deliberately partnered alcoholic men in order to satisfy their own unconscious psychological needs for control (Kalashian, 1959; Whalen, 1953). It was also believed that women deliberately undermined their alcoholic partner's attempts at change in order to preserve this need (Futterman, 1953). This idea that the spouses of problem drinkers controlled their loved ones in this way was demolished by the research of Edwards et al. (1973). This research found no evidence to support the view that spouses of alcoholic partners suffered from an underlying psychological condition of their own. Instead, Edwards et al. (1973) findings reiterated that the phenomenal stresses caused by the partners drinking caused immense psychological distress in their spouses.

Despite this comprehensive rebuttal, the treatment industry in the 1970s remained overtly focused on the idea that problem use was located in the family. It drew inspiration from the emerging Systems Theory that surmised that human behaviours were the product of the social systems which they occupied. Problems were not so much located in the individual but locked into the dysfunction systems that they belong too. Hence addiction in a family member was the expression of the dysfunctions in the wider family. This broadened the focus from the spouses of problem drinkers to include their children and gave rise to the Adult Children of Alcoholics (ACoA) movement, founded in 1977. They suggested that the alcoholic parent had a huge impact on their children, creating distinct family roles that would be perpetuated into adulthood. These roles would inevitably mean that the children of alcoholics were unable to sustain intimate relationships, become overtly perfectionist and embroil themselves in relationships with problem users in later life in order to feel needed. This necessitated treatment for the adult children of alcoholics.

The meaning of co-dependency was now being substantially revised. It no longer described the consequences of living with a problem user. It was now understood to be an ingrained dysfunctional behaviour that was inter-generational. This new formulation of co-dependency was to be extended further by a small cabal of recovering addicts such as John Bradshaw and Melody Beattie, along with family members of alcoholics such as Sharon Wegscheider-Cruse (Steadman-Rice, 1998). As part of their recoveries they began training as addiction counsellors in the 1980s. Through their studies they were heavily influenced by several counselling traditions. They began to re-configure co-dependency within elements of the Twelve Step disease model, Systems Theory and the deep individualism iterated in the work of Carl Rogers. This formulation began to create a new movement that was to dominate treatment services for concerned others for the next twenty years.

In this new co-dependency movement, the concept of co-dependency was revised even further. These writers came to advocate that co-dependency was the *primary* disease of which chemical dependency is but one facet. Co-dependency now describes the family conditions that give *rise* to addiction. As Wegscheider-Cruse and Cruse (1990: 12) state, 'Many have thought that co-dependency has been due to life's problems, such as living with an alcoholic or addict, having low self-worth, being from an alcoholic family, etc. But it's the other way around'. This redefinition revives the discredited 1950s concept of co-dependency. Co-

Caretaker: A personification of the partner of an alcoholic. They take care of the alcoholic, soothe their worries and clear up their destruction. They are destined to marry an alcoholic in later life and continue this role as they seek approval and validation through taking responsibility for others.

Hero: This individual is a source of pride to the family which is achieved through external achievements in school or work. At home they take on roles abdicated by their parents. Whilst they appear confident and driven, they suffer from a deep sense of inadequacy and are destined to become workaholics.

Scapegoat: As wider family members sublimate their anger, the scapegoat fails to learn healthy expressions of anger. Instead they act out anger in self-destructive behaviour which diverts attention from any problematic user in the home. They run the risk of developing alcoholism themselves as their behaviour is so self-injurious and they have a disregard for risk.

Lost Child: This child withdraws from the dysfunctional family into their own world. Often the family believes them to be happy and content. This distance is achieved through the use of television, internet and computer games. They lack social interaction with their peers. They are believed to be vulnerable to the development of bulimia and eating disorders.

Family Clown: They bring comic relief to the family. Often the youngest, they act cute or make jokes as an outlet for tension. As a result they fail to mature and experience difficulties in school.

Figure 2.   The sub-groups of co-dependency

dependency has become understood as an underlying personality disorder forged in the family. This inherited disposition means that the co-dependent will inevitably re-create their childhood family experience in their adult relationships. They attract and will be attracted to the alcoholic spouse due to the childhood roles they were forced to adopt. This will express itself in the establishment of a range of predictable personality types that the co-dependent will assume in adult life (see Figure 2).

Even addiction is subsumed into this broader definition of co-dependence. Addiction is actually 'counter-dependence,' an aggressive form of co-dependence exhibited by the problem user that originates in a childhood where they had battled for attention and validation from emotionally unavailable parents. Hence co-dependence and counter-dependence are facets of the same underlying disorder patterned in childhood.

The fusion of these ideas has lead to redefining co-dependency as a family disease that is as fatal as chemical dependency itself. In this revisionist movement, even non-alcoholic families could create these conditions. A sick family can be characterised by even mild invalidation, the upholding of family laws or the emotional unavailability of the parents. Any parenting style that is less than nurturing will create co-dependency. As leading co-dependency advocate John Bradshaw (1988) summarised 'All addictions are rooted in co-dependence and co-dependence is a symptom of abandonment.' Furthermore, as we are all prone to seek validation from others, leading advocates of co-dependency now suggest that everyone in Western society is co-dependent and in need of treatment, especially those who criticise the approach or fail to adopt their methods. Ann Wilson Schaeff (1986: 95) states 'The mental health field has simply not identified the addictive process and the syndrome of co-dependency because people in the field are non-recovering co-dependents who have not recognised that their professional practice is closely linked with the practice of their untreated diseases'.

The new formulation of co-dependency was institutionalised in the traditions of the Alcoholics Anonymous in October 1986 at the first meeting of Co-dependence Anonymous (CoDA). At the First National Conference on Co-dependency in 1989, co-dependency advocates defined the condition as 'a pattern of painful dependence on compulsive behaviours and on approval from others in an attempt to find safety, self-worth, and identity.' Recovery is achieved through breaking the pattern of subservience to family, partners, social and community oppression. Instead, the person must express their individual wants and needs first and foremost. In line with Carl Rogers' ideas, this expression of self will always *tend* to the good. Total individuation is the ultimate goal of recovery from co-dependency.

Information about this fatal disease that afflicts everyone was not disseminated through medical or research journals. Instead, these ideas were championed by the American chat show circuit of Oprah, Donahue and Geraldo. This led to a boom in book sales that publishers were keen to capitalise on. The ideas were marketed directly to a receptive but largely uninformed audience. None of the ideas propounded by this movement received any scientific scrutiny at all. Academic journals require submitted material to be reviewed by a panel of experts to assess the validity of any claims that authors make. This was considered symptomatic of co-dependency and therefore this level of accountability was wholly ignored by the movement. Instead of research and evidence the movement adopted an evangelical zeal in disseminating the ideas directly to the treatment industry. Miller (2003: 5) describes a typical experience of this. 'In the 1990s I saw a distressed young woman who had agreed to attend 'family night' at a private residential program where her father was being treated for alcohol dependence, which had developed years after she left home. The staff had invited her to come to 'help and support' her father's treatment. She found herself surrounded by staff telling her that she had a potentially fatal disease of co-dependence and desperately needed residential treatment herself. When she protested that she had had a happy childhood and felt quite normal, the staff told her she was so far out of touch with reality that she couldn't possibly recognise normality'.

Despite the endorsement of the popular-media, defining the condition of co-dependency is very difficult. The symptoms co-dependent advocates describe in their literature are not recognised by any professional psychiatric or psychological body. They employ a new language to define this disease. Vague but emotive phrases such as 'toxic shame,' 'healing the inner child,' 'women who love too much,' 'poisonous pedagogy' and the central source of the disease in 'emotional abandonment' characterise the disorder. There is also an overt preoccupation with the self-esteem levels of individuals. There have been 140 identified characteristics that describe the co-dependent individual. This is striking when we consider that there are only two defining symptoms of physical dependence on alcohol itself. As a result, co-dependency has been criticised as a poorly defined concept that lacks any clinical utility (see

Sher, 1991). The consequences of living with a problem drug or alcohol user can cause severe mental and physical health problems in the family that are recognised by professionals. There is a danger that the fuzzy label of co-dependency distracts from profound mental illness and distress which family members actually experience and which could go untreated.

Whilst the co-dependency movement has closely aligned itself with the Twelve Step tradition there are important differences between them. For example, Al Anon and Ala Teen attribute the problems that family members experience to the loved one's 'disease' of addiction. Accepting the concept of the disease demands no further reflection on why the loved one behaves in the way they do. This can liberate the concerned others from the torturous analysis of why their loved one behaves a certain way. This offers a degree of acceptance of their situation and allows them to invest their energy in the present healing of self. An important aspect of this healing process is making reparation, and therefore re-integration, with others. In contrast, CoDA and ACoA meetings remain overtly focused on the past in an attempt to distil blame and recrimination from the family of origin. Furthermore, as recovery is based upon the overcoming of oppressive or invalidating laws imposed by others, CoDA and ACoA members must separate from the influence of others rather than re-build relationships. Finally, whilst the Twelve Step tradition has emphasised that the movement remain anonymous and should not be a vehicle for personal gain, the co-dependency movement has created media stars of its chief proponents, who have capitalised on their new found fame through book, DVD's and television appearances.

Despite the broad dissemination of these ideas it is important to recognise that there is no scientific evidence to support the concept that co-dependence exists or that people enact the patterns of behaviours that co-dependency advocates describe. As Steadman-Rice (1998: 201) observes '. . . co-dependency advocates take repeated recourse to a rhetoric marked by excessive and inflammatory imagery, and all exhibit an all-but-total indifference to supporting empirical evidence'. Parental substance abuse invariably affects child development and may influence their subsequent behaviour in adult life. But this is not to suggest that this leads to a predictable adult personality disorder. There is considerable evidence that children of problem users do make significant life adjustments as they get older, despite the profound problems they have experienced. For example, a study by Velleman and Orford (2000: 229) of adult children of problem drinkers found the adverse effects they suffered as children tended to disappear in adult life. 'Yet one of the most striking features of the results presented here is that the large differences between the two-subgroups of offspring and comparisons relating to their recollections of childhood, are not reflected in young adulthood in differences between the groups in self-reported adjustment – there were very few significant differences between offspring and comparison groups when respondents described present adult adjustment'. Children raised with problem drinkers appear as well adjusted as their peers once they reach maturity.

The dissemination of the modern concept of co-dependency has been through popular mediums such as the Internet where there is little accountability or quality control. This means that many concerned others who are seeking help will have encountered the idea of co-dependency and be tempted to apply such a diagnosis to themselves. This makes it essential that practitioners working with the concerned others have a clear grasp of the multiple definitions of the term and its evidence base. The programme described in this manual explicitly acknowledges the pressures and stresses that families experience due to a loved one's problematic use. The programme is designed to assist concerned others to rebuild their impoverished lives. Within this, it does not assume that the concerned other is suffering from pre-existent disorder or that seeking help is a symptom of the family's sickness. As such, the ideas purported by the modern co-dependency movement are wholly incompatible with the treatment approach outlined in this manual. Concerned others who hold these beliefs to be true may be better served in the self-help movement that shares these beliefs.

The co-dependency movement is a paradox. On the one hand it has spawned a multi-million dollar publishing industry and its leading advocates are revered. At the same time the ideas innate in the movement remain unpalatable to many seeking help for their loved one and may dissuade many from pursuing assistance. This was reflected in callers' experience when presenting for a large-scale study of an alternative approach for concerned others. 'For example, CO (concerned other) callers in the present study often indicated to the ARISE clinicians that they had tried other agencies without receiving encouragement to apply their interest in a positive way. Many mentioned the anger they experienced at being labelled 'co-dependent', 'controlling', 'a victim', or an 'enabler' and the helplessness at being told that there was nothing they could do until their loved one 'hit bottom.' (Landau et al., 2004: 739).

Whilst the modern co-dependence movement has based itself on unsubstantiated claims and displayed an almost total disregard for clinical evidence, the movement did offer support to families who had been long ignored by professional services. The modern co-dependency movement's ethos tends to appeal to two distinct groups. Those already involved in the Twelve Step Fellowship where the extension of the disease concept to relationships appeals to an already receptive audience. It also appears to resonate with those individuals who lack assertiveness in their relationships who may feel empowered by the movement's vehement advocacy of individualism. However, professional practitioners should remain cautious of these ideas until empirical evidence is presented that supports these concepts and the treatment interventions that they purport are demonstrated to be effective.

1.9 The Intervention

Not all treatment within the co-dependency movement has suggested that concerned others are helpless to address a loved one's consumption. A second established model for assisting concerned others is the Johnson technique (Johnson, 1998). Popularly known as 'the intervention', this model was developed in the 1960s as a bold and pioneering approach which has remained influential in the development of new models of assisting concerned others. The intervention maintains co-dependency is a progressive, fatal disease. However, this is not assumed to be an underlying disorder but is dependent upon the length of exposure to the problem drug/alcohol use. 'When talking about family recovery, the point at issue is this: Because chemical dependency develops into a family illness, virtually *all* family members need some kind of help in recovery. Furthermore, if the chemical dependency has existed in the family over a long period of time, it is most likely that *all* family members will need some kind of outside help in restoring themselves to a state of health and happiness.' (Johnson, 1998: 107, *original italics*).

Johnson (1998) stresses that the concerned other cannot blame the problem user for their situation as they are suffering from a disease of addiction. In this way it hopes to depersonalise problems. In order to address the disease, the process to facilitate treatment entry is relatively simple. The concerned other recruits as many meaningful people in the problem loved one's life as possible. Collectively, and in secret, they then plan a surprise intervention where they will confront the loved one with overwhelming evidence of problematic use.

After careful planning this intervention is delivered to the 'victim' [sic] with everyone present. This meeting is chaired by one person who explains the reason for the meeting and orchestrates proceedings. Each group member takes it in turns to read a prepared speech outlining their concerns and describing specific incidents where their loved one's alcohol or drug use has caused them pain or hurt. These must be concrete events and the family member describes their emotional reactions to these moments. Responses to any objections that the problem user may make are anticipated and rehearsed in advance. The loved one is then corralled into leaving the party and attending a pre-booked appointment at a treatment centre of their choice, whilst the rest of the family seek professional help for their co-dependency (see Figure 3). 'There is a shorter, simpler way to define intervention: *presenting reality to a person out of touch with it in a receivable way.*' (Johnston, 1998: 61).

Johnson states that the intervention is effective in every case where it is delivered correctly. However, the degree of conflict that it entails can make it an unappetising strategy to many families. This approach is often felt to be too under-hand and even shaming for concerned

---

1. Meaningful persons in the life of the chemically dependent person are involved.

2. All the meaningful persons write down specific data about the events and behaviours involving the dependent person's chemical use which legitimise their concern.

3. All of the meaningful persons tell the dependent person how they feel about what has been happening in their lives, and they do it in a non-judgemental way.

4. The victim is offered specific choices – this treatment centre or that hospital.

5. Where the victim agrees to accept help, it is made available immediately.

Figure 3. Principles of the intervention (Johnston, 1998)

others to follow through to completion. For example, in the Liepman et al. (1989) experimental study of 24 cases, only seven families reached the stage of delivering the intervention, and of these six problem users subsequently entered treatment. Logan's (1983) study found better results for the intervention when combined with extensive social networks. This study also found the intervention assisted 95 per cent of 60 problem drinkers into treatment after a family intervention and has been widely cited as the definitive success rate of the intervention. However, as Landau et al. (2004) point out, this figure does not include those that declined to enter the programme or refused to commit to the intervention. They cite other studies that have demonstrated huge drop out or non-implementation rates in this approach, which can range from 70–100 per cent. Many families simply will not implement the intervention because of fear of emotional damage to both themselves and their loved one. As such, Logan's (1983) figures must be treated with caution.

Fears regarding the application of the intervention may be well-founded. The intervention appears to increase estrangement from family and higher relapse rates are found in loved ones that have had the intervention (Feinstein and Tamerin, 1972; Mattrick et al., 1998). As Stanton (2004) observed 'Too often, however, I have seen people who were the target of the Intervention describe the experience with tears welling up in their eyes. Years later, the humiliation, and the pain of betrayal, are still with them, still palpable. You can hear people read you their well-meaning letters and all, but the fact an aggregate of the folks to whom you are closest colluded to spring a tribunal on you may not easily fade away, and that is not a positive side effect.' Again, whilst the intervention was a pioneering approach to assisting concerned others facilitate change in their loved one, its intrusive and underhand approach has made it unappealing to many families and may acerbate problems of use when it is applied.

1.10 Recent Approaches for Concerned Others

It was not until the 1980s when support for concerned others was developed systematically and based on sound empirical research. This has seen a dramatic increase in the number of modalities to assist concerned others. For example, Stanton (2004) identified that only seven outcome studies were reported between 1983–1990. This figured increased by a further twelve between 1995–2004. The most influential model in the second generation of programmes for concerned others has been Community Reinforcement Training. This unilateral family therapy evolved from the emerging interest in the application of behavioural therapy techniques to the treatment of problematic substance abuse.

In the 1970s Nathan Hunt developed the Community Reinforcement Approach for problem drinkers as an alternative psychiatric admission. This model drew upon behavioural principles in an outpatient programme that tried to engineer improvements in the user's own community to reinforce abstinence from drinking. This included improving family life, employment and social and recreational life amongst others. These rewarding alternatives were contingent on the user not drinking in order to maintain change. A key development in this programme was the involvement of the concerned other, usually the wife. Initially this became part of behavioural marital therapy to increase levels of satisfaction in the drinker's relationships. However, this role was expanded further in the 'disulfiram assurance technique.' Spouses were trained to monitor and reinforce a daily dose of disulfiram, a sensitising drug that if taken in combination with alcohol causes punishing side effects such as nausea. The first study (Azrin et al., 1982) comparing standard treatment with the disulfiram assurance technique identified a dramatic effect on outcomes. Clients in the disulfiram assurance programme achieved 97 per cent days abstinence compared to 45 per cent abstinence in the traditional group. Subsequent research has shown lower outcomes, but the idea of spouse involvement in treatment has become increasingly important in the development of this approach.

These ideas were to be extended in the 1980s when a prototype intervention called Community Reinforcement Training (CRT) was developed to see if the treatment procedures developed for problem drinkers could help concerned others who's loved ones were not seeking treatment. In the very first study, Sisson and Azrin (1986) randomly assigned twelve concerned others to either the prototype Community Reinforcement Training or Al Anon treatment. The Community Reinforcement Training assisted six out of seven resistant problem drinkers to enter into treatment after an average of 7.2 sessions (58.2 days). They also found that these individuals had halved their drinking during this period. None of the drinkers in Al Anon treatment arm took up treatment. Kirby et al. (1999) multi-site study of CRT found that 64 per cent of the concerned others of problem drug users were able to motivate their loved ones into treatment compared to 17 per cent in the Twelve Step treatment arm. The possibility that treatment approaches for concerned others could be effective in motivating non-treatment seekers into treatment stimulated interest in this hitherto neglected corner of addiction work. CRT would provide the inspiration for a plethora of new approaches. The proliferation of these new models can be categorised by division into two distinct sub-groups. Some of these treatment approaches work with the concerned other to facilitate their loved one's treatment entry alone. Others combine the facilitation of treatment entry with a structured approach to improving the quality of life for the concerned other as well. For an overview of the leading models, treatment lengths and entry success (see Table 2).

1.11 Approaches Facilitating Treatment Entry Only

Treatment approaches that focus solely on supporting treatment entry remain influenced by the principles asserted by the Johnson Intervention. However, they have attempted to circumvent its more humiliating aspects by using it within a stepped care model as in the A Relational Sequence for Engagement (ARISE) programme. Formerly known as the Rochester Albany Intervention Sequential Engagement model, it dropped 'intervention' from its name due to the negative public and media opinion that has evolved regarding the Johnson intervention. ARISE utilises a slower paced and staggered approach to intervening (Landau et al., 2004). This comprises three stages of increasingly directive interventions to change. Stage I offers an informal intervention without professional assistance. Concerned others contacting the service

Table 2. Comparison of treatment outcomes for concerned other approaches

Model	Substance used	Sample size	Relationship of CO	No. sessions/ weeks	% Engaged
Community Reinforcement Training (Sisson and Azrin, 1986): A behavioural approach providing skills to assist treatment entry without confrontation, improve the CO's own life and assist the loved once in treatment.	Alcohol	12	9 wives 2 male siblings 1 daughter	7.2	86%
Co-operative Counselling (Yates, 1988): An outreach programme in response to CO calls. Loved one invited to advice service which includes information, counselling and educational materials.	Alcohol	30	11 spouses 1 partner 4 daughters 3 mothers 8 other relatives 3 friends	1–6	21% of the 19 that entered treatment
Unilateral Family Therapy (Thomas et al., 1987): Refined from CRT, the skills programme develops behaviour training and enhances coping skills. Incorporates a programmed confrontation to facilitate treatment entry combined with extensive training in relapse prevention post treatment entry.	Alcohol	25	spouses (96% female)	11–30	32%
Pressures to Change Models (Barber and Crisp, 1995): A brief intervention based on CRT and UFT, it aims to facilitate rapid treatment entry of the loved one. This is achieved through incremental pressure on the loved one building to a Johnson style intervention without secrecy. Also reinforces non-using activity with rewards.	Alcohol	23	spouses 97% female	4–6 weeks	38% of one-to-one format. 50% of group format
CRAFT (Meyers et al., 1999): An advancement of CRT, incorporates problem-solving, skills development and role-play to rehearse communication and strategies for change. Facilitates a non-confrontational treatment entry; reduces stress on CO and improves quality of life of the CO.	Drugs	62	33 mothers 2 fathers 21 spouses 4 siblings 2 offspring	12 sessions	74%
Second CRAFT study (Miller et al., 1999)	Alcohol	130		12 sessions	64%

Strategic Structural Systems Engagement (Szapocznik et al., 1988): Six levels of engagement from joining the family to ecological models of intervention based on families-of-adolescents approach.	Young drug users	108	90% mothers	1–3 sessions	93%
Intensive Parent and Youth Intervention (Donahue et al., 1998): Based on the CRT, the programme aims to increase attendance of youth offenders and parents in treatment within 2-7 days. Includes standardised telephone induction, selling advantages of engaging in treatment including positive feedback of workers and programme and benefits in alleviating punitive court sanctions. It has also been combined with telephone reminders two days prior to the appointment.	Dually diagnosed young people.	39	parents	2-hours	89% of reminder group. 60% of IPYT only group
A Relational Intervention Sequence for Engagement ARISE (Landau et al., 2001): This rapid response intervention aims to assist the quickest entry into treatment of the concerned other. A stepped intervention where the CO is coached on making contact to invited other COs and the loved one to a first session. Refusal increases intervention to a network problem-solving session and leads to a full intervention where necessary.	Drugs and alcohol	84 drug users (13 adolescents), 26 alcohol users	40% parents spouses or partners 31% offspring 4% relatives 19% non-relatives 5%	1–6 sessions	83%

are invited to attend a joint appointment accompanied by significant others as well as inviting the problem user to this first meeting. Hence there is no secrecy involved in any of the approaches. If the problem user does not attend this first session then Stage II is introduced. Working with this group of concerned others the practitioner helps them collectively assess useful strategies that may motivate the problem user into treatment. The problem user is then contacted directly by telephone at this meeting. If this fails, a gentler intervention in the Johnston mould is then implemented at Stage III. A study by Stanton (1997) found that the three step ARISE method enabled 55 per cent of drug users and 70 per cent of problem drinkers to enter treatment.

Barber and Crisp's (1995) Pressures to Change approach also recommended increasingly intensive levels of coercion on the loved one but combines them with many of the principles first developed in the CRT programme. Level 1 involves information on how people change and how to apply pressure without conflict. Level 2 consists of providing alternative sources of satisfaction to compete with use. Level 3 teaches how to exploit alcohol-related crises. Whilst Level 4 involves the establishment of a drinking contract that set limits and consequences to use.

Where these lower levels of intervention fail, the approach is stepped up, ultimately leading to the implementation of a fully-fledged intervention in the Johnson mould. Again, as none of the families in one study were willing to implement a full-blown intervention, they too softened the approach. Instead of benign confrontation by a group, the concerned other was taught to write a letter. This letter explicitly describes the concerned other's love for the problem user, how use had diminished their relationship and proffered a simple plea that the loved one should seek help. This was more acceptable to the concerned others and successful in improving the behaviour of 60 per cent of problem users within a five-week period. These alternative approaches demonstrate that an intervention can be effective, and indeed, may offer a last resort for the resistant problem user. However, it works best when the stress levels are low and the approach is mitigated by explicit gestures of love and concern for the problem user. Hence many models now prefer the term 'carefrontation' in interventions of this kind (see Fearing, 1996; 2000).

The advantage of the Pressures to Change model is that it can be delivered effectively in a variety of formats including five to six sessions of group work. Barber and Gilbertson (1998) were also able to deliver the same programme as a brief intervention. Their results confirmed that behavioural interventions were superior to traditional approaches in fostering treatment entry and improving the quality of life for the concerned other even when delivered in a variety of formats (see Table 3).

Barber and Gilbertson (1998) also demonstrated that the behaviour-based intervention could be delivered equally as well in bibliotherapy formats. Bibliotherapy describes a self-help book or manual which clients use without the assistance of professional practitioner. In this study, 12 concerned others were assigned to counselling; 15 were assigned to the self-help manuals and

Table 3. Drinkers seeking help post test (Barber and Gilbertson, 1996)

Experimental condition	Sought help	Cut down	No change
PTC Counselling	4	6	2
PTC Groupwork	4	2	6
No Treatment	0	0	12
Al-Anon	0	0	12

11 concerned others were held on a waiting list as a control group. They found little difference between the counselling and the self-help outcomes. Six of the counselling group achieved significant behavioural change; seven of the bibliotherapy group did; whilst only two of the control group achieved significant change.

The strength of these models is that they have the potential to instigate rapid treatment entry with minimum professional intervention. For example Landau et al. (2004) were able to instigates 50 per cent of their sample to go into treatment within one week, 76 per cent by the second week and 84 per cent by the third week of the intervention with the ARISE approach. The average intervention length was only 88 minutes of practitioner time. This may be more likely when a recent event has triggered crises, leading the concerned other to seek help and the loved one to contemplate change. However, a longstanding finding is that when the loved one enters treatment this event alone does not translate into improvements in the concerned other's life. As Barber and Crisp (1995: 335) noted, that despite their treatment entry successes, the Pressures to Change model failed to improve the concerned other's life. 'A disappointing result of the present study is that none of the experimental conditions reported any significant improvement in general wellbeing'. This is a very important finding. Concerned others often assume that the loved one entering treatment will resolve many of the problems that they experience. It is essential to convey to them that this is not the case and that wilful effort is still required for them to reconstruct their own lives after extended periods of stress and pressures.

1.12 Dual Approach Models

The early, promising results of the CRT model led to further development and refinement of this approach. This resulted in the Community Reinforcement and Family Therapy (CRAFT) (Meyers and Smith, 1995) a skills-based programme comprising techniques and procedures which have three principle aims. The first aim is to enable the concerned other to assist their unmotivated loved one into treatment. The second aim of CRAFT is to reduce the stress and suffering of the concerned other themselves. This includes diminishing conflict, domestic violence and stress. The third aim is to improve the quality of life of the concerned other, regardless of whether the loved one enters treatment. CRAFT incorporated additional procedures which were more focused on the needs of concerned others compared with the original CRT model.

Table 4. Comparison of family interventions (Miller et al., 1999)

	CRAFT	Johnson Intervention	Al-Anon
Treatment seekers	64%*	30%	13%
CO attendance	89%	53%	95%

The CRAFT programme has continually demonstrated superior outcomes to traditional approaches in assisting concerned others. In one study, 130 concerned others of problem drinkers were randomly assigned to CRAFT, Al Anon or the Johnson Intervention (Miller et al., 1999). Each programme was based on 12 hours of treatment with a manual-based approach. CRAFT significantly out-performed the other approaches in securing treatment entry for the problem loved one. This was achieved within 47 days of the first appointment, with the concerned others having completed 4.7 sessions on average. The CRAFT groups also showed considerable improvement in stress reduction and improvements in quality of life (see Table 4).

In comparing these outcomes it is important to note issues regarding attendance to the sessions. In the Johnston Intervention just under half of the sample dropped out of treatment. This correlates with findings that have already been reviewed: that many families are not comfortable in instigating the high degree of secrecy and conflict necessary to carry out a full-blown intervention. Interestingly, the Al Anon group showed the highest attendance rates in the study even though this did not translate into improved rates of treatment entry for the loved one. It must be recognised that Al Anon was not specifically designed to facilitate treatment entry of problem users. But the high attendance rates maintained by these families does suggest that the concerned others did find sharing their experiences with others in a similar position invaluable even if this does not in itself change their current situation.

In a second, non-controlled, CRAFT study, 62 concerned others of problem drug users were recruited into the treatment programme (Meyers et al., 1999). In this trial, 74 per cent of problem users were engaged in treatment. This was achieved within 4.8 sessions over 48 days on average. All the concerned others demonstrated significant reductions in anger, anxiety, depression and in other problems. Other studies based on CRAFT have been conducted with similar results. A more recent study (Meyers et al., 2002) compared CRAFT with CRAFT + CRA aftercare and an Al-Narc Facilitation programme based on Al Anon principles but for drug users. This research found that the CRAFT conditions successfully engaged 67 per cent of problem users and the Al-Narc engaged only 29 per cent. This study included measurements of the concerned other's functioning prior to and after treatment. Significant reductions were found in the levels of depression, stress and anger. It is important to note that these dual models, which address both treatment entry and seek to improve the life of the concerned other, significantly increase the length of the intervention. These interventions are more likely to take 3 months or more in order to achieve both aims.

In the new generation of approaches for concerned others, general patterns have been observed in the spread of treatment outcomes. Meyers et al. (2001) found that the approach was more likely to succeed when the concerned other was a parent. Not all studies have replicated this but it is a common finding. Chan's (2003) comprehensive review identified three critical features necessary for effective intervention through concerned others: the identified patient was male; the family were prepared to make a significant investment in the intervention; and the concerned other was supportive of abstinence as goal. The gender bias suggested here might simply be a reflection of the fact that it is usually the wife or mother who seeks constructive help in the majority of studies. We have found that the intervention is more successful where there is a high incentive value on the relationship with the concerned other and that women are more likely to present for the approach to intervene with male drug or alcohol use.

Within the PACT programme we have consistently found that longstanding relationships which existed prior to the onset of the problem tended to be more effective than shorter relationships that are formed after the problem use was established. At the same time these models appear effective for a range of family relationships. Programmes are effective for parents of adult problem users as well as teenage users. It has also proved effective for the partners of problem users. Currently we have not applied the programme to young carers attempting to change their parent's use. The programme could be successful for this younger group depending on the current cognitive maturity of the young person. If the young person is able to provide a psychological explanation of their parent's use, attributing it to inferred internal motivations at assessment, they may be able to implement the full programme. Components of the programme that address the young person's support needs and quality of life could be usefully adapted for young carers.

Parent and Carers Training Programme (PACT)

1.13 PACT: Programme Aims and Structure

The research reviewed demonstrates that interventions can be highly effective in assisting concerned others to facilitate their loved one's entry into treatment and simultaneously improving the concerned other's life. The approaches and research informed the development of the Parents and Carers Training programme. The existing research base suggested that it would be possible for the concerned other to influence treatment entry either through a rapid entry process (Pressures to Change) or through the development of an ongoing intervention (CRT/CRAFT). Furthermore, as treatment entry did not improve the concerned other's life by default, it would be important to include a focused programme to assist them to reconstruct their own lives (CRT/CRAFT). Once the loved one did enter treatment, the concerned other could support them in this role (Unilateral Family Therapy). And where these interventions failed, it was possible to offer a more dramatic intervention, which if delivered in a less stressful manner, could influence the most resistant loved one (Carefrontation). As such, the PACT programme synthesises elements of a wide range of disparate approaches into a more seamless

- Assist the concerned other to facilitate their loved one's entry into treatment as quickly as possible

- Support the loved one in treatment

- Reduce the stresses and pressures that they are under

- Improve the quality of life of the concerned other

Figure 4. Goals of PACT

model of intervention. This has led to the development of a skills-based, behavioural programme with a wide range of goals focusing on the concerned other and the loved one's needs. The acronym PACT was adopted in homage to this lineage for the CRT and CRAFT model to which it owes a significant debt. The goals of PACT are outlined in Figure 4.

Whilst existing models had shown significant outcomes it was felt that these models could not be imported directly into the UK treatment system without significant modification. The success demonstrated by the variants CRT/CRAFT suggested that it would be feasible to restructure these pioneering models to accommodate local factors of service delivery without compromising treatment gains. Reviewing the alternative models with varying degrees of intensity suggested that they might not necessarily be understood as separate approaches, but rather interventions that occurred along a continuum. Therefore the PACT programme can be understood as a synthesis of these highly effective approaches whereby the strengths of each modality is utilised at the most apposite moments. For example, the Pressures to Change can initiate change very quickly where existing motivation exists in the loved one. However, it does not improve the concerned other's life and may forestall should there be no motivation in the loved one. CRT/CRAFT models have demonstrated their effectiveness in offering the skills that can rally motivation in an unmotivated loved one and improve the concerned other's life. But the programme does not offer guidance on how the concerned other can support the loved one in treatment nor offers a response should this skills set fail to initiate treatment entry. Unilateral Family Therapy has devised an extensive programme to offer concerned others a relapse prevention skills base which has proven effective in supporting change. Whereas 'carefrontation', if delivered in a low stress environment, can offer a final attempt to initiate treatment entry should all other strategies fail.

Therefore, in order to accommodate the possibility of rapid treatment entry, a stepped care approach was adopted (see Sobell and Sobell, 1993). This approach stratifies treatment options into levels of intensity. This ranges from brief interventions at the treatment entry point and encompasses layers of ever intensifying levels of intervention beneath. Within this framework individuals seeking help are offered the least intensive approaches first. If these prove ineffective, the level of support is 'stepped up' with a more intensive approach (see Figure 5). In this stepped care arrangement, the concerned other presenting for services undergoes a comprehensive assessment of their needs. Within this assessment, the loved one's current levels of motivation for change are assessed. Often a crisis in the relationship between the concerned other and their loved one precipitates their seeking out professional help as well as raising concerns in the loved one regarding their own use. As such, close examination of the loved one's current readiness to change during the initial assessment might reveal a high level of current motivation to engage in treatment. If the loved one is contemplating change, it may be an opportune time to make a direct plea for them to seek out professional help whilst this internal motivation is high. This may only be possible within a short period of time. Research demonstrates that a perceived conflict between current behaviour and self-image can trigger treatment entry (see Miller and Rollnick, 2002). This occurs when an individual's actions are in contradiction to their self-image. The internal psychological discomfort this generates can drive people to amend these behaviours in order to restore their self-image. This dissonance may last up to two weeks but decreases rapidly after the initial realisation (Draycott and Dabbs, 1998). Therefore, if the loved one has made statements about the need for change within the two week period prior to the concerned other seeking help, they may be suitable for a direct request to seek out help.

If the loved one enters treatment through the rapid intervention the concerned other will still be supported by helping them reduce their stress and improving the quality of their own life. It must be remembered that the loved one's entry into treatment will not necessarily improve the life of the concerned other. Should the loved one refuse to enter treatment, or they have no current motivation, the support for the concerned other is 'stepped up' into the skills programme. CRT and CRAFT approaches have demonstrated that the concerned other can acquire the skills to precipitate treatment entry even where there is no obvious motivation in the loved one. The programme then teaches them skills to increase motivation for treatment in the loved one whilst continuing to work on improving the concerned other's life. Should the implementation of these skills still fail to elicit treatment entry the programme can be stepped up again to a carefrontation between the loved one and concerned other. Termination of the relationship may result after all options have been exhausted. The concerned other will at least know that they did all they possibility could for their loved one should this occur. However, termination may present as an issue earlier in the programme. Many concerned others come to realise that the effort required may not be reciprocated in the value of the relationship that they are fighting to restore. Termination is not seen as a treatment failure but a legitimate option for the concerned other. The programme can still continue to support them in rebuilding a new life after the relationship has ended.

This formulation can also be used in a group programme. Again, using similar principles, a group format would still require individual assessment of the concerned other's needs. Once again this may indicate the rapid treatment entry procedure where the loved one is currently demonstrating existing motivation to enter treatment. If the treatment entry is successful the concerned other may still find use in graduating up into the group work programme. The group work programme consists of two key components. The first hour of the group is open, offering the mutual support, ventilation and peer understanding that concerned others value so highly. The second hour then offers the group a range of structured interventions in order to assist them to make changes in their lives using the same techniques as described in the

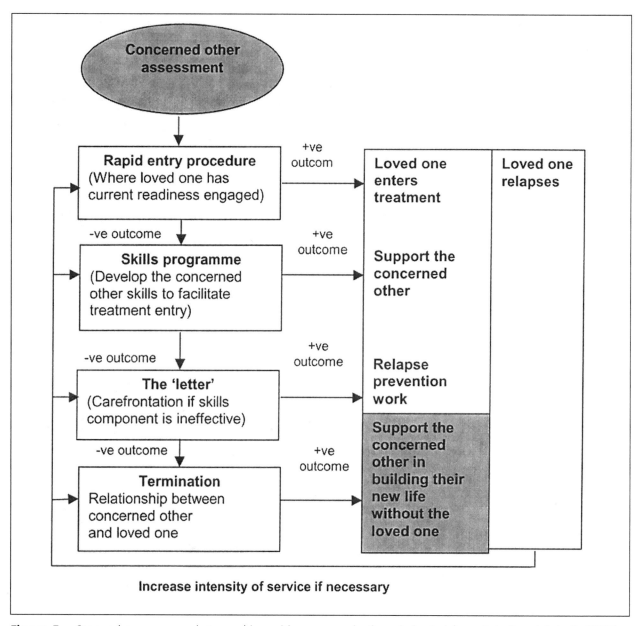

Figure 5. Stepped care approach to working with concerned others (adapted from Sobell and Sobell, 1993)

one-to-one manual. This second hour is optional for those who desire a more structured response to their situation. Individuals who need more support can then receive additional coaching in the methods should they need it. The advantages of the group format are that it offers treatment to a wider number of people when resources are limited; includes the broader mutual support that is helpful and allows the group to learn from each other's experiences in implementing the programme. The drawbacks can be that individuals get less one-to-one time; there may be issues of confidentiality and the reality is that some people do not like groups. (Please check the Russell House Publishing website for the latest details.)

It is important to recognise that concerned others do not have to work their way through every level of treatment. They can commence the programme at a higher level of support where indicated. The structure of this programme is to ensure that the opportunity of existent motivation in the loved one is not missed. The stepped care model also allows for greater flexibility in service provision as the number of levels of treatment can be modified. For example, where resources are scarce, the one-to-one skills programme could be substituted for a group skills programme using the same tools. An additional level of support could then be included to provide extra coaching for those who struggle in the group programme.

Stepped care models question the traditional notion of treatment length. The length of treatment may vary according to the needs of the presenting client. Within a stepped care framework, the PACT programme could initiate rapid treatment entry that would dramatically reduce the length of intervention to as little as six weeks or even less. This might prove to be the case where the programme is delivered early in the loved one's substance misuse career or where use has had minimal impact on the concerned other's own social functioning. Conversely, the full programme, from assessment to carefrontation should be possible in eighteen weeks. However, sometimes there are structural reasons why this is not always possible. For example, many concerned others have other responsibilities such as employment or child care which makes regular weekly meetings difficult. Many concerned others find sanctuary in employment or other aspects of their life which they are loathe to compromise. In these situations we have offered shorter time slots than an hour or have agreed to meeting over longer periods of time. For example, with some cases the frequency of appointments has not been weekly but monthly to accommodate other priorities in the concerned other's life.

We have also found that in complex cases the intervention can take longer. This is particularly true where the loved one has experienced some neurological damage, usually from alcohol abuse, which impairs their cognitive ability. These cases have taken up to two years to precipitate change. In such circumstances, practitioners are advised to offer the full programme and then retain contact with this much smaller population of concerned others who may be addressing more entrenched problems than simply drug or alcohol abuse. Again, in these cases we have offered these concerned others monthly meetings in order to continue to support them in what are often very difficult circumstances. This allows for the opportunity to review the continued application of the skills and assess progress across this period of time. Whilst these cases have demanded a greater investment of treatment time they have been successful with loved ones with more complex needs. So, in general terms the programme should be considered as an 18-week programme. Any clients exceeding this time frame should be recorded along with the therapeutic reasons why any contract has been extended. This is important in reporting figures to commissioning services and in developing consistent practice across a team.

Core elements of these programmes have also had to be adjusted or changed due to a number of factors. Firstly, the National Treatment Agency's requirement to recognise the unique and distinct needs of the concerned others demanded that any programme developed in the UK needed to provide the dual function of treatment entry and offer considerable attention to improving the concerned other's life. Further to these policy requirements, there was the need for a comprehensive clinical assessment of the concerned other's needs and structured care plans that paralleled the models of care for problematic drug and alcohol users seeking treatment. Elements of these requirements were not intrinsic to many of the evidence-based concerned other approaches. Secondly, the language used in many US models did not translate well for a more reserved British sensibility. Finally, whilst a great deal of research existed on the effectiveness of the models, the methods of application were not always articulated in a manner that lent themselves to direct practice. Any programme that works with concerned others often breaks with many of the accepted practices of the field. Practitioners require that any approach is as concrete and specific as possible in order to direct them when working. Over the course of three years of evaluation of the original PACT programme, numerous amendments were also made in the light of feedback from clients, practitioners and by reviewing trends and patterns in the clinical outcomes.

An initial twelve-month study was implemented to assess whether the PACT programme would be effective in addressing the needs of concerned others. This study was not intended to be a gold standard, random control trial. Instead it was a pilot to examine the feasibility of delivering services for concerned others in a community setting, both in terms of demand for the service and its efficacy in general practice. Concerned others could elect for either the PACT programme or generalised counselling models. The same worker delivered both interventions in order to account for any alliance differences. During this period only 20 per cent of clients in the generic counselling arm assisted their loved ones into treatment compared to the 100 per cent of the PACT clients. The generic counselling figure was probably artificially high. The clients often reported feeling stuck and so occasional use was made of elements of the PACT programme in these situations. Whilst this did cause some treatment contamination, it also suggested that elements of the PACT can be incorporated into other counselling approaches but better results are achieved when delivered as complete programme.

The outcomes of the PACT programme have declined slightly over time but remain comparable to other studies, helping 90 per cent of clients to get their loved ones into treatment. The programme has also demonstrated significant reductions in stress and dissatisfaction in the concerned other, even amongst family members who reported chronic depression at the outset of treatment. The programme has also contributed to substantially improving the life of the concerned other. In one sample measure, over 70 per cent of concerned others demonstrated clinically significant improvement in social function. A proportion of loved ones could not initially access treatment because of pre-existent brain damage caused though long term alcohol abuse. However, with extended support even these loved ones initiated changes in drinking. In such instances, formalising a psychiatric diagnosis is necessary to seek financial and respite support for the concerned other. Elements of the programme which are designed to improve the concerned other's life remain very important in assisting them manage the profound stresses that this can generate.

In our initial trial the programme was delivered from a manual to ensure a high fidelity to the model. This meant that the procedures had to work well on the page and provide a clear framework to deliver each intervention. The success of the previous concerned other programmes which had utilised a bibliotherapy format alone made us confident that this was possible. This conferred greater attention to the use of work sheets in sessions. The concerned others in the feasibility trial reported that having a workbook provided a useful focus in the session. Furthermore, the fact that they could take the workbook home, write up notes and refer to it, was invaluable in helping them maintain interventions. So this element of the programme has been retained even in the expansion of the service. Each concerned other can have their own workbook where they can continue to practice the core skills and review session content.

1.14 PACT: Assessment

It will be necessary to conduct a comprehensive assessment of the concerned other's needs. This should only be conducted after induction processes are completed and the concerned other has made an informed choice to enrol in the programme. Induction procedures involve several key elements. The concerned other should be invited to describe the circumstances that led them to seeking professional help first before initiating any structured procedure. It is likely that a crisis precipitated their entry into treatment, even after battling with the problem for a long time before seeking help. They may be in shock, feel overwhelmed or even fatalistic regarding their situation. Normalising these responses is important. Once the concerned other's emotional charge dissipates, it is possible to explain the programme to them. This can done by encouraging them to review what they have tried already and how helpful these proved to be. This will also give the practitioner some insight into where the concerned other is in terms of their response to the loved one's use, whether they are in the active, passive or withdrawal phases. Considering the energy that the concerned other has expended so far, it is important to ask them whether they feel it is time to try another strategy. Any data collected on the success of the programme can be given to the concerned other. This should be followed by an explanation of how the programme works and, more importantly, what will be expected of the concerned other in this process. Any policy issues such as confidentiality or data-protection can also be explained at this point. It should also be emphasised that at no point will the concerned other ever be asked to do anything that they do not feel completely comfortable with. As a skills-based programme it does demand sustained, wilful effort on their part. They should not be pressured into accepting the offer of the programme. Instead, the possible benefits and costs of engaging should be evaluated objectively. If the concerned other is still uncertain, they can be advised to sample the programme to see if it helpful for them without any long-term commitment.

The concerned others should always be informed of the purpose of the assessment, how long it takes to conduct and how it will help them, prior to starting the process. This will help them understand its necessity and relevance. Assessment should not be considered a one-off activity but provide the framework for subsequent treatment of both the concerned other and the problem user. It should be explicitly recognised that the concerned other has invaluable insight into their loved one's using behaviour, which often establishes itself in highly predictable

Table 5. Functions of comprehensive assessment

Assessment	Function
Relationship between the concerned other and the loved one	This may reveal the relationships that are most likely to impact on the loved one's use
The evolution of the substance misuse problem	Allow the concerned other to ventilate emotional responses and have their experience acknowledged
The loved one's social function	This will give an indication of treatment progress. The poorer the loved one's social function and longer-term exclusion the longer treatment required. Offers insight into the factors that the concerned other feels are sustaining their loved one's use
Current pattern of loved one's use	Estimates the frequency of the loved one's use in order to create a baseline measure which can be compared to follow-up score during treatment
Dependency	This criteria will help establish whether the loved one exhibits any sign of physical dependency that will need to be accounted for in any subsequent treatment. It can also offer the concerned other feedback on the severity of the loved one's problem
Key indicators for the concerned other	Identifies the hardships that the concerned other currently faces and forms the basis of their care plan
Dependents and abuse	Identifies any issues relating to child protection, POVA or the protection of the concerned other as a priority
Readiness and treatment history	May indicate whether current motivation exists in the loved one and whether any previous treatment experience needs to be accounted for
Concerned other's priorities	Allows the concerned other to prioritise those aspects of the programme that they feel are most important

patterns. Obtaining the most exact indicators and precise detail is helpful in creating deep understanding of the current situation for both the concerned other and their loved one. The comprehensive assessment has several functions (see Table 5).

Some commentators (Edwards et al., 2003) have warned that the concerned other are susceptible to distorting their loved one's use to ventilate their own feeling or co-opt the practitioner. This has not been evidenced in our experience where concerned others have produced very detailed and specific information that has proved invaluable and reliable in basing interventions. However, this possibility should not be totally discounted where discrepancies and inconsistencies arise in their representations.

An assessment that is conducted well can be therapeutic in itself. It offers the concerned other a chance to organise their own understanding in a structured and coherent manner. The assessment will allow for the identification of, and exploration of critical issues that are affecting their life and can enhance their understanding of the exact nature of their loved one's problems. Whilst the assessment process will not reveal anything new to the concerned other, the methodical organisation of this material can be emotionally overwhelming. It is important to remember that the act of seeking professional help is often interpreted by concerned others as having already failed their loved one, eliciting a profound guilt. Assessment must be handled with sensitivity, empathy and acknowledgment. Explicitly recognising their struggles, normalising their experiences and reminding the concerned other that the programme is helpful in changing this situation can help stop them from feeling utterly defeated at the outset. Whilst demanding, if the assessment process is handled well, it can be a cathartic experience of ventilating thoughts, feelings and frustrations that have been contained, sometimes for years, and establish the critical bond between client and practitioner.

Often the concerned other is seeking explanations as to why their loved one uses. This issue often emerges in the assessment process. In Western societies there is a popular assumption that drug and alcohol using behaviours are either driven by the biology of the individual or are a result of upbringing. Research has consistently failed to provide one causal explanation that can account for the development of drug and alcohol problems. The evolution of addictions is a complex interplay of many variables. Psychology, family history, family consumption, lack of alternative sources of satisfaction, social environment, peer influence, circumstance, trauma, disconnection from others and coping deficits all contribute. The more risk factors an individual is exposed to the greater their vulnerability to problematic use (see Harris, 2005). These risk factors are located in a wide range of sources from the biological, psychological, social and cultural niches which we inhabit. Popular explanations of addiction are attractive because of their simplicity rather than their accuracy. This information can be helpful to concerned others who are often racked with a sense of guilt for their loved one use. It is also worth recognising that even if we understood why a loved one was taking drugs or alcohol problematically, it would not necessarily change that reality or automatically alleviate the concerned other's emotional response to the hurts that substance abuse has caused them. Regardless of this, concerned others are tempted to pour over the causes of the behaviour and implicate themselves as responsible. Too much introspection may acerbate depression and feelings of helplessness even further. It is important to stress to the concerned other that they are not to blame for their loved one's use, but they can help influence it. It is more useful to invest their energy into this influence than the imponderable enterprise of establishing why there is a problem.

1.15 PACT: A Behavioural Ethos

The PACT programme itself is based upon a behavioural approach to treatment. Behavioural approaches originate in a very different tradition to introspective or emotionally expressive counselling that attempt to reconcile the inner conflicts in the clients mind. Early pioneers of behaviourism advocated that the study of human nature should be subject to the same rigorous observation and testing as any other scientific discipline. They were concerned that the central focus of psychology and psychotherapy was based upon speculative ideas and intangible concepts such as 'mind.' They were concerned that these inferences were not open to scientific testing or validation. Instead of mind, behaviourist looked to what could be objectively assessed and measured. This meant that they would limit themselves primarily to the observation of actual behaviour itself.

At the simplest level, they suggested that human action was not driven by unconscious conflicts but by the consequences that behaviour produced. In an overly simplified example, a farmer goes into his orchard in autumn and begins to shake one of his apple trees forcibly. A traditional psychotherapist might interpret this action as a metaphor of unresolved unconscious conflicts in the farmer that are deep 'rooted' issues relating to their family 'tree.' As such, the behaviour is a reflection of these inner turmoils. A behavioural therapist would instead ask what are the consequences of the farmer's behaviour? The behaviour of shaking the tree causes apples to fall, which he then sells. As such, they would suggest that the farmer's behaviour is governed by the desired consequence of harvesting apples. Behaviour approaches are therefore primarily concerned with specific behaviours and the consequences that these actions produce. If the consequences of a behaviour are desirable, it will increase the frequency of the behaviour that produced them. If the consequences of the behaviour are undesirable, it will decrease the frequency of the behaviour that produced them. The more profound the desirable or undesirable consequences, the greater the influence it exerts on the frequency of behaviour.

We refer to the influence that consequences have on behaviour as *operant conditioning* (Skinner, 1938). Operant conditioning describes a learning process. As we explore the world around us, we identify and repeat behaviours that bring us desired rewards and we learn to identify and stop behaviours that cause us undesirable discomfort. Behaviour can become so automatic that it acquires the status of a habit. Hence memory and expectations do play a role in this process. However, the important distinction of the behavioural approach is that it does not assume that behaviours are the expression of unresolved conflict in the person's mind as in the Freudian tradition. Rather, the individual has learned that certain behaviours in certain environments bring about rewards or punishments. As such, behaviours are seen as functional. The function of any given behaviour is determined by the consequences that they generate. If we wish to understand a specific behaviour we can simply analyse where it occurred, what behaviour was enacted and what consequences were elicited. Careful analysis of the behaviour can isolate its function. This functional analysis can then be used to change the target behaviour (see Figure 6).

This suggests that behaviour is not purely a product of the client's own thought processes but is governed by the interaction between the individual and their environment. Behaviour can be understood as the activity that links the individual to their environment. This is because the individual behaves in certain ways to bring about specific consequences from the environments they inhabit. This distinction is important. Understanding human behaviour in this way

1. Identify the external and internal triggers that reliably occur with the presence of the behaviour.

2. Identify the consequences that reliably follow the problem behaviour.

3. Identify whether the environment influences the control exerted over both antecedents and consequences.

4. Formulate a hypothesis of the factors maintaining the behaviour.

5. Identify alternative behaviours that can perform the same functions as the behaviour target for change.

Figure 6. Assessing the function of behaviour (Based on Repp et al., 1997)

broadens the terrain of possible interventions because behavioural therapy is not only interested in the person but also in the behaviour and the environment in which they operate. As such, we are no longer restricted to having to engage the mind of the individual in a way that fosters their insight into the necessity of making change. Instead we can change the behaviour by influencing the environment where the behaviour occurs. This is because if the environment is altered to produce a different range of consequences, the behaviour will decrease regardless of the intentions of the individual. For example, if we return to the over simplified example of the farmer tending his orchard. Let us suggest it has been a terrible season for apple growing and his trees produce no fruit at all. The farmer soon learns that the behaviour of shaking trees no longer produces the desired consequences of apple falling. He may check several trees. He may become increasingly aggressive in his tree shaking. But after a short period of time with no fruit falling he will cease the behaviour regardless of his desire for apples. The behaviour stops because it no longer produces the desired consequences. A change in the environment can therefore change an individual's behaviour regardless of their personal intentions.

In this case example, the behaviour ceases because of fluke weather conditions. But the farmer's behaviour could also be changed through the interventions of others. Let us say that during one season there is a global apple mountain but a global shortage of pears. Governments wish to discourage farmers from growing yet more apples and instead increase pear production. They do this by introducing an exorbitantly high apple tax. Every apple that is picked will incur a prohibitively expensive tax levy. On the other hand, every pear produced is exempted from any tax and financial incentives are offered to plant pear trees. The farmer will soon change his crop regardless of how much he loves growing apples. The consequences of apple harvesting are no longer desirable but have become positively punishing because of these changes in the environment (taxation). When once rewarding behaviours bring about increasingly punishing consequences, their frequency will decrease regardless of the internal hopes of the person. Instead our farmer grows pears because the consequences of doing so are simply more desirable.

Our behaviour is constantly influenced by external forces all the time. We can increase a given behaviour by making it more rewarding and we can decrease a given behaviour by making the consequences more punishing. Coupons, two for the price of one, loyalty cards and discounts are all consequences aimed at increasing purchasing behaviour. No one shows great interest in a new supermarket opening, but when a celebrity launches it, it may attract a crowd. Wages, bonuses, time-and-a-half for overtime, performance-related pay are all forms of consequences designed to increase work behaviours. Pocket money, borrowing the car, treats for passing exams, cooking a meal for a friend who has done you a favour may reward a host of behaviours in our personal life. Conversely, heavy taxation and a smoking ban on cigarettes, green taxes on aeroplane flights, grounding children, fines for speeding, decreases in pay for frequent sickness at work or prison sentences for criminal behaviour are all punishing consequences that are aimed at decreasing certain behaviours. In this way we are not introspective beings that act out our deep conflicts. We are all locked into a dynamic relationship with the environments we occupy. Here we act and react to events, opportunities and people that surround us. The medium of this activity is our behaviour. Our behaviour links our wants to the environments we occupy. And in return, it is the rewarding or aversive consequences that follow our actions that establish, shape and sustain these behaviours.

The same principles apply in addressing drug and alcohol use. There is a strong tendency to assume that it is either the powerful effect of drugs and alcohol on the human brain or a deep psychological problem which accounts for problematic use. These causes locate consumption solely in the problem user and beyond the reach of any concerned other. Certainly these are contributory factors but they are not the only factors in consumption. Drugs and alcohol use produces a wide range of consequences that spans every area of the problem user's life. There are biological and psychological aspects to use but also relational and social dimensions. These consequences are not located in the user but in their social environment. As such, they are susceptible to the influence of others.

This has been demonstrated in a number of experiments. In a study by Cohen et al. (1971), it was possible to moderate alcohol consumption even in the case of chronic alcoholics. Problem drinkers who restricted their alcohol consumption to under five ounces a day were rewarded with access to privileges such as being able to earn money, use a private telephone, have reading material or engage in recreational activities. If they drank heavily, these privileges were withdrawn. By modifying the consequences in this way alcohol consumption dropped significantly. Interestingly, when these problem drinkers were allowed free access to all these alternative rewards, regardless of their drinking level, it did not produce any reductions in consumption. Only when these rewards were contingent on moderate drinking did this have the effect of reducing consumption.

The same principles have also been successfully applied to informal environments. For example, in a pioneering experimental study by Mertens and Fuller (1964), it was possible to stop a problem drinker's consumption of alcohol by making changes to his natural social environment. When the identified patient drank, he had enjoyed the desirable consequences of intoxication *and* the social interactions with others. However, by having people in his social environment 'cold shoulder' him when he consumed alcohol, they introduced a negative consequence to drinking. In these new conditions, drinking is causing the undesired consequence of social withdrawal. Alternatively, consuming soft drinks did produce the desirable consequence of social interaction. The persistent application of this new set of favourable consequences associated with consuming soft drinks began to influence behaviour. Hence, alcohol consuming behaviour decreased whilst soft drink consumption increased because of this change in environmental consequences. This occurs without having to engage the identified individual in an explicit dialogue in order to elicit change. By simply altering the consequences of consumption the behaviour declines.

These studies demonstrate that despite popular opinion, problematic consumption of drugs and alcohol can be greatly influenced by altering the environmental consequences in which they are consumed. As the concerned other shares the same environment as the problem using loved one, or has a high frequency of contact within them, they are in an ideal position to implement changes that alter the consequences of use. In this way they can have a significant influence on their loved one's consumption. To support concerned others to develop the skills to achieve this, practitioners must have a deep understanding of the specific consequences that sustain or diminish drug and alcohol consumption. The more we understand these consequences, the greater influence we can exert over changing them.

1.16 Reinforcement and Substance Misuse

Drug and alcohol consumption can be considered to be driven by the consequences that follow the use of drugs and alcohol. The most obvious consequence of using is the feeling of intoxication that substances produce when drank, smoked, injected or swallowed. However, these powerful psychoactive effects are not the only consequences. Drugs and alcohol can also alleviate stress or relieve pressure. They can cause physical sickness and withdrawal. And they can exclude the individual from important relationships and social networks. Whilst these consequences are both rich and varied, it is important to note that they are always specific to the individual user. What is rewarding for one person is not necessarily rewarding to another. For example, one person appreciates their alcohol use because it offers them social contact. Another person drinks in isolation because alcohol soothes the pressures of a failing business. One young cannabis user enjoys the buzz of smoking weed, whilst another feels the drug makes them more creative. Likewise, the punishing consequences also vary from individual to individual. One person may experience the threat of losing an important relationship in their life as punishing. Another person might experience the loss of social status as difficult. Whilst another person finds that deterioration in their health compels them to stop using. Drug and alcohol use creates a cascade of multiple consequences, some of which the user experiences as enriching and others as damaging. Each individual is unique in what consequences they value in their using experience and in what consequences they abhor.

These types of consequences are very distinctive and affect the user's motivation in different ways. The desire to feel the pleasure of intoxication or to alleviate stresses can both increase consumption of drug and alcohol use but for very different reasons. Likewise, physical withdrawal or social rejection may decrease use but once again for different reasons. Understanding these different types of consequence is essential if we are to have the optimum influence over consumption. In behavioural therapy the consequences of behaviour are categorised into sub-types, depending upon whether they increase or decrease behaviour. *Reinforcers* are the specific consequences that *increase* the behaviour that preceded them. *Punishers* are specific consequences that *decrease* a behaviour that preceded them. For example, if you were given a chocolate M & M for each page of this book that you read, and this increased your rate of reading, M & Ms would be a reinforcer. If M & Ms had no effect on your reading then it would not be a reinforcer. However, if the receipt of M & Ms reduced the rate at which you read, it would be a punisher for you. It is important to note that this is not saying whether it should or should not, or whether it is a good or a bad thing. Behavioural approaches are simply concerned with the frequency of behaviour. If the frequency of a behaviour increases, it is being reinforced. If the frequency of a behaviour decreases, then it is being punished.

The consequences of behaviour can be divided again, based on whether these consequences add or remove something from the individual's environment. Consequences that add to the individual are defined as 'positive' whilst those that subtract are defined as 'negative.' Hence 'positive' reinforcers increase behaviours by adding a desirable consequence. Whilst negative reinforcers increase behaviours because they remove undesirable consequences. In contrast, 'positive' punishments decrease the frequency of behaviours by adding undesirable consequences. 'Negative' punishments reduce the frequency of behaviour by removing something desirable. This can be more than a little confusing at first glance. Review Table 6, which describes examples of different consequences in order to understand these categories fully.

Reviewing this table we can see the difference between positive and negative reinforcers. Items in Box A and B both increase the behaviour but positive reinforcers do so through adding a reward. Negative reinforcers do so by removing a negative consequence. Punishers always decrease behaviour (Box C and D). Again, they do so by either adding a hostile consequence or removing a desired reward from the individual. The classic mistake practitioners make is confusing a negative reinforcer with a punisher. A negative reinforcer increases behaviour precisely because people are motivated to *avoid* the negative consequence. So, we would not consider applying sun cream as punishing as it enables us to avoid an undesirable consequence of sunburn. As we wish to avoid such painful consequences we *increase* the rate in which we apply sun cream.

Based on this perspective, we can understand the frequency of drug and alcohol consumption as the net result of these competing consequences. For example, when the reinforcers of consumption are high and the punishers are low, individuals will increase or maintain their use. Conversely, as the punishing consequences of use rise and the reinforcers decline, use will decrease (see Figure 7).

Table 6. Examples of different reinforcers and punishers of use

A. Positive Reinforcers *increase* the behaviour by *adding* desirable consequences.	C. Positive Punishments *decrease* the frequency of behaviour by *adding* undesirable consequence.
The consequence of drinking alcohol adds a desirable taste.	The consequence of taking drugs can add the undesirable feeling of withdrawal.
The consequences of drinking alcohol adds a desired feeling of intoxication.	The consequence of drinking alcohol can add the undesirable experience of blackouts.
The consequence of taking a drug adds a desirable feeling of invincibility.	The consequences of drug use can add the undesirable prison sentence.
The consequence of drinking alcohol adds a sense of belonging with other drinkers.	The consequences of alcohol can add the undesirable physical illnesses.
The consequence of taking a drug adds a desirable feeling of excitement and danger.	The consequences of taking drugs can add undesirable conflict with loved ones.
B. Negative Reinforcers *increase* a behaviour by *removing* something undesirable.	**D. Negative Punishments *decrease* a behaviour by *removing* something desirable.**
The consequences of taking a drug removes undesired pain.	The consequences of drug-taking may result in the loss of desired social contact.
The consequences of drinking alcohol removes undesired boredom.	The consequences of drinking alcohol can cause a loss of desired self-respect.
The consequences of taking a drug removes undesirable feelings of stress.	The consequence of taking a drug can lead to the loss of desired wider life experience.
The consequences of drinking remove the undesirable consequences of physical withdrawal.	The consequence of drinking alcohol can result in the loss of desired driving licence.
The consequences of taking a drug removes the undesirable awareness of conflict.	The consequences of taking a drug can result in a loss of desired cherished beliefs.
The consequences of drinking alcohol removes the undesirable feeling of guilt.	The consequences of drinking can result in a loss of desired self-control.

1.17 Reinforcement and Change

Consequences of drug and alcohol use are not static. They shift and change over time. Initially the user may only feel the positive rewarding benefits of use such as having fun with friends, feeling the excitement of intoxication or enhancing their identity. Over time the increasingly punishing consequences begin to emerge and take over the experience. This might include physical withdrawal, conflict with family, rejection or the loss of a job. Now use can take a different form, drugs and alcohol can become increasingly negatively reinforced as people continue to use in order to stave off these hostile consequences. They use to alleviate stress, pain or emotional overwhelming. As we saw earlier, using a substance to alleviate withdrawal symptoms is an indication of the severest form of physical dependence. These shifts in consequences may occur gradually and drive the individual through a succession of stages regarding their awareness of their need for change and their ability to sustain it. This can be

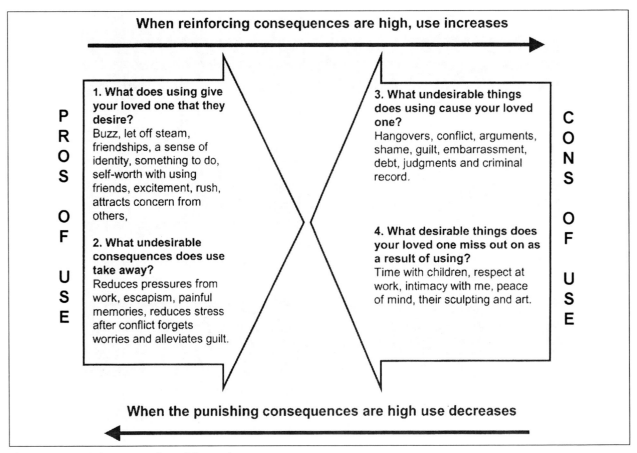

Figure 7. Reinforcers and punishers of use

understood as the Stages of Change (Prochaska et al., 1994). The Stages of Change has been widely accepted in the treatment field as a framework to understand change processes. It describes an invariant sequence of behaviours that people engage in when making change. These patterns of behaviour are defined by stages. Initially people are regarded as *Pre-contemplative* towards change as they are not making efforts or recognising the need for change. Increasing awareness of the consequences and problems of use elicits increased awareness and self re-evaluation of the behaviour as they enter *Contemplation*. Here they must make a commitment to change and then establish how they will implement it. This *Preparation* stage is defined by planning and reviewing options before trying out these plans in the *Action* stage. In the action stage people must actually implement these plans and act differently. Finally they must *Maintain* these behaviours despite obstacles and setbacks. However, it is important to note that most people are not successful in their first attempt at change. Many will *Relapse* back into the behaviour several times before they successfully manage stable recovery. Research shows people tend to cycle through these stages, making increasing gains with every change attempt. The Stages of Change provides an important conceptual framework in understanding recovery processes and, as such, practitioners should ensure that they are familiar with the detail of the model (see Harris, 2007).

Within the realm of working with concerned others whose loved ones are unmotivated, it becomes increasingly important that the practitioner has a clear understanding of this change process, especially the early stages (Prochaska et al., 1994). However, it is important to recognise that the model is limited. The Stages of Change describes the sequence of behaviours exhibited by individuals who are at various stages of implementing change. It does not describe what drives the need for change.

The need for change is influenced by a shift in consequences. Initially individuals are pre-contemplative about change because they either experience no negative consequences or they do not recognise the negative consequences of use. For example, many people drink too much because they are unaware of safe drinking limits or the long-term problems associated with higher consumption. People may drink or use drugs with other high-consuming peers which normalises many of the adverse reactions that they experience. Alternatively, heavy users may also fail to recognise the consequences because they experience negatively punishing consequences from consumption as opposed to positively punishing ones. It is not that bad things happen when they are using but rather the good things in life stop. Promising relationships end prematurely, they are passed over for professional advancement because they are not perceived as reliable, friends begin to disassociate with them as the user becomes an alcohol or drug bore. This is a more insidious process where people do not recognise these better opportunities passing them by as vividly as they might notice stresses, trauma or profound physical consequences. This sub-group of pre-contemplators are referred to as *reluctant* pre-contemplators. As these individuals primarily lack awareness of their situation they are often highly responsive to objective feedback and information (DiClemente, 1991).

Other pre-contemplative users recognise the consequences of their consumption but understand the consequences in different ways. It is important to remember that reinforcers and punishers are unique to each person. What is punishing and worrisome for one person is desirable and rewarding to another. For example, some pre-contemplative users recognise the punishing consequences of their consumption but appreciate these risks as part of their identity. These *rebellious* users are often younger and attached to a youth sub-culture that characterises itself by being very 'street.' In these peer groups, risk-taking offers status in a deviant lifestyle. Hence the punishing consequences of consumption become valued as a badge of honour for these individuals. High-risk combinations of substances, near-miss overdoses or dangerous volumes of consumption may positively reinforce a sense of self as the 'outsider' in these peer groups. Treatment's failure to help them can also serve to support their outsider role and provide further reinforcement in portraying them as too hard to reach.

In opposition to this, some pre-contemplators are individuals who do not see themselves as the type of person who has a problems with drugs or alcohol. These individuals tend to have a higher social status and find the idea that they would be the type of person who has problem with use as simply too unconscionable to bear. These *rationalising* pre-contemplators are liable to justify, diminish or argue with any evidence that they have a problem because it feels too injurious to their sense of self. They fear treatment because it is stigmatising to their social status.

Finally there are the *resigned* users. These are individuals who have recognised that they have problems, have made strenuous efforts to change but failed in that process and returned to use. Ironically the *resigned* users are those who did really well in the previous change attempt. This success can increase the magnitude of their despair when they do subsequently lapse. In an attempt to diminish this sense of crushing personal defeat the individual user can fall into the trap of attributing their failure to fate or to forces beyond their control. Hence their failure becomes perceived as evidence of their true nature which cannot be changed. This is the individual who presents as the 'addict' or 'junkie' or lays claim to an 'addictive personality.' As such, they have come to define themselves by what they do rather than who they feel they really are. This resignation alleviates a deep sense of failure. It is not that they do not see they have profound problems, but they lack of belief that they can change them which disables their motivation. These individuals tend to have extensive previous treatment experience and report having tried everything to no avail. These individuals are therefore pessimistic about treatment and see themselves as beyond reach (see Table 7).

The shift from pre-contemplation to contemplation of change occurs when the consequences of use outweigh the perceived benefits of consumption. Research that examines why people changed their problematic drug and alcohol use continually reiterates this shift. For example, in Klingemann's (1991) study of individuals who initiated change without professional help, these alcohol- and heroin-using individuals described several varieties of this process. For some it was the experience of an extremely negative event, such as a life threatening experience or the experience of profound deprivation. This is similar to the idea of hitting rock bottom: a

Table 7. Typology of pre-contemplation (based on DiClemente, 1991)

Sub-groups	Definition
Reluctant	• novice users • lack awareness • not yet experiencing negative consequences of use
Rebellious	• risk is a badge of identity • affiliated to distinctive sub-culture lifestyle • common in adolescence • drug and alcohol offer identity where a sense of self is weak
Rationalising	• diminish or justify their use • problems are attributed to others • tend to have a higher social status, which is threatened by problem
Resigned	• longer term users • aware they have severe problems • lack the confidence that they can change • define themselves by their behaviour as opposed to their values • label themselves as 'addict,' 'junkie' or 'alcoholic'

profound crisis that demands the user change. Others described a more gradual process, such as the 'pressure sensitive' cases. They experienced an ultimatum from an important relationship. Here the individual had to choose between their use or a loved one. Other individuals described being at a 'cross-roads' where a life-changing choice had to be made. Down one road was life and being substance-free, whilst the other road led to drugs, alcohol and death.

In these examples, the decisional balance to change was tipped by increasingly punishing consequences. However, others also describe how access to a more rewarding life opportunity influenced their decision to change. New relationships or job offers were more important than using and so drugs and alcohol were disregarded in favour of these more enriching alternatives. External pressures figured highly in these accounts of change, which were similar whether they were problem drinkers or drug users. These shifts have also been reported in numerous other studies (see Touchfield, 1981; Ludwig, 1985; Stall and Beirnaki, 1986). It appears that problem use changes when either the punishing consequences of use outweigh the benefits, or when the user perceives that they are losing out on opportunities which they value more highly.

1.18 Principles of Treatment Entry

It is important to remember that in contemplation people still have not made a decision to change but are still evaluating it. The competing rewards of use versus the increasingly punishing consequences tends to leave the individual user feeling torn regarding change. We describe this as ambivalence, where the individual has contradictory emotions about the need for change. On the one hand drugs and alcohol have damaged their life and yet at the same time it is their only source of comfort and alleviates their pain. Miller and Rollnick (2002) observed that ambivalence is the initial signal that change is unfolding. However, when the status quo of benefits and cost of use remains evenly balanced the problem user can get trapped in a terminal contemplative state. In this way the problem is not the drug or alcohol use in itself but the fact that the user is stuck between the equalised forces of attraction and dissatisfaction with use. Resolving ambivalence is the central problem in motivation for change because it paralyses the change process. If we can shift this ambivalence we can trigger change. This provides the foundation for concerned others to tip the balance. As they share the same environment with the problem user, it is possible for them to influence the consequences of use. If they can reduce the benefits of use and increase the punishing consequences, they can disturb the status quo of consumption. We can do this by the application of four broad strategies (see Figure 8).

It is important to examine these four principles in detail as they are the engine of changing a loved one's use. Drugs and alcohol have very powerful and reinforcing properties. We cannot readily negate these effects. However, we can compete with them by programming alternative rewarding activities that coincide with times of use. It is important to ensure that we identify

---

- The concerned can *reduce* the positive reinforcers of consumption by providing competing rewards at times when their loved one typically uses.

- The concerned other can *reduce* the negative reinforcers of consumption by reducing conflict between the problem user and themselves.

- The concerned other can *increase* the positive punishments of use by identifying and disabling interventions that reduce, diminish or alleviate the stresses associated with their loved one's use.

- The concerned other can *increase* the negative punishments of use by withdrawing themselves and planned rewards in the light of their loved one using.

Figure 8. Principles of initiating change

alternative activities that the loved one finds reinforcing. This demands a careful assessment of the kind of activities the loved one enjoys. This will differ from person to person but the concerned other's knowledge of their loved one can provide a rich resource for ideas. In order to do this, the practitioner must remember that reinforcers are extremely specific. The classic mistake practitioners make is to confuse a category with a reinforcer. For example, we might consider food as a reinforcer but it is not. Food is far too broad a category. There is a vast difference between Belgian chocolate and boiled cabbage. The reinforcer would be the exact item of food that an individual most desired, whether it be an English breakfast, homemade pop corn or chicken chow mien. 'Spending time with a spouse' is not a reinforcer as it is too general. 'Taking my partner to the restaurant where we got engaged' is far more specific. Working with the concerned other to identify the specific reinforcers that are motivational for the loved one becomes essential in constructing attractive alternatives. Consider Table 8, and the distinction between a category and a reinforcer. Also notice how we can enhance the reinforcer to make it even more desirable to ensure maximum affect. This ability to maximise the value of specific reinforcers is important in identifying rewards for the concerned other and loved one alike.

These rewards can be enhanced to try to maximise the experience and generate sufficient attraction to compete with use. Once identified, these other rewarding activities can be offered when the loved one would typically use drugs and alcohol. The loved one now faces a dilemma: to use drugs or alcohol or engage in the non-using but desirable behaviour. This compromises the hold that drugs or alcohol may have over the loved one's life as a sole source of satisfaction, impeding the monopoly of consumption. It is important that these rewards are only made available when the loved one does not use. As we have seen, consumption will only decrease when rewards are contingent on non-use. Giving rewards and allowing consumption will not diminish use.

Reinforcers are not limited to the material but include relationships, beliefs and commodities (see Table 9). A reinforcer is simply a consequence that is valued by the individual and therefore can be drawn from a wide range of sources. The application of competing rewards is

Table 8. Examples of categories and reinforcers

Category	Reinforcer	What would make this even better?
Books	New Terry Pratchet novel	Reading it in bed with a mug of hot chocolate
Gardening	Building a pond	Going to a specialist centre for fish
Food	Steak	Barbeque on Saturday night with family
Sport	Going to see your football team	Tour of the ground before the match
Time with young children	Watching them imagine stories	Taking them to the park with the dinosaur statues
Peace of mind	Going to church	Sunday Mass at the cathedral

Table 9. Types of reinforcement

Types	Examples
Commodities	Goods such as books, food, objects, trophies
Social	Affection, respect, praise from a loved one, encouragement, intimacy and closeness
Activities	Hobbies and pastimes, such as listening to music, collecting or watching TV Can extend social reinforcement by engaging in activities with others such as camping, team sports, dinner party
Tokens	Money or vouchers that can be redeemed for reinforcers of another kind, ie pocket money to buy a desired toy
Covert	Thoughts, beliefs and self-evaluations that encourage us to act, persevere or feel good about ourselves

demanding on the concerned other. Therefore they must feel comfortable in delivering the alternative reward and they should enjoy the activity as well.

The use of rewards in treatment does attract a great deal of controversy. It is often seen as a morally dubious form of bribery. The assumption is that people 'ought' to change for higher moral reasons not because there is a pay-off for doing so. It should be recognised that bribery is applied to the pay off for offensive behaviours. Rewarding pro-social behaviour is common in our society through salaries, bonuses, recognition, promotions and other forms of approval. As such, the use of rewards is no more a bribe than wages for working are. Secondly, clinical research has demonstrated that people who make successful changes rely heavily upon rewards to reinforce the changes that they make for a short period of time. For example, women who do not put on weight when giving up smoking are at higher risk of relapse. The temporary substitution of an unhealthy behaviour for a less damaging one appears to be an essential transitory phase in the change process. Within traditional psychotherapy this has been interpreted as 'symptom substitution.' It is assumed that the underlying psychological problems of the individuals are just being expressed in a different way and so the person remains actively problematic. However, this is just an assumption. There is no evidence to support this idea as a clinical reality. The use of alternative rewards for a short period of time is an essential component in effective change (Prochaska et al., 1994). By use of the rewards the concerned other will begin to shape a new behaviour that will continue to strengthen over time. The reward can then be staggered or removed and the new behaviours will remain stable without continued reinforcement. Furthermore, the establishment of a new behaviour in this way is highly predictable. Whereas most therapies operate on interpreting events with the benefits of hindsight, behavioural models can make very strong predictions about future behaviour.

Secondly, the negative reinforcing consequences that drive use can also be decreased. Teaching the concerned other communication skills can dramatically reduce conflict and arguments. The concerned other can vent their frustrations at the loved one in powerful ways. Whilst this is often well-deserved and wholly understandable given the pressures they are placed under, it generates stresses in the loved one which they then alleviate through increased consumption of drugs or alcohol. The concerned other is then accused of driving the loved one to use because of their incessant nagging or aggression. Research demonstrates that unpleasant emotions and conflict are the most important determinants of relapse in long-term users (Marlatt and Gordon, 1980). This pattern is seen clearly in the relationship between marital conflict and problem drinking. As we have seen, conflict can both promote change as well as trigger relapse and higher consumption. Conflict tends to be counter-productive and exhausting for the concerned other. The elimination of conflict can have a profound effect on the loved one's consumption and the concerned other's own stress levels.

The principle tool for reducing conflict is the use of assertive communication. Assertiveness is misunderstood as a communication style. It is often believed that assertiveness is concerned with assertion of our rights. Assertiveness should be understood more broadly than this. Being assertive is simply saying the right thing to the right person at the right time in the right way. Telling someone that you love them is just as assertive as taking an item of clothing back to a shop because it is faulty. There are a number of approaches to formulating assertive communication to varying degrees of sophistication. However, under the pressure of the moment simplified approaches tend to work better. In the first instance the concerned other should develop 'I' messages. The 'I' message approach entails telling the loved one how they feel as opposed to commenting on their behaviour. Instead of focusing on the loved one's action – 'You always let me down' – the concerned other focuses on conveying their own feelings: 'I feel disappointed that we could not do this together.' This can be enhanced by making positive statements, where the concerned other tells the loved one what they want them to do as opposed to telling them what they do not want them to do. For example, 'I like it when we can talk' rather than 'I am sick of finding you drunk.'

Developing these skills is difficult. Concerned others are under immense pressure. They are often fatigued and exhausted by the demands of their life. Composing these statements in the moment is not easy so identifying when to use the approach and rehearsing of their statements becomes important. Identifying typical flashpoints of conflict in advance helps prepare the 'I' messages. The same conflicts tend to arise repeatedly so mapping them in detail can assist concerned others to pinpoint exactly when they should use the skills. Within this, it is important to explore any provocation that the loved one deploys in order to undermine the concerned other. To some degree it is in the interest of the loved one to initiate conflict as it offers them the excuse to use and then attribute all the blame on the concerned other. They may therefore actively manipulate the conflicts in order to achieve this. Identifying the ways in which they provoke the concerned other can be very helpful in increasing the resilience of the concerned other to resist quarrelling. In addition, exploring the subsequent impact of conflict on the concerned other's own health and wellbeing can increase their motivation for applying the skills.

Once the typical flashpoints of conflict are established, the concerned other should be encouraged to reframe the conflicts that they are drawn into. They must be able to focus their attention on conveying their own feelings about these situations rather than focusing the loved one's behaviour. The concerned other expresses their feelings to the loved one as opposed to criticising their behaviour. For example, if the loved one has let the concerned other down, focusing on their behaviour will trigger conflict 'You always let me down, you only think of yourself. You are a selfish bastard!' When these statements are made it will automatically trigger defensiveness and rebuttal from the loved one. However, if the concerned other focuses on their feelings it becomes increasing difficult to contradict. 'I feel that I am not important to you anymore.' This allows the concerned other to express their feelings without conflict as it is difficult to contradict these 'I' statements. For example, if a concerned other said 'I get anxious and worried when you disappear.' It is hard for the loved one to refute this by saying 'No you don't'.

Mastering these statements is very difficult especially in an emotionally charged situation. We can formulate these statements in advance of any conflict but the concerned other will still have to deliver their lines with conviction under the pressure of a real life situation, often with a loved one experiencing a craving tantrum. Rehearsal and role-play are essential components in the development of these communication skills. These role plays should be restricted to a couple of lines at time, with the practitioner taking the role of the loved one. Giving balanced feedback and showing where the concerned other can refine their communication can increase confidence. Pitch and tone are important in this as it is easy to transform the most positive of statements into sarcastic dismissal with the slightest inflection.

Visualisation techniques can also help the concerned other to contain their own emotions and focus on the task when they are under duress. For example, conceptualising their loved one's aggression as the addiction defending itself can be a useful device. Explaining to the concerned other that addiction loves conflict as it will always increase consumption, can help them visualise that they are in a battle for their loved one. It is a battle where their anger only strengthens the enemy. Whilst it is very difficult to deliver a more positive communication style under the pressure of a loved one's use and the chaos that comes with it, the mastery of these skills has the single biggest impact on stress for the concerned other as well as reducing consumption in the loved one.

In terms of increasing the punishing consequences of use we will do this in two ways. Instead of teaching the concerned other to actively apply positive punishments, which only alienate the problem user, the concerned other is taught to simply allow the undesirable consequence of the loved one's use to occur. This is achieved by reviewing the punishing consequences of use for the loved one and exploring whether the concerned other is doing anything to reduce them on the loved one's behalf. This is most likely to occur where the loved one's pattern of problem use has become established and the concerned other's active attempts to curtail use have failed. The concerned other's attention tends to switch to minimising the consequences of use rather than curtailing consumption itself. Enabling can be explicit in terms of reducing the immediate impact of use on the loved one. Or they can be implicit in protecting the loved one from the influence of others through defending, concealing or diminishing their use (see Table 10).

The process of allowing the loved one to feel the consequences of use is referred to as disabling enabling. This demands scrutinising the concerned other's responses to the loved one when they are intoxicated, recuperating or facing the consequences of their use and identifying anything that they might do to minimise these impacts. Reducing a loved one's suffering is a natural response for any family member. However, the concerned other who diminishes the punishing consequences of use may inadvertently diminish the loved one's motivation. As many concerned others will not recognise the term enabling we refer to this as 'helping' in the programme.

Table 10. Types of enabling

Explicit enabling: minimising the consequences of use	Implicit enabling: protecting the loved ones from others
Got out of bed in the middle of the night to help your intoxicated loved one	Convinced yourself your loved one uses less than others
Paid a debt caused by their use	Made excuses to your family about your loved one's behaviour
Nursed injuries caused by use	Refused to make plans with friends or family because you fear the consequences of your loved one's behaviour
Helped soothe a hangover/comedown	
Cleaned up your loved one's mess as a result of intoxication	Hide problems from family and friends
Soothing and calming the loved one when they demonstrate guilt or remorse	Minimised your loved one's poor behaviour as being 'not that bad'
	Defended your loved one against criticism

It has often been supposed that any assistance offered to the loved one could be deemed as enabling behaviour and therefore tough love is the only option. This is not the case. Enabling is where diminishing the negative consequences of the loved one's use comes at a cost to the concerned other. For example, buying drugs for a loved one costs the concerned other money as well as placing them at risk of legal repercussions. Hiding the loved one's drug or alcohol problem from other family members compromises the concerned other's relationship with their family structure. Not going out with friends anymore because of the loved one's boorish and embarrassing behaviour when drunk costs the concerned other their social life. Enabling becomes an insidious process where the concerned other's own life becomes decimated through the sacrifices they make for the loved one. This can affect every aspect of their life, compromising them socially, emotionally, physically, spiritually and financially. It can even tear their own family relationships apart as genders may differ in their willingness to enable use. A common point of conflict between parents is how far each of them will go to reduce the consequences of a loved one's use. Enabling erodes the important social attachments in the concerned other's own life in a similar way that drug and alcohol consumption can erode the problem user's relationships. The greatest impoverishment in the concerned other's life stems from these well-meaning attempts to protect the loved one. This damage is often so profound that the loved one's entry into treatment will not restore these relationships by default.

Enabling is not an ingrained mental health problem in the concerned other. As we have already seen, modern definitions of co-dependency have little evidence to support the notion that enabling is a symptom of an illness in the concerned other. It is an entirely understandable response to a loved one's suffering. Enabling is an act of love in a desperate situation which becomes institutionalised over time in the relationship. It also serves an important function for the concerned other in reducing their fear, anxiety and worry. This can make changing the established pattern difficult. Assessing enabling can be deeply guilt-inducing in the concerned other as if they have been doing wrong. They have not. They have been expressing compassion for their family member and trying to reduce their own anxiety in the best way they could. Understanding that this comes at a price for both themselves and their loved ones is the first step in revising their responses. What is important is whether they can stop responding to their loved one's use in this way. Can they stop getting up at 4.00 a.m. to mop up their vomit-splashed loved one who is sleeping off the night's excesses? Will they stop paying their fines or debts? Getting the loved one up in time for college or school in the morning? Buying in alcohol in the hope that their loved one stays at home?

This is not to suggest that all enabling behaviours cease. Enabling can reduce the concerned other's stress in the short term though it banks increasing emotional fatigue in the long term. The concerned other must feel comfortable in stopping any given enabling behaviour that has been identified. If they feel that ceasing an enabling behaviour would put their loved one at risk then they should not stop this particular response. For example, if a mother always collects the children from school because their partner's drinking makes them too unreliable, it would be fine to continue with this because of the risk involved. In any event, if the concerned other feels unsafe in ceasing any enabling response they simply will not stop doing it anyway. It is therefore better that the practitioner recognises the value of the concerned other continuing, in order to maintain an explicit collaboration with them.

A further complication is that the loved one may be receiving support from other family members or, as in the case with a young person, both parents might seek out the programme in order to facilitate change. If there is more than one parent involved, it is essential that they agree on these new boundaries and they stick to them. This is because if two or more people seek help, the loved one will automatically attempt to play one party off against another for reasons we shall explore shortly. It is essential that these changes are consistently applied by all involved parties. An additional problem can arise when a male concerned other presents for help. We have noticed that when men attempt to implement the programme, they are very good at setting these new boundaries. However, it is common for another member of the family, usually female, to step in and take over the vacant enabling role. We have seen this phenomena only with male concerned others but it is possible that female concerned others experience similar problems. For example, the father that refuses his son money for drugs may deflect the young person to their grandmother who does. Therefore, the comprehensive assessment should identify any other supportive others in the loved one's life. The concerned other has the choice of either preparing an approach to this involved other asking them to desist from enabling the loved one or they can invite this other person to attend the one-to-one PACT sessions with them.

The negative punishers of use can be increased by teaching the concerned other to retract themselves and alternative rewards in the light of the loved one using. This is done without conflict using prepared positive communication if the loved one shows signs of intoxication or engages in use at any point. Alternatively, they may give the loved one the reward but withdraw and leave the loved one to engage in it alone. For example, a mother might plan a 'girls night in' with her daughter who drinks and uses drugs. The night's itinerary might include beauty products, comfort foods and watching a film. However, at the appointed time, the daughter turns up intoxicated. In this instance, the mother could give the beauty products, food and the film to the daughter and invite her to go ahead and enjoy them, saying that she will leave her to enjoy it as she finds it difficult to see her daughter under the influence. In this way, the negative punishments that withhold a reward are very powerful without being aggressively or conspicuously hostile. It should be remembered that the concerned other is a powerful reinforcer themselves. Their withdrawal has a dramatic affect on the loved one. It means if the loved one wants to use, it becomes solely their choice. They cannot attribute blame on the concerned other. The anger and hostility that is elicited by the concerned other's confrontation cannot fuel their consumption. In other words, the loved one cannot indulge themselves into thinking about their poor relationships with the concerned other. Instead they are forced to consider their relationship with the substance. The consequences of the loved one's use suddenly shifts from escaping conflict and stress to losing out on more important relationships and dwelling on their own choices. This leads to a very different experience of use. It is one of isolation, loneliness and entirely the loved one's own responsibility. It is often these periods of withdrawal that trigger discussions regarding treatment entry.

The rate of change that can be generated in the loved one may be dependent on two principle factors. The first of these is the reinforcement value of the concerned other. As we have seen, problem users place a high premium on immediate kinships relationships: mother, father and siblings. Even when these attachments are characterised by difficulties that existed prior to the onset of problem use, they are still highly valued by the user. Long-term relationships with spouses are also likely to have a high value attached to them. The more prized the relationship, the greater the leverage in influencing change. In our experience, the programme does not appear to produce consistent treatment entry in relationships that were initiated after the problematic consumption was established, though it does remain effective in improving the concerned other's own life and reducing their stress. A second factor affecting the duration of the intervention is the severity of the consequences of use. Research shows the socially stable but heavy drinkers who are not experiencing consequences are the least likely to change (see Vaillant, 1995). As the punishing consequences of use increase, so does the impetus to change. However, this impetus may be diminished by the concerned other if they are unwilling to stop all enabling behaviours. This may be because it feels unsafe for them to so and this should always be respected. However, they need to recognise that the programme may take longer to influence their loved one's behaviour as the intervention becomes a more protracted process of attrition.

1.19 Functional Analysis Logs

At the outset of treatment the concerned other often needs a great deal of support to identify the background material in which to apply the four principles of treatment entry. For example, the concerned other will have to consider alternative rewards for the loved one deeply, assess specific situations where conflict occurs, screen for possible enabling behaviours and practice withdrawing from using situations without conflict. However, as they become more conversant with these elements of treatment entry, it becomes easier for them to identify each principle and begin to apply them in new and diverse settings. Once the concerned other grasps these principles it is possible to utilise them in a simple and more focused intervention. The functional analysis logs are designed to allow for the planning of interventions with the concerned other who is becoming increasing skilled and confident in the approach. Based on the functional analysis of behavioural therapy, the practitioner and concerned other can explore a specific situation where the loved one uses. It is important that the analysis is conducted on a specific incident as people's use can vary enormously from one situation and time to another. Motivation to drink is very different at a Saturday night social event than it is after a disciplinary meeting at work.

The functional analysis needs to be conducted in a warm and empathetic way with concerned others. Whilst it explores many aspects of the loved one's use, it should be completed as if the concerned other is telling their story about these events. In this way, the structure of the functional analysis is there to guide the practitioner to focus on specific elements of this episode that can be drawn upon to develop a subsequent planned response. The art of the functional analysis resides in the practitioner's ability to elicit the concerned other's view whilst at the same time establishing the specific detail of these events. The more specific the detail established, then the more effective the subsequent response will be.

The functional analysis is based on the concerned other's understanding of the situation. This accepts the situation to the best of their knowledge. It is important to remember that any functional analysis is a working hypothesis that is refined over time. Within this, the concerned other should identify the external triggers to use prior to their loved one's consumption. This might involve certain people, places or times of the week. Then the concerned other should explore what they feel the internal triggers for use were in the loved one. This does involve an element of second guessing but very often the concerned other will know the loved one so intimately that they become fairly easy to read in this way. Internal triggers include mood, thoughts, stresses or even physical discomfort, like a tension head ache for example.

Once these internal and external triggers are defined, the concerned other should identify how much the loved one consumed on this occasion. Again, this will not always be known. The best guesstimate on any measure is helpful at this stage. The guesstimates can always be marked with a (g) in order to account for a degree of uncertainty. Using a wide range of measures can be helpful here, including time spent using the substance, money spent, amounts that people used or even the degree of intoxication the loved one exhibited at the time. Any measures which can help track the loved one's use across the duration of the programme will be helpful when consistently applied in subsequent functional analysis.

The concerned other should then consider what the short term benefits of use for the loved one are. These are the immediate pay-offs from using that the user experiences when intoxicated. Research suggests that there are eight principle determinants (Marlatt, 1985), though people may use for a combination of reasons. In general, long-term users are more likely to use for negative reasons (unpleasant moods and conflict) whilst young people are more likely to use on positive occasions (pleasant mood or pleasant time with others) (see Table 11).

When all the immediate short-term benefits of use are identified, the concerned other should then map the long-term negative consequences of use. These are the punishing consequences that tend to occur after the intoxication has subsided. As we have seen, these consequences can be wide-ranging and include both the physical and social complications of use. Physical consequences can include withdrawal, heath problems and accidents under the influence. Social complications can include how the user feels about themselves after use, the impact use has on family and friends, problems in work/college, legal or financial problems and housing problems.

The functional analysis of a loved one's use has been well established in other models of treatment for concerned others such as in the CRT and CRAFT programmes. In the PACT programme we have adapted its use in two ways. Firstly, the functional analysis is conducted as a log. Having multiple functional analyses laid out on one page allows for greater comparison between the loved one's previous using events and their current ones. This allows any patterns

Table 11. Determinants of relapse (based on Marlatt et al., 1980)

Determinant	Descriptions
Unpleasant moods	Feeling bored, depressed, lonely, isolated or anxious
Conflict	Arguments with others, feeling as though people are interfering in our plans or undermining us, harbouring unspoken resentments, over reacting to others and feeling guilty
Physical pain	Physical discomfort from withdrawal or cravings but can also include illness and feeling unwell. Food substitute may be an issue for young women too
Positive moods	Feeling optimistic, problem free, complacent and that you are in control
Positive occasions	Shared moments with others at a party, social gathering or getting out of prison. Can include the desire to be intimate, sharing with a partner or friend
Social pressure	Includes direct offers of drugs or alcohol from someone who coaxes the person to use or can be more indirect such as seeing others drink
Temptations and urges	This is a desire to re-create an old experience, to feel as they once did. Usually linked to positive expectations of drugs and alcohol to induce a feeling of relief or enhance a positive mood
Testing control	Believing that you have control over the substance, trying to demonstrate to others that you can manage use or believing that this time will be different to previous occasions

or differences in response to be identified and incorporated into future planning. For example, it is easier to identify whether the programme is decreasing the loved one's use or which interventions have a high or low impact on the loved one's consumption. This reviewing process can greatly assist in fine-tuning effective responses or eliminating ineffective ones. Secondly, PACT maximises the information identified in the functional analysis in order to plan. Based on the completed functional analysis, the sister interventions sheet allows the concerned other to plan a treatment response quickly using the four principles of treatment entry. This makes direct use of this information possible with a simple to use format.

The functional analysis intervention plan allows the concerned other to base their responses on the identified triggers of any using episode in the loved one. For example, if the external 'when', 'where' and 'who' that triggers the loved one's consumption are known, then the concerned other can plan alternative rewards at these times and account for outside influences. If the internal triggers are identified, then the concerned other can intercede and offer support using communication skills that allow the loved one to vent any frustrations they are experiencing. The determinant column may indicate the underlying patterns of the loved one's use, based on the key determinants of relapse.

The behaviour column indicates how much the loved one used by rating their level of intoxication. This can be useful when viewed over the course of the programme. Reductions in intoxication can signal whether the programme is affecting the loved one's consumption. It can also be used as a cue for any prepared statements of withdrawal that the concerned other will make in the event that the loved one uses regardless of their efforts. In terms of the short term benefits, these indicate an unmet need in the loved one. These needs will need to be expressed in some form. As such, these needs can be used as an acid test to evaluate whether any planned reward for the loved one would meet these same needs. The closer the fit between the alternative rewards and these unmet needs, then the better the outcome. Finally, the long term consequences will highlight any specific enabling patterns that are occurring. This will allow the concerned other to review any current enabling and help them identify which ones feel safe for them to disable. For a summary of how the functional analysis logs and intervention plans marry see Table 12.

1.20 Extinction Burst

It is important to recognise that any attempt to change the loved one's behaviour can result in a short period of intensifying their anti-social or undermining behaviour. This process is referred to as an 'extinction burst' and occurs when *an anticipated reward is withheld*. Any given behaviour is eliminated when it repeated fails to elicit a desired consequence. However, this takes a period of time to occur. In the interim, the individual will often increase the frequency of the behaviour in order to acquire the desired response. For example, in a laboratory experiment a rat receives a dose of cocaine every time it pulls a lever. Overtime the rat learns to expect cocaine administration every time the lever is pulled. One day the supply of cocaine is stopped. As the anticipated reward is withheld that rat will engage in a short period of frantic lever pulling. This burst of behaviour will continue for a short period of time until the rat finally gives up and no longer bothers with the lever.

We see the exact same burst in behaviour in human beings too. For example, a young person continually nags, throws tantrums and screams until their parents give them money. When the parents give-in they are inadvertently rewarding pressurising behaviour. The young person soon learns that aggressive pestering brings rewards: money. One day the parents tire of this and so make a pact that no matter what their child does, they will not give them a penny. Confronted by this sudden stone wall of unity, the young person will be shocked that the anticipated reward for their theatrics is not forthcoming. They will not simply resign themselves to this new order though. They will increase the intensity of their nagging and moaning with the addition of tears, anger, accusation and threats. They may also alternate between this and a charm offensive to seduce the reward from the parents. Promising to be good, offering favours, making promises, and flattering may ensue. In the light of this onslaught, the parents may be increasingly liable to give in. They misinterpret the child's response as indicative that their approach is not working. However, by doing so, they will inadvertently reward even more extreme behaviour. It is in this way that many concerned others end up shaping behaviour in

Table 12. Example of a functional analysis log and intervention plan

Domain	Functional analysis log	Functional analysis intervention
External triggers	When: Sunday-1.00 p.m. Who: after visiting parents Where: on the way home stopping at the Red Lion Pub	Planned reward: suggest going to his favourite cafe for a fry-up straight after leaving parents' home. Be more vocal in supporting him if parents criticise him.
Internal triggers	Thoughts: 'My parents always criticise me.' 'My partner always sides with them.' Feelings: stressed, put upon, not heard. Physical sensation: tension in voice and hands-wringing	Communication skills: Recognise his stress and frustration at his parents' comments. Remind him of the positive things that he does.
Determinant	Unpleasant mood	Parents always stress he feels got at. Could defend him more.
Behaviour	Intoxication | nc	1	2	3	4	5 | x	Prepare for Withdrawing: 'I would really like us to get something to eat. If you want to go to the pub, then it is up to you. I am not going to argue. I will head home and maybe see you later.
Short term benefits	Relief Lifts mood Feels accepted by drinking friends.	If I listen to his stress at the meal, it will lift his mood. I could then talk about things we both enjoyed, or funny moments with his parents in the past.
Long term positives	Feels depressed and self-loathing Incontinence in the night Struggles to get ready for work Feels he makes a fool of himself in public when drunk	Stop getting him to bed late at night. Not cleaning up his clothes before he wakes. Not dismissing his feelings about what others say about him. Ask him what he thinks other people say or how they respond to him when he drinks.

the wrong direction. Succumbing to the pressures of the loved one does offer respite in the short term but will lead to further demands in the long term.

Understanding this process from the outset is important as it will assist the concerned other to reframe the loved one's reactions to change. It is important to reiterate that the extinction

Table 13. Examples of threats and temptations when anticipated rewards are withheld

Threats	Temptations
I will kill myself	Promises to change
I will leave you	Reminders of what they mean to each other
I will tell people what you are really like	

burst only occurs when anticipated rewards are withheld. As such, a loved one's antagonistic or undermining responses are a signal that the implemented changes are having an effect. However, there is a danger that if the concerned other does not understand this response then their confidence can be undermined. Evaluating the threats and temptations that the loved one has used historically can assist the concerned other to prepare for the loved one's reaction to change. It will also demand that concerned others on the programme remain consistent in their deployment of the skills and are not swayed by either temptations or threats designed to undermine their efforts. If more than one person is seeking help for a loved one, such as both parents, it also means that they too must be agreed on their responses and both adhere to the same boundaries lest they undermine each other (see Table 13).

Within the programme, the extinction burst can appear at several points in the process. Specifically, it can often occur when the problem user is told, or discovers, that the concerned other is seeking professional help. Initial curiosity about the help sought can take the form of indirect questions and apparently indifferent enquiries. However, this can soon escalate into snipes, jibes, undermining and mocking. Alternatively, a charm offensive may ensue to convince the concerned other that this professional assistance is not really necessary. The implementation of a new boundary can also trigger these responses. For example, the concerned other who has always made the loved one's excuses for not attending a family event may tell the loved one that it is fine if they do not want to attend but they must telephone and make their own excuses. This will elicit a similar short burst before subsiding and they make the telephone call. Interestingly, extinction burst behaviour may also occur when the concerned other responds to typical flashpoints with communication skills. Their unwillingness to engage in a conflict deprives the loved one of an anticipated reward, that is an excuse to use. Hence the loved one may increase the pressure on the concerned other to argue with undermining statements, classically, 'I suppose your counsellor told you to say that' and such comments. If a loved one does display increased determination to initiate conflict in this way, it signals that this is a strategy they employ to justify consumption. If the practitioner can predict these responses it will increase the concerned other's confidence in the programme. Furthermore, if the concerned other can understand the loved one's responses occur because the programme is effecting change, it can help them remain focused.

The extinction burst is a tiresome response to have to deal with. If the concerned other can endure sitting through this response the behaviour will subside and be eliminated in future. The reaction can be softened in the short term by the offer of an alternative reward. For example, the child that pesters their parents for money could be offered a substitute reward instead, such as the offer of a lift later that week if they are quiet. The availability of an alternative reward may diminish the burst because the individual still has some needs met. The general exception to dealing with the extinction burst is when physical violence is a very real threat. It is recommended that in the light of a potential or imminent assault that the concerned other yield to the demand and escape the situation as quickly as possible. Domestic violence will be reviewed in detail later.

1.21 Bringing up The Subject of Treatment

The consistent application of these new boundaries will quickly shift the balance of rewards and consequences, making continued use increasingly untenable. This in turn will stimulate internal motivation for change in the loved one. The concerned other should prepare in advance for the most opportune moment to broach the subject of the loved one seeking professional help. There are two important components in this process. Firstly, it is important to assess and identify when the loved one would be most receptive to the suggestion of treatment. This entails reviewing the prompts that are most likely to trigger concern in the loved one and identifying any possible barriers or objections that might prevent them from entering treatment in advance. Problem solving any roadblocks to treatment entry will smooth the path. Secondly, the concerned other should gather information on different treatment packages that are available locally. The range of options will vary depending on the local provision. Familiarity with the treatment landscape will assist the concerned other to present options to the loved one as well as inform the conversation in dispelling any fears the loved one might have. It is also important to ensure that treatment is proportionate to the loved one's current level of use. A young person at college, whose recreational use has increased, is going to find a 12-month rehabilitation programme unappealing.

Deciding on the timing of when to raise the subject of treatment will vary from person to person. Assessing past incidents where the loved one has shown remorse, experienced discomfort or dissatisfaction with use can provide important clues into their internal motivation and the most apposite time. It is important to recognise that individuals are motivated by different factors. Health, self-image, loss of important relationships or crises may motivate change to varying degrees in the same person. The more accurately the concerned other can identify previous events that have prompted change then the more effective their subsequent request will be. Again, the concerned other may be able to anticipate objections from the loved one. Research has shown that there is a very broad spectrum of barriers to treatment entry. These can range from the purely psychological barriers, such as difficulty in accepting help; structural problems making it difficult to physically attend, such as child care; assumptions about what treatment will entail; fear of judgement from others or previously bad experiences.

Screening possible objections in advance will help the concerned other troubleshoot practical problems. Alternatively, understanding the treatment process will enable them to allay fears or inform the loved one of the demands of treatment. Should the concerned other broach the subject with the loved one and they decline, their reasons for doing so can be recorded and refined for a future opportunity. How the concerned other raises the subject of treatment is as important as when they raise it. It must been couched in a sensitive and positive communication style. Underselling treatment can assist the problem user to consider sampling treatment without commitment. Should the loved one decline the invite to get help, it is important that the issue is not pressed. The concerned other should accept the loved one's position and allow the shift in consequences to continue until another opportunity presents.

1.22 Selecting Treatment Options

In reviewing appropriate treatment, it can be helpful to advise the concerned other on what works in treatment. Getting the right treatment from the outset is important. As Emrick (1983) observed in a follow-up study of 384 treatment problem drinkers, it appears easier for treatment to impede a client's progress rather than assist it. Facilitating entry into the wrong treatment will induce a major setback and deter any other attempt to seek help. Treatment must be appropriate to the intensity of the presenting problem and must address the two aspects of problem use: physical dependence and addiction. The comprehensive assessment conducted with the concerned other should indicate where a physical detoxification needs to be included in the loved one's treatment to address physical dependence.

It is important to recognise that prescribed medications, whether for detoxification or as part of relapse prevention, can only address issues of dependence. Substitute prescribing alone can reduce the harm the loved one experiences but will not improve their social situation. In general, loved ones with severe levels of physical dependency and a long history of extensive social exclusion will require longer treatment. Reviewing the available information on the problem user's social function prior to the onset of problems, the current severity of their physical dependence and their access to non-using social groups should offer a good indication of the treatment intensity that is most appropriate for them. It should be remembered that the least intrusive treatment options can be trialled first and if these prove unsuccessful the treatment can be 'stepped up' into more comprehensive packages.

Brief interventions can be highly effective for a lower range of substance-related problems. Loved ones experiencing problems with drug or alcohol use without physical dependence and who have intact social relationships are more appropriate for brief interventions of one-to-three sessions. For more complex, long-term problems, comprehensive interventions that increase social integration show superior outcomes. In general, early onset problematic drug use often requires more intensive interventions (six months plus), whilst problem alcohol users can show a much wider range of social functioning from poor to good. For example, Edwards et al. (1977) randomly assigned hospitalised problem drinkers to either one session of advice where they were told they would be offered no more support or referred to a six month group-work programme. Outcomes were the same for both groups. Long term weekly counselling can be

Table 14. Indications of treatment prognosis

Short-term treatment (1–12 sessions)	Long-term treatment (12 weeks+)
No signs of physical dependence	Long-term Class A drug user
Good social functioning prior to the problem (family, relationships, housing, employment, training)	Profound physical dependence
	Poor social functioning prior to the onset of the problem
No or limited social exclusion	Protracted social exclusion
Access to non-using peer groups	No access to non-using groups
Currently employment	Long-term unemployed

far too much for drinkers with milder problems and not intensive enough for more entrenched problems (see Table 14). The severest end of alcohol problems will demand the same intensive treatment that is required for problem drug users.

Holder et al. (1991) reviewed 200 control studies of 33 treatment modalities. They found that social skills, marital therapies and community reinforcement showed the best outcomes for problem alcohol users. Miller et al. (2003) have also been engaged in periodic reviews of research on the outcomes demonstrated by different treatment approaches in addressing alcohol problems. These findings are compiled in a large table – the *mesa grande* – where 381 controlled trials of treatment are summarised. The *mesa grande* accords with Holder et al. (1991) in many aspects, specifically in high ratings for treatments that are design to address specific aspects of use (see Table 15).

This research strongly suggests generalised counselling interventions do not appear to be very effective in addressing substance misuse problems (see also Pattison, 1976; Barbor et al., 2003; Emrick and Hanson, 1983). This is because they tend to focus on general issues in the client's life as opposed to specific areas. For example, clients in a general counselling approach may experience reduced severity of depression but this does not automatically confer any benefits to

Table 15. Evidence of treatment effectiveness for alcohol problems (Holder et al., 1991)

Treatments with good evidence	Treatments with promising evidence	Treatments with no evidence
Social skills training	Covert sensitisation	Chemical or electrical aversion therapy
Self-control training	Behavioural contracting	
Brief motivational interviewing	Disulfirum (antabuse)	Education films or lectures
Behavioural marital therapy	Antidepressant medication	Anxiolytic medication
Community reinforcement approach	Non-behavioural marital therapy	General counselling
	Cognitive therapy	Residential milieu therapy.
Stress management training	Hypnosis	
	Lithium	

other dimensions of their life. Simply because an individual is less depressed does not mean that they are more employable or able to resolve family issues or create a fulfilling social life. This may be why 'psychotherapy', 'generic counselling' models, 'treatment as usual' and even 'personal centred' counselling did not perform well in these studies. In the UK, these broader interventions represent 'treatment as usual.' These models prioritise personal insight and emotional expression. This can neglect the development of specific behavioural skills necessary to master change as well as the necessity for the client to reconstruct wider social relationships that have been compromised by their consumption. Treatment works well when it expands its focus to address the specific social factors that sustain use. The concerned other should contact service providers to explore what they offer, the length of these programmes and the extent to which longer programmes help the loved one to restructure their life rather than explore the emotional needs alone. Having the practical details of opening times, if there are waiting lists and problem-solving any obvious impediment to treatment can ensure swift entry to the most appropriate and assessable service.

Treatment can also focus on a variety of different goals. For those with milder problems and younger people, controlled use may be a valid option. Young people in general are ten times more likely to relapse in total abstinence programmes rather than in treatment programmes that advocate controlled use (Polich et al., 1981). Conversely, severely dependent drinkers are three times more likely to relapse on controlled programmes. Despite common perceptions of the problem user being unable to exert any control of their use, controlled behavioural programmes have been extensively studied and demonstrate very good outcomes with lower order problem populations (Miller, 1983). The indicators for controlled use are described in Table 16.

It is important to remember that many heavier drug and alcohol users will attempt controlled use several times before they realise that abstinence is the only option for them. So, even for

Table 16. Factors relevant to controlled drinking (Edwards et al., 2003)

Factors unfavourable to controlled use	Favourable factors to controlled use
Severe dependence	Mild or no signs of dependence
Previous failures at controlled drinking	Recent sustained normal drinking
Strong desire in the drinker for abstinence	Strong preference for normal drinking
Commitment to AA	Evidence of self-control in other areas of life
Poor self control in other areas of life	No mental illness or concurrent drug abuse.
Mental illness or drug misuse	Mild or no physical complications from drinking
Severe organ damage from alcohol abuse	Supportive family and friends
Heavy drinking family and social group	Drinking does not affect work performance
Heavy drinking in work settings	Non-violent when drinking
Social isolation	
Employment jeopardised by drinking problems	
Violence when drinking	

people with higher levels of dependence controlled use may serve as an attractive option to enter treatment, but they may find as a result, that the difficulty in doing so prompts a commitment to abstinence. Should the problem user fall outside the categories for controlled use, the concerned other may need to understand that future drinking or drug use may no longer be an option for their loved one. This reality is not always appreciated by the concerned other or the wider family.

Many concerned others and the wider family are tempted to pay for private treatment for the loved one. This may range from residential rehabilitation to rapid detoxification in private hospitals. Such a move should be considered carefully. Addictions are a chronic relapse condition. It may be unlikely that private treatment, no matter how expensive, will be successful first time. A subsequent relapse in the loved one can be amplified by any substantial investment that the family has made from their own private funds. Most experts in the field warn against rapid detoxification methods. These should only ever occur as part of a comprehensive treatment package if they have any chance of success. The implications of relapse in the loved one should be considered carefully, especially if the money is an issue for the family. Should the family agree to fund private treatment, then the aims of the treatment should be made clear to those who are financing it and they should be kept informed of the loved one's progress.

1.23 Supporting the Loved One in Treatment

A loved one entering treatment is an important landmark in the recovery process but it is not necessarily the definitive one. It raises many issues, such as whether the concerned other will continue to support the loved one and how best to do this. Soyez and Broekaert (Undated: 131) observed in their study of social networks' responses to loved ones entering into residential treatment that 'First, it seems a number of network members are simply unaware of how to provide support. To them, providing support is equal to giving money or material help. And this is not what residents are expecting. The difference in expectations may create new frustrations and consequently hamper further contact'. Helping the concerned other to identify the best means of supporting their loved one becomes important. Research suggests that supportive families are more likely not only to initiate change but also to help people successfully maintain it (Moos et al., 1990). The process of supporting their loved one in treatment must begin with an open discussion of what the loved one would value in terms of support. However, it is not appropriate or expected that every concerned other will wish to continue to support their loved one once they do enter treatment. Anger, exhaustion or the immediacy of their own problems may preclude many family members from continuing to prioritise the loved one once they are in receipt of professional help (Soyez and Broekaert, Undated). This should be respected and concerned others should not be pressurised into offering support if they feel unable to do so for any reason.

For those that do continue to support their loved one, it is important that they have a realistic understanding of the treatment process. Simply because the loved one enters treatment does not necessarily mean that the process ends. The dropout rates from treatment can be high. An important finding in treatment research is that early subject improvement in the treatment seeker tends to predict long-term outcome (Brown et al., 1999). The first three weeks of treatment are vitally important. If the loved one enters into treatment and does not feel any subjective benefit within this period there is unlikely to be any improvement at all. The fact that treatment tends to work quickly means that encouraging the loved one to sample treatment is often enough to give them a taste of it. If the loved one is finding their treatment unsatisfactory this should be reviewed and other options explored before they become sceptical or disillusioned. Whilst this can be disheartening, it is not uncommon. If it is not for them, there are other options available. Even bibliotherapy should not be discounted as an option. Self-help manuals can be as effective as professional help.

Even if treatment attendance is helpful, it can be an unpalatable experience to many problem users. However, it is possible for the concerned other to influence attendance. Firstly, the concerned other should enquire with agencies as to what information will be made available to them regarding their loved one's progress. Some agencies may release information if the problem user signs a waiver of confidentiality to allow attendance rates and other 'hard' information to be available to family members. This can circumvent the potential for the problem user to misrepresent the treatment provider to the family through triangulation. Some treatment services may invite the concerned other to play a role in the treatment itself. This may include providing wider information, monitoring progress and assisting in the daily administration of medications such as naltraxone or disulfiram. Many agencies remain reticent to involve the concerned other in any way. Whilst they see providing information to a concerned other as breaching confidentiality, they remain happy to offer information to other professionals. This double standard is unsatisfactory and neglects the reality that it is the concerned other who provides the majority of support for the loved one outside of their treatment hours.

Outside of treatment, the concerned other can support attendance by shifting the focus of the rewards. Prior to treatment, the concerned other has provided rewards to compete with use. Once the problem user enters treatment the rewards are adapted to augment attendance in the same manner. This is referred to as the Premack Principle named after the experimental psychologist David Premack (1965). His research showed that 'for any pair of responses the more probable one will reinforce the less probable one.' In everyday language this translates into 'Grandma's Law': *first you work then you play* (Homme, 1971). The consequences of going to treatment can feel punishing. People might feel shame, explore painful experiences or provide a constant reminder of the loved one's own fallibility. Treatment attendance can be improved if it is rewarded with desirable consequences. These rewards can be modest, such as cooking a favourite meal, going to the cinema or offering praise and encouragement. However, once again the rewards are only administered when the problem user attends treatment and the concerned other must also enjoy the activity. The Premack principle can also be extended to cover high risk times for the problem user, such as Saturday nights or when they are alone. Programming in a busy schedule that provides alternative satisfaction at times when the loved one is vulnerable to lapse or relapse can help minimise relapse potential and augment non-using life. This necessitates the creation of a strong support network who can help the concerned other and the problem user to increase their social contact.

1.24 Treatment Outcomes and Relapse

In alcohol studies, the percentages of those achieving long-term abstinence post-treatment vary considerably from 64 per cent (Sundby, 1967) to 13 per cent (Bratfos, 1974). Addictions are a chronic relapse condition. The majority of drinkers and drug users will slip within the first three months of quitting (Hunt et al., 1971). Despite this, there is an embedded assumption explicit in support services and amongst families that individuals who are successful in treatment curtail all drug and alcohol use immediately. This does not appear to be the case. Even those who successfully overcome their addictions experience setbacks and slips in their use along the way. For example, studies of treated drinkers who are successful in their long-term recovery reveal a sporadic pattern of use for at least the first two years. Research suggests that over the course of first year follow-up there will be considerable variation from abstinence to problem drinking post-treatment, which eventually stabilises over time (Taylor, 1994). Hence it is not possible to identify who is likely to succeed in treatment for two to three years. In general, Vaillant's (1995) longitudinal study of problem alcohol users suggested the incidence of relapses dropped from 41 per cent in the second year of recovery to 7 per cent after six years. This risk did not decline any further after this point.

In US drug abuse studies, Drug Abuse Reporting Programme (DARP) followed over 6,000 drug users in the first six years post-treatment. A second wave interviewed 697 drug users up to 12 years post-treatment. Similar rates of decline were found in their consumption. In daily opiate users, 53 per cent reported no daily opiate use at one year follow-up. This fell to 40 per cent of 'any use' and only 25 per cent of daily use at six year follow-up (Simpson and Sells, 1990). At 12-year follow-up, three quarters had lapsed back into daily use at some point, but 63 per cent had not used opiates daily in three years. In the UK based National Treatment Outcome Research study (NTORS), 1,075 drug users were recruited and followed-up at two and four to five years post treatment. Frequency of heroin used halved at one year follow-up. In residential rehabilitation treatment groups, 49 per cent were abstinent at four to five year follow-up. High drinking levels were also reduced in the residential treatment populations, but not in methadone treated patients (Gossop, 2000). In both studies outcome was related to treatment length for problem drug users.

As a result of these continued findings, eminent researchers in the field have called for the abolition of the word 'relapse' from the vocabulary of the substance misuse field. Where setbacks and slips are the norm, the concept of relapse creates an artificial standard that suggests complete failure or a total regression in the individual's progress. This is wholly unrepresentative of the natural development of the recovery experience. It means that the loved one, who is actually making very good progress, can interpret a minor setback as total failure, which in turn sets up a chain reaction that drives continued use. Likewise, the concerned other is likely to interpret any setback as a sign of total failure regardless of its magnitude. This can evoke powerful emotional responses and reaction in concerned others leading to conflict that may also exacerbate further use in the loved one. We have found that setbacks in the loved one's progress can have a devastating effect on the concerned other's treatment gains, even in cases where the loved one goes on to achieve full recovery. The unrealistic expectation that their loved one will stop using at the first attempt and never slip is a serious threat to the long term outcome for both the loved one and the concerned other.

In order to minimise the damage that setbacks can invoke in both the concerned other and the loved one, it is essential that they have a clear understanding of the lapse process. This process should be normalised as typical of the recovery sequence and is to be expected. Familiarity with the Stages of Change can be a great asset to the practitioner in explaining how change unfolds; how it is often characterised by setbacks and that treatment gains tend to be cumulative with each change attempt (Harris, 2007). Further to this, it should be recognised that there is no common agreement on what constitutes a relapse. Some literature classifies 'any use' as a relapse whilst other studies use the return to pre-treatment levels of use to classify it. Whilst the classification described here is not an officially recognised classification system, it can be helpful to alert the concerned other to varying degrees of setback so they can discriminate between them and respond accordingly. Their responses should build in proportion to the severity of the setback (see Table 17).

Slips are part of the process of change and where they occur it is important that the concerned other has strategies in place to help the loved one and to maintain their own motivation. In general, young people are often more vulnerable to setbacks due to positive life events such as enhancing positive moods, identity and enjoyment with others. Long-term users are more likely to lapse to alleviate negative moods or conflict. Assessing the individual users previous pattern of use and lapse can help anticipate and forewarn the concerned other about potential setbacks. These can be met with emergency plans or specific techniques. Normalising setbacks

Table 17. Typology of setbacks

Setback	Definition	Response
Slip	One off using event	Preserve the concerned other's motivation
Lapse	Less than three days continuous use	Apply core principle of the PACT programme
Relapse	More than three days continuous use	Increase social support for the concerned other
Reinitiating	Conscious decision to resume use after a period of abstinence	Review motivations for resuming use, consider stepping up the programme to carefrontation or even termination

with the concerned other is equally important, otherwise the loved one that is making otherwise good progress can be deemed as failing when measured against unrealistic expectations. It should be re-iterated that the main outcome of treatment is a reduction in use. Treatment gains tend to be accumulative with each treatment attempt tending to reduce consumption rather than end it. However, rapid re-entry into treatment within three months post-relapse substantially increases people's chances of long-term success (Prochaska et al., 1994). Should relapse occur, the basic principles of the programme are re-instigated. Often this is done against a backdrop of frustration on the part of the concerned other, who will need support in maintaining the changes anew whilst dealing with their own disappointments.

1.25 Carefrontation and Termination

Despite the best efforts of the concerned other and the systematic approach of the programme, the skills to facilitate treatment entry may not always be enough to secure treatment entry or the long term recovery of the loved one. Although the programme will help the majority of loved ones, the programme should offer assistance to the minority who are not successful at this stage. Should the concerned other reach this point they have two options left. Firstly, they can step up the programme into a carefrontation or secondly, they can terminate the relationship. The carefrontation is the last option available to the concerned other. From the wider research it has been demonstrated that a more confrontational approach can be successful in facilitating change in the loved one. This is under certain important provisos. Firstly, the confrontation should be couched in genuine terms of love, affection and concern. In order to be effective in this, it must draw upon the most shared and highly valued elements of the relationship between the concerned other and the loved one. Secondly, it needs to be delivered in a non-stressful environment. Finally, recruiting significant others to form an ambush should be avoided at all costs. Instead it is a direct appeal from the concerned other to their loved one in the form of a letter which spells out the importance of the relationship and the loved one to the concerned other. It should include the loved one's contribution to the relationship and the cherished past that they have shared. The letter should describe the hoped for future that the concerned other wants with their loved one. Should the loved one not be able to meet this request to enter treatment and work with them to build that future, there should be a clear statement of the consequence of their decision. The concerned other should emphasise that this is not what they want but explain why they must take this course of action. Once the letter is written, the concerned other should give it to their loved one at an appropriate time when the loved one can read it and consider their response.

Termination can be called upon at any time when the concerned other feels that separation from the problem user is now necessary. This should not be considered a poor option or a bad outcome. Should the concerned other consider termination, then this should be explored deeply and without bias by the practitioner. Ultimately, the concerned other will have to consider whether their life and future will be better without the loved one in it. This is a difficult question but an important one and will demand that this is considered empathetically from all angles. If the concerned other does decide to terminate, they will do so with good heart. Knowing that they have done as much as they possibly could in order to salvage their relationship can offer some comfort in the face of a difficult separation. The termination sheet is designed to review progress and evaluate the decision to end the relationship in order to allow the concerned other to make this choice in good faith. Even if the concerned other does end their relationship with the problem user, they should still be supported through this difficult moment. The section on improving their life will remain just as important in the light of this loss.

1.26 Improving the Concerned Other's Life

The use of reinforcers is also important in improving the quality of life for the concerned other. Their lives are often hijacked by the loved one's problems. An established pattern of enabling will soon begin to compromise the concerned other's own relationships as they prioritise the well-being of their loved one. The focus of their life becomes the loved one and their own needs become neglected to this end. Fear of social embarrassment or stigma means their own social life evaporates. Work can become a sanctuary to many but accompanying this is the worry that the impact the loved one has on them may affect their performance. Depression, anxiety and emotional exhaustions are already well advanced by the time many concerned others present for help. It is not uncommon for some concerned others to re-present once their loved one does enter treatment regarding their own consumption of alcohol. Increasing their motivation, enriching their life and diminishing their stresses is the priority.

Reinforcement is used to enhance the concerned other's engagement in the programme and in their own life. Within the programme this is achieved through several means. Firstly, the concerned other's primary motivator is to change the loved one's behaviour. Secondary to this is their own improvement in quality of life. Therefore if the concerned other can recognise that the effort they are investing in the programme brings about the desired changes in these areas, it will reinforce their motivation. This can be done through the use of the clinical assessments that are conducted throughout the programme. A number of domains are assessed at the outset of treatment. These include estimates of the loved one's use, the concerned other's mood, their functioning and their overall life satisfaction. Whilst these assessments offer useful insight into the current situation of the concerned other, they can also provide important baseline data. As the programme progresses or if the concerned other's motivation begins to flag, these tools can be repeated. These results can be compared to those at intake to assess whether the loved one's use has decreased and the concerned other's quality of life has increased. These assessments can be conducted periodically, such as part of a monthly review process.

We also use reinforcement principles to improve the quality of life for the concerned other. Central to this aim was the adapting of the CRAFT Happiness Scales (Meyers and Smith, 1995) and Hassle Scales (Kanner et al., 1981). Modifications were made for a number of reasons.

Firstly, the name 'Happiness Scale' did not translate well with UK populations. Secondly, it was felt that frequency of problems in each domain would help prioritise care-planned goals. And thirdly, concerned others on the programme tended towards suggesting that the absence of pressures would improve such as being 'less stress', 'less anxious' or 'less busy' and so on rather than positive goals. Splitting the domains between current dissatisfactions and what would improve this area thus offered more scaffolding in identifying the stresses that might negatively reinforce change and the rewards that might positively reinforce change. Within this framework, concerned others are invited to rate their current levels of satisfaction in every specific domain of their life. This includes their own drug and alcohol use, family, environment and social life amongst others. The purpose of this exercise is to generate possible positive reinforcing leads that might improve the concerned other's life across every domain of social functioning. This can assist concerned others to examine their own needs after extended periods of neglect. This is then used as reference material to inform a structured care plan (Hoggans, 2008). This care plan means that the PACT programme meets the requirements of UK recommendations (see Figure 9).

Relationships are a primary source of reinforcement for concerned others and social networks tend to be the first level of enrichment sacrificed in caring for a loved one. Improving the concerned other's social life has a major impact on reducing their stress. This network can provide support in a number of areas. Firstly, they can provide a respite for when the concerned other withdraws from the intoxicated loved one. In more drastic circumstances, they may

Domain	Score	Mth Freq	What makes it x?	What is it like when it is higher than x?
Drugs/Alcohol	1 2 3 4 5 6 7 8 9 10	30	Started smoking heavily again	Not smoking, feeling healthier.
Partnering	1 2 3 4 5 6 7 8 9 10	15 days	Arguing because of son's use, tend to take frustrations out on each other.	Closer, have more time to spend together doing things that we enjoy like eating out or going to the caravan.
Family	1 2 3 4 5 6 7 8 9 10	30	Feel that we are neglecting the younger siblings.	Supporting youngest son with school work. Taking daughter out shopping.
Employment	1 2 3 4 5 6 7 8 9 10	N/A	Feels like a sanctuary where I can escape the mess at home.	I am able to focus more when things are easier at home.
Housing	1 2 3 4 5 6 7 8 9 10			

Figure 9. Example of life audit

provide a safe haven in the light of domestic violence. The network can play a critical role once treatment entry is achieved by helping support the newly substance free individual occupy their time. As importantly though, the network can offer the concerned other increased social contact and recreation to improve the quality of their own life. Different individuals within the network may be more appropriate for different functions. Research studies indicate indirectly that larger social networks are more effective in supporting both the concerned other and the loved one (Landau, 2004). This can be especially useful if there is a high degree of tension between the loved one and the concerned other. Broadening the network with involved others can break the established tensions, alleviating any polarisation in the relationship. The problem in extending the social network is the lack of confidence or the deep reticence that many concerned others feel in asking for support from others. They may fear rejection or worry that they are burdening people. Reviewing the possible responses, rehearsing approaches and considering how the concerned other would feel if people close to them ask for their help can encourage them in their approach.

An important aspect of the concerned other's quality of life is recreation. Recreation can be sacrificed for any number of reasons. Firstly, the cost of enabling may impinge on people's ability to do so. Secondly as the concerned other battles with their loved one's use their energy becomes increasing depleted. When people are fatigued they are liable to sacrifice their leisure as it is expendable in a way that other demands of life are not. This can be very double edged. Research suggests that the more rewarding activities we sacrifice then the more depressed we become (Lewinsohn et al., 1992). This becomes a vicious cycle where people retreat from other sources of enrichment. However, the reverse also appears to be true. The more we engage in activities we enjoy or are passionate about, the more it stimulates our appetite for other things.

Identifying sources of recreation can be fairly straightforward for many concerned others. Reviewing what they used to enjoy or wanted to do but have not been able to may elicit a wide range of activities. However, in other cases where depression is a feature, some concerned others may find it very difficult to identify anything that they find pleasurable. This is because many people with depression also suffer with over-generalised memory. Over-generalised memory occurs when people can describe all the things that they are not looking forward to or worry about, but find it difficult to identify what they are looking forward to or what they enjoy. For these concerned others memory prompts and exploration can be helpful in generating leads and suggestions. The practitioner should model enthusiasm and genuine interest in the recreational pursuits that the concerned other does identify. Exploration of these areas can deepen the concerned other's own ideas about what they enjoy and can make desire for the tasks even more contagious.

1.27 Reducing Pressure on the Concerned Other

Reducing the stresses that the concerned other experiences is a vital component of the programme. This can be achieved in several ways. Firstly, by developing communication skills the concerned other can reduce the incidence of conflict which has such a negative effect on the concerned other and the loved one. A second area which will reduce the stress that the concerned other is under is in terms of domestic abuse. This may take several forms from physical, emotional or psychological aggression to threats, name calling, blackmail and other more insidious varieties. Should the concerned other identify domestic violence as an issue at assessment, then reducing domestic abuse will always be the first priority of the intervention. It is essential to protect the concerned other's well-being first and foremost.

Procedures for the reduction of domestic violence include an emergency plan in the light of imminent assault. In these circumstances, the concerned other is advised to plan any withdrawal in advance by having clothes, cash, documents and toiletries deposited in a safe place in order to facilitate an immediate exit. Whilst those that are subjected to violence (usually women) are advised to leave the aggressor, many do not want to or feel even greater guilt and loss of self-worth by being pressed into doing so. Where the concerned other wishes to stay in a relationship that has become increasingly abusive, it should be respected. The practitioner's role is to support the concerned other to reduce the incidence of aggression. Any child protection procedures will obviously need to be considered as part of this process. The second line of intervention is to conduct a detailed functional analysis of any incidents of violence. Based on this analysis, it is possible to tailor a response that can defuse potentially threatening situations before they occur in the future. This approach has been effective within the CRAFT model (Meyers and Smith, 1995) though we have adapted it further by presenting it as a log rather than as an isolated assessment. This allows for greater comparison of incidents over time in order to ensure that the aggression is being reduced. This is also used in combination with a treatment plan to develop responses to aggression.

This approach can be effective in cases of situational aggression which is triggered by current environmental pressures or instrumental aggression where the loved one wants something. However, when conducting this assessment it is important to note when pre-meditated violence is a key feature. Planned or pre-meditated assaults are indicative of more complex underlying issues and re-arranging external triggers or consequences is unlikely to have any impact on this behaviour. Ensuring this approach is reducing incidences of aggression is vital for the concerned other's safety. Should it be clear that environmental or situational triggers do not contribute to the incidence then termination and the wider safety of the concerned other is a priority.

Outside of any domestic abuse, the concerned other will have cultivated many coping strategies to deal with the pressures that they live with everyday. However, as human beings tend to be drawn to their problems in the first instance, it is not uncommon for many concerned others to focus on the most difficult times. This is not to suggest these times are not demanding. However, the fact that they deal with incredibly difficult problems; that they are able at times to switch off from their loved one's problems or that they simply battle on regardless, indicates that they have a wide range of resources they may not consciously be aware that they have. Solution focused therapy (Berg and Miller, 1992) suggests that many people in adverse situations have more coping strategies and skills than they realise; it is simply that they neglect these in favour of reflecting on their problems. Solution focused therapy would always suggest that the client's story is two-sided. On the one hand there are the problems they describe and on the other there are the coping strategies they use which go unreported. It is not possible to experience difficulties without meeting them with equally adept coping strategies. For example, the concerned other cannot tell a history of great pain without telling of their fortitude. They cannot describe a story of trauma without telling about great resilience. They cannot tell of the years of battling without revealing terrific endurance. The concerned other may be barely coping but they are coping in more ways than they realise.

Some programmes for concerned others suggest that they train themselves in new coping skills. This can be a viable option but has a drawback. It can take a great deal of time to acquire new skills and perfect them. As the PACT programme is already rich in skills which the concerned other must practice and rehearse, it can feel like an additional burden to then expect them to learn to cope as well. Instead, the practitioner can draw upon what solution-focused therapy defines as the 'exception' (Berg and Ruess, 1998). This exceptional time invites the client to describe the times when the problem is **not** happening. The fact that the problem is not occurring suggests that the client is doing, thinking or feeling something different at these times in order for the problem to recede. Many concerned others are tempted to answer that the problems do not occur when their loved refrains from using. This is understandable. However, even when the loved one does use, there will be times when this feels more manageable than others. There will be times when the loved is more responsive to the concerned other than others. There will be times when, despite the multiple pressures they face, the concerned other is able to switch off. It can be invaluable to explore these times further to identify how the concerned other manages to do this *despite the pressures that they face*. This can illuminate the coping skills that the concerned other has already (and often unknowingly) cultivated. The fact that the concerned other can already perform these coping strategies – having done so already – means that they do not have to learn new skills but simply deploy the skills they already have more deliberately. The less confident the concerned other is, the smaller the exceptions will be to begin with. The practitioner should encourage them to try to use whatever positive coping skills they have found useful and refine those skills over time.

1.28 Closing Treatment

Endings in working relationships are powerful moments for both the practitioner and the concerned other. The concerned other has often reached a trough of utter hopelessness at the point when they seek professional assistance. The process of initiating change in their loved one, the reduction in the pressures in their own life and positive improvement in their social functioning may feel untenable at the outset of the programme. This can be compounded by the concerned other's previous attempts at seeking support being rebutted or ineffectual. As the programme unfolds and the glimmer of change begins to take form and solidify, it offers the concerned other new hope. By treatment completion the majority of the concerned others will have restored many core aspects of their lives which they once felt were irretrievable. This is not to suggest that the concerned other's lives will be perfect and most are not hoping for such. The restitution of a normal life and a loved one is sufficient. During such a transitional period a deep bond forms between the practitioner and the concerned other that makes endings emotional for both participants in the process. Formulating a positive ending in the final session provides closure for both parties. It should be viewed as an opportunity to review the processes and finalise any treatment outcomes and, as importantly, to say anything that needs to be said.

The closing session should include a review of the treatment outcomes of the programme. This should involve taking repeat measures that were conducted at the assessment baseline. This includes the frequency of the loved one's use in the comprehensive assessment, CES-D and Mood Screener. A review of current satisfaction with a repeat of the Life Audit is also helpful. These figures can be compared to those that the concerned other reported at intake and form the basis of their own assessment of their progress during the programme. It can be helpful to explore these scores from a more personal perspective by investigating what these changes mean in terms of the concerned other's actual experience and quality of life. This can then inform a broad discussion of how the concerned other found the programme. This should include feedback on what they found helpful and what they did not find so useful. Whilst it is expected that each concerned other will express idiosyncratic preferences, should any patterns appear in the feedback from a wide number of concerned other treatment groups, this should be considered carefully and responded to in order to ensure the programme evolves based on concerned others' experience. The closing session is also an opportunity for the practitioner to share their feedback on the concerned other's progress through the programme. Every concerned other is unique. They bring with them new insight, experiences and challenges. They test our practice and their responsiveness or unresponsiveness to the practitioner is the arena where practitioners really learn their craft. I have never worked with a client that did not teach me something, even if it was what not to do. Offering this feedback to the concerned other can demonstrate how they have contributed to the programme and help the practitioner to reflect on their own development within the normal course of practice.

1.29 Outcomes and Measures

Taking outcomes measurements is an essential feature of the delivery of all treatment programmes. Baseline measurements should be taken at the commencement of treatment and at its completion. Periodic evaluation and longer-term follow-up can be invaluable but difficult with limited resources. This outcome monitoring can assist service development in a number of areas. As we have already seen, measuring the impact of the programme on reducing their loved one's behaviours reinforces the concerned other's participation in the programme as objective feedback demonstrates their progress. Sustaining motivation in the concerned other is essential, as they may experience a period of increased strain or setbacks before the targeted behaviours change. Precise outcomes measures can also be used to inform other concerned individuals who are considering whether to enter into the programme. Providing these curious but often sceptical others with data on how the programme has helped others, can reinforce the value of entering the programme. This can be very important as many concerned others arrive at a point of hopelessness before seeking help. Such data can challenge negative expectations sufficiently for them to try the programme.

Finally, collecting data has a dual purpose. Besides allowing concerned others to assess their progress, collecting data is important for the development of services from a wider perspective. All treatment services are now expected to collect data to demonstrate not just the number of individuals who have been seen, but what was achieved with these individuals. This has introduced new levels of accountability within treatment services that must demonstrate their effectiveness. Collecting data that measures the impact of the programme on concerned others is especially important. It is imperative that services for concerned others demonstrate their value if they are to attract the financial support to initiate, continue or expand the range of provision. Failure to do so may contribute to the failure of adequate service provision for concerned others. This makes the gathering of outcome monitoring a priority. The best outcome monitoring is embedded within the framework of the treatment itself rather than in addition to it. A range of tools are included within the programme, each corresponding to the goals of the service. Practitioners should take these measures of the concerned other's functioning at intake as a baseline measure prior to treatment and then repeat the same measures at treatment completion. A pro forma for recording the initial baseline results in comparison to the repeat measure is included in the final review conducted at treatment completion. This will demonstrate how successfully the programme has met its aims for each concerned other (see Table 18).

Table 18. Principle outcomes and their measurement in the PACT programme

Outcome	Measurement at intake	Measurement at completion
Assist the loved one into treatment	Is the loved one in treatment?	Did the loved one enter treatment?
Support the loved one in treatment	Loved one's weekly drug and alcohol use Length of previous treatment episodes	Loved one's weekly drug and alcohol use Length of current treatment episode
Reduce the stresses on the loved one	C.E.S. Mood screener	C.E.S. Mood screener
Improve the quality of life for the CO	Life audit scores	Life audit scores

The most obvious measure for treatment entry is whether the loved one did indeed seek professional help and engage with these services. The comprehensive assessment tool asks whether the loved one is currently seeking help and their subsequent entry into treatment services is recorded at the treatment completion review. Previous treatment episode lengths identified at the comprehensive assessment stage can also be compared with the loved one's current engagement levels, in order to assess whether the programme assisted the loved one to remain in treatment. Further differences in terms of the impact of the programme on the loved one's consumption can also be established by repeating the Loved One's Weekly Use table in the final review session.

Measuring the improvements in the concerned other's own social functioning is difficult. In general, improvement in social functioning is a difficult area to assess. Historically, research in this area has been sparse despite being of critical importance in a wider range of social, medical and psychological interventions. As Tyrer and Casey (1998) summarised in their review of social functioning research: '. . . the subject of social functioning is in a developmental phase. In fact, it is reasonable to conclude that it is at a very early phase of development, summed up in the words of Groucho Marx, 'risen from nothing to a state of absolute poverty'.' One measure of the concerned other's progress is the Life Audit. Having recorded data at the assessment stage this measure can be repeated at treatment completion and the differences in a raw total score or the difference between sub-scores will be indicative of the progress made in improving the concerned other's life. It should be recognised that this would not be a validated assessment tool. Should any purchasers of the service require a validated outcome tool then the Outcome Rating Scales and Session Rating Scales referred to earlier also provide an accurate measure of improvements in the concerned other's functioning and are validated for a wide range of treatment populations.

In terms of reducing the stresses that the concerned other experiences measured as a programme gain, a number of assessment tools can be used. One important tool is the Mood Screener (Robins et al., 1981). This assessment tool is designed to assess the historic or current experience of clinical depression in the concerned other. This tool was introduced after the initial feasibility where it became apparent that many concerned others present with significant depression and some with suicidal thinking. It is felt to be an ethical obligation to ensure effective screening of more profound levels of depression in order to provide the concerned other with wider medical support if necessary. The Centre of Epidemiological Studies-Depression Scale (Radloff, 1977) is also used to establish baseline mood of the concerned other at treatment entry. This assessment tool does not indicate the existence of depression but identifies variance within general mood. Repeating these assessments at treatment completion will give a reliable indication of reductions in negative mood states and whether the programme has reduced the stress the concerned other is under.

1.30 Conclusion

Despite prevailing assumptions in the field of addiction treatment, it is evident that the concerned others of problem users have a significant, if not defining, influence on change. Indeed, when the problems of substance misuse are clarified, it becomes apparent that external pressure to change is an inevitable consequence. These pressures relate to the type of social complications with the users' relationships. When relationships are placed under pressure, concerned others respond in kind to restore the previous equilibrium. As such, addiction and pressure to change are two sides of the same process. Conversely, pressure to change does not relate to the substances used or the amount consumed. The field should no longer regard these external pressures to change as imposing upon the rights of the user but rather as a proactive attempt to prevent the violation of important relationships. This is echoed in research into family responses whereby the effort of the family appears to be the greatest single influence on treatment entry and further demonstrated by the reluctance of the family to sever contact with the problem user entirely. When pressure to change becomes an inevitable consequence, and the concerned other remains the central force in the problem user's life, the question becomes how to best orchestrate family efforts to precipitate change. By evaluating the consequences that drive or curtail use in the individual problem user, it is possible to shift the balance of consequences in favour of change. This demands sustained effort in equipping the concerned other to do so whilst maintaining a relationship with their loved one. The strong suggestion from the current research is that families may vary in their willingness to invest in this process. Where the concerned other has become increasingly emotionally drained through many years of trying to change the loved one, termination and support from other services may be more appropriate.

The concerned other should not be understood as a mere adjunct to treatment. They are not an additional resource for an agency to extend their own aims. Concerned others remain individuals in their own right, with their own unique hopes, needs and wants. The enormous collateral damage inflicted on their life through a loved one's use is not resolved simply by getting the problem user into treatment. The concerned other requires support and assistance to rebuild their own lives. This is no easy task after many years of self-sacrifice and effort. Assisting the concerned other to overcome a profound sense of personal defeat, revive an appetite for a richer life and foster the belief that they can act and influence those around them takes wilful and sustained support. Within this process it is essential that the practitioner offers them the respect, understanding and empathy that the immediacy of any helpful relationship requires. This demands that the practitioner exorcises prevalent and invidious assumptions about the concerned other being the source of the loved one's use, or that these problems satisfy deeper unstated wants within them. There remains no evidence to support these theories which should be regarded as therapeutically speculative at best.

Instead, this programme assumes that the most effective way to help concerned others is to translate substantiated research findings into practical strategies and solutions that assist concerned others to achieve their own personal and relational goals. It respects the concerned other's efforts as symptomatic of the importance of the relationship with the loved one and not an affliction. It supposes that the best way to achieve this end is to provide concerned others with a broad spectrum of possible responses to their loved one and an expansive range of support to address their own needs. This programme is designed to give the practitioner a framework within which to deliver on this ethos, but it is by no means complete. Instead it should be considered as a foundation for the practitioner's approach which should be continually informed by the insight, experiences and qualities that the concerned others bring themselves. Ultimately it will be their feedback that will allow the practitioner and programme to mature. A programme that is closed to this will remain in its infancy. It is sincerely hoped that the ideas and techniques described in this manual can offer a new beginning for concerned others, their loved ones, and those practiioners tasked with their assistance.

Parents and Carers Training

Client Manual

Name _____

Date _____

Agency _____

Key worker _____

Phil Harris

Russell House Publishing

RHP

Part Two: The Programme

Part Two of this manual (*The Concerned Other: How to change problematic drug and alcohol users through their family members* by Phil Harris [RHP, 2010]) contains the compete programme, including the pages of copiable material identified by the footer © Phil Harris, *The Concerned Other*, www.russellhouse.co.uk.

Notes for the Practitioner

This page contains notes on copying certain pages in this manual for use in your direct work with clients. Only the identified pages may be copied. If you want more copies of other pages please note that *multiple copies* of the complete manual are available direct from the publisher. To discuss *discounts* please contact us on 01297 443948 or jan@russellhouse.co.uk.

RHP and Phil Harris recommend that concerned others be supplied with a 'booklet' of the 66 worksheet pages along with the cover (opposite) and a copy of this page.

A number of assessment and outcome tools are included in the programme for the practitioner to use in their work with concerned others:

- Comprehensive Assessment (pages 105–112)
- Mood Screener (page 115)
- (CES-D) Depression Scale (pages 118–119)
- Life Satisfaction Audit (page 123)
- My Better Life (pages 126–127)
- Closure and Review (pages 269–270)

Notes for the Concerned Other

If you have received these pages, either as a photocopy or as a printout, please note that they may not be copied in any form.

Please see your key worker or practitioner if you need further copies of the worksheets.

Induction and Assessment for the PACT Programme

Induction

2.1 What Have You Tried so Far?

Overview: The induction programme is to be utilised when first meeting with the concerned other. Besides gaining background information about why the concerned other has sought professional help, it can assist concerned others to assess the value of their previous strategies to change their loved one, gain insight into the demands of the programme and to be aware of how their loved one may respond on learning that the concerned other is seeking professional help. This can help the concerned other to make an informed decision as to whether they should enter into the PACT programme prior to comprehensive assessment and care planning. The practitioner should be mindful that the concerned other may be in a state of shock having recently discovered that the loved one is using drugs problematically or distraught by a recent crisis that has triggered treatment entry. Time should be spent investigating this trigger event empathetically prior to drawing upon worksheets to explain the programme.

Aim: To review the strategies that the concerned other has previously tried in order to change their loved one's use. This will help the concerned other evaluate whether these previous attempts have been useful and whether it is time to try a different approach.

Rationale: The concerned other will have presented for help after the shock of discovering their loved one's problem or having battled with it for a protracted period of time. It is not uncommon for family members to take up often dramatic and well-intended approaches to change their loved one. This should always be seen as understandable in light of the intolerable situation they find themselves in. At the same time, many of the interventions we will teach them, such as targeted rewards, will seem counter-intuitive to many concerned others. Therefore it is important to review the success, or lack of, of their current repertoire of approaches and the emotional cost of pursuing ineffective approaches. By the programme's very nature, concerned others are seeking help precisely because their strategies are not working. If the concerned other's current strategies can be seen to be both high effort and unproductive, it may increase their openness to consider other options.

The broad framework of typical family responses has been used (Worksheet 2.1) to serve as a prompt for the concerned other. The individual mechanisms that families use to pressure their loved ones to change have not been listed but grouped into typical phases of response. It is likely that the concerned other will disclose many dramatic failed strategies which were well intended but counter-productive. Normalisation and non-judgmental listening is essential in these instances. The spread of responses may also be revealing. Concerned others who identify primarily active phase responses may have recently discovered their loved one's use and are highly motivated to address it. Concerned others who are investing effort into diminishing consequences will have significant impairment in their own social functioning. Concerned others who identify more withdrawal approaches may be more jaded and pessimistic regarding their ability to change the loved one.

Step 1: Explain that the purpose of the worksheet is to review the strategies that they have previously used, or are currently using, to try to influence their loved one's pattern of use. This will help assess what is working, whether anything needs to be modified or whether it is time to revise their approach.

Step 2: Work through each phase, one at time. Explain that while not all families are the same, they often go through a sequence of responses in battling with a loved one's use. Explain each phase on the table and offer examples. For example, the active phase might include challenging the loved one, getting others to threaten them, taking drugs and alcohol to 'show them' what it is like or a wide array of inventive shock tactics. Invite the concerned other to identify specific approaches that they have tried in order to change their loved one's current consumption of drugs or alcohol. This may be offered as a list or presented as one item at a time. Either way, record each strategy succinctly in the table under the heading describing the approach. It is important to remember that many concerned others can interpret help-seeking for their loved one as signal of failure in itself. Furthermore, they may feel even more exposed revealing the desperate measures they have taken. They are likely to punctuate their explanations with discounting statements such as, 'I know it was not the right thing to do' or, 'It was probably wrong but . . .' These punctuations should be met with empathy, acknowledgment of the desperation they felt at the time and the normalisation of their responses. This provides the opportunity to build non-judgmental rapport and to demonstrate immediate acceptance of the concerned other, contributing to the safe environment necessary for productive work together.

Step 3: Once each strategy has been identified, we can review the effort and cost to the concerned other of implementing this approach. For example, many concerned others may be tempted to corral their loved ones into private treatment before they are ready to engage. Others may sustain high levels of conflict to force change. Sustaining these efforts is demanding. Evaluating the effort of implementing this approach may help the concerned other understand the source of their emotional exhaustion, especially when compared to the second domain, which defines the degree of success. Reflecting on how useful the approach was in effecting change should help them recognise not the futility of trying to help, but the limits of their previous strategy. This can be broadened with the wider consideration of their own feelings in response to the lack of progress. In contrast to the emotional exhaustion that results from immense effort, the subsequent failure of this investment compounds their situation by generating powerful feelings. Failure, guilt, disappointment, anger, helplessness, frustration and impotence can follow the most well-meaning but misdirected approach. Therefore, it is important that we extend our exploration beyond the outcome of the adopted strategy and into the concerned other's response to this outcome.

Step 4: Once the major strategies have been reviewed systematically, the issue of whether the concerned other feels ready or emotionally able to implement another approach should be discussed. Again, this may be met with a range of responses. Families in the active phase of constructive helping and who have not yet exhausted themselves may be more willing to invest in the programme. The long-suffering family whose loved one has drained them of resources and hope may be more ambivalent. Remind them that they do not have to make a decision until they see how the PACT programme works and what will be expected of them. In the worst case scenario, they should always be reminded that they are able to sample the programme and review whether it works for them as they go along.

Treatment goal:	Induction
Associated worksheets:	**2.1 What Have You Tried so Far?** 2.2 How PACT Changes Your Loved One's Use 2.3 Temptations and Threats
Further context:	1.4 Family Coping

2.1 What Have You Tried so Far?

Approach	Details	How much effort? Low High	How much changed? None A lot
Active phase: Includes purposeful efforts or attempts to change your loved one			
		1 2 3 4 5	1 2 3 4 5
		1 2 3 4 5	1 2 3 4 5
		1 2 3 4 5	1 2 3 4 5
Inactive phase: Includes accepting their use but trying to reduce the consequences of it			
		1 2 3 4 5	**1 2 3 4 5**
		1 2 3 4 5	**1 2 3 4 5**
		1 2 3 4 5	**1 2 3 4 5**
Withdrawing phase: Getting on with one's own life regardless of the loved one's use			
		1 2 3 4 5	1 2 3 4 5
		1 2 3 4 5	1 2 3 4 5
		1 2 3 4 5	1 2 3 4 5
Considering these past approaches, do you feel it is time to try something new?			

2.2 How PACT Changes Your Loved One's Use

Aim: To initiate greater understanding of the loved one's use and introduce the core principles of the programme in order to assist the concerned other to make an informed decision regarding committing to the programme.

Rationale: The PACT programme is a demanding skills-based approach where the concerned other will have to make a sustained effort to facilitate change in the loved one. These demands will entail taking a counter-intuitive approach to their loved one by offering alternative sources of enrichment and reducing conflict. This is an opportunity to explain the mechanics of the programme to the concerned other so that they can gauge whether it is appropriate for them. Understanding the rationale of the approach as simply as possible allows them to make an informed decision as to whether to commit to the programme and what will be expected of them if they do.

The rationale of the programme is based on the assumption that people take drugs and alcohol, even problematically, because of the consequences that these substances produce. These consequences are not simply the physical effects of the drugs but are more wide ranging. The more that we understand the consequences that the loved one desires and the ones they abhor, the greater the influence we can have on their use. This is because we can influence these consequences, decreasing the benefits of use and increasing the cost of use. In order to demonstrate how this works, the practitioner should invite the concerned other to map out the current consequences of the loved one's use to the best of the concerned other's knowledge. This should be done one area at a time, identifying as many reinforcers and punishers in each area as they can. This is also an opportunity to affirm the concerned other's knowledge of their loved one and their use and how important this insight will be throughout the programme.

Step 1: Introduce the exercise by explaining how it will illustrate the key principles of the programme and how it will teach the concerned other to influence their loved one's use. Remind them that this is in order for them to make an informed decision regarding whether the programme feels right for them. Once the concerned other understands how the approach works they can consider whether it feels right for them and whether they believe that they can apply the approach.

Step 2: Inform the concerned other that the programme does not suppose that the loved one is using because of a single deep-rooted psychological problem. Rather, consumption is driven by the many consequences of using drugs and or alcohol. These consequences not only vary from person to person but can vary over time. For example, if they consider why the concerned other first drank an alcoholic drink themselves compared to why they might drink now will demonstrate how consequences can shift over time. These consequences can be of different types. Some of the consequences of use are felt as rewarding by the individual and others are felt as punishing. The first type of consequences that will be explored are those aspects of use which their loved one finds rewarding.

Step 3: Start by identifying the positive reinforcers in area A. These are the desirable consequences that drug and alcohol use offer the user. The concerned other is invited to consider what positive things the loved one gets out of their use. These can range from the taste, effects, identity, esteem from peers, offering them something enjoyable to do with their time, being close to a partner and so on. As the concerned other bears witness to so much pain and chaos in the loved one's life, it can be hard for them to see these positive benefits at first or they can find such an investigation to be justifying the loved one's use. They should be reminded that if there were no benefits to counteract the bad things, then their loved one would not still be using. Furthermore, it is important to understand the use first rather than agree with it. Identifying as many positive rewards as possible with the concerned other fosters deeper empathy and insight into the problematic usage.

Step 4: The exploration of rewards then turns to the negative reinforcers in area B. These are the consequences that remove or nullify unpleasant consequences. These include consequences such as escapism, the relief of stress, the alleviation of boredom, the reduction of pain, the sedation of conflicts, or the removal of withdrawal symptoms. It is important to remember that these are not punishers. People engage in these behaviours in order to *avoid* punishing consequences. Where the concerned other identifies areas such as reducing stress, pressures or conflicts the practitioner must ensure that the particular stresses are identified, whether they are from specific aspects of work, school, or tension with particular people.

Step 5: Once all the reinforcers are identified, the practitioner can sum up these benefits of use for the loved one. A useful way of explaining how these rewarding consequences contribute to consumption is by saying to the concerned other 'If you were offered a substance that could do all these good things for you and remove all these bad things would you be tempted to take it right now?' In this way the concerned other can appreciate that the greater these rewarding consequences are for the loved one then the more they will use.

Step 6: The practitioner should then explore the punishing consequences of use starting with the positive punishers in area C. These are the actual undesirable consequences of use. These can include hangovers, illness, negative judgements from others, depressed moods, shame, arguing and guilt amongst others. Again it is important to assist the concerned other to identify specific positive punishers that relate to their loved one. Some people are more sensitive to social judgement or health concerns than others for example.

Step 7: We now explore the negative punishers in the same way in area D. Negative punishers describe the loss of important things that occurs because of use. This can include example such as social rejection, loss of important relationships or breakdown in other interests. What hopes, ambitions or promising relationships is the loved one missing out on as a result of their use?

What are their substance-use free peers doing with their lives in contrast to the loved one? Has the loved one ever remarked upon this?

Step 8: The practitioner should summarise these punishing consequences with the reverse of the question put to the concerned other before. If they were offered a substance that did only these punishing things, would they take one? The answer is usually no. The practitioner should explain to the concerned other that if the negative consequences of use are greater than the positive ones, people's use decreases. They can understand their loved one's use as a balance between these two forces. They may have noticed that there are times when the loved one has used more or used less, and this is often caused by a shift in balance between the rewards and the punishing consequences of use. When these competing forces remain balanced, the loved one will continue to use until the consequences get better or worse. As such, the rewards must decrease and the punishers must increase in order to shift the loved one towards change.

Step 9: This is important as it is possible for those close to the problem user to shift this balance of consequences. This involves reducing the positive rewards of use and increasing the negative consequences of use. This can be done by:

- We can decrease the positive benefits of use by providing alternative rewards at the times when the loved one would typically use.

- We can decrease the negative reinforcers by reducing the conflict between the loved one and the concerned other by improving communication skills.

- We can increase the positive punishment on the loved one by allowing the natural consequences of their own use to affect their lives.

- We can increase the negative punishment on the loved one by removing planned rewards and the concerned other should they use drugs or alcohol.

Step 10: In order to do this the practitioner and the concerned other must work together to identify these consequences and develop clear strategies to shift this balance. It is essential within this that the concerned other is very consistent in the approach. At the same time they will never be asked to do anything that they do not want to do but applying these strategies consistently is important for success. At the same time the programme will also focus on the concerned other's needs by reducing the pressures that they are under and improving the quality of their life.

Step 11: The practitioner should now explore whether the concerned other feels that the programme will be relevant for them and discuss any issues that they might have in the applying the programme.

Treatment goal:	Induction
Associated worksheets:	2.1 What Have You Tried so Far? **2.2 How PACT Changes Your Loved One's Use** 2.3 Temptations and Threats
Further context:	1.15 PACT: A Behavioural Ethos 1.16 Reinforcement and Substance Misuse 1.17 Reinforcement and Change 1.18 Principles of Treatment Entry

2.2 How PACT Changes Your Loved One's Use

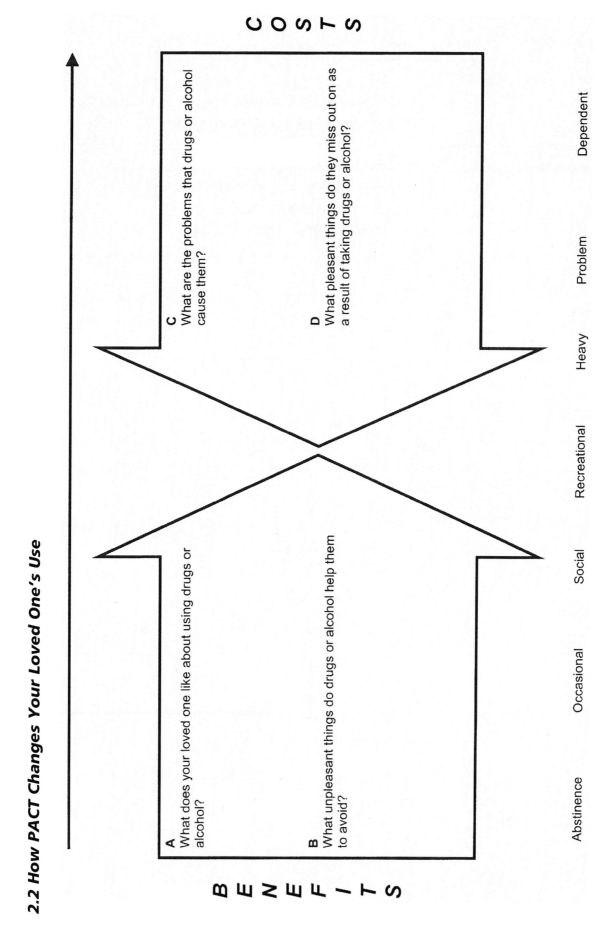

COSTS

C
What are the problems that drugs or alcohol cause them?

D
What pleasant things do they miss out on as a result of taking drugs or alcohol?

A
What does your loved one like about using drugs or alcohol?

B
What unpleasant things do drugs or alcohol help them to avoid?

BENEFITS

Abstinence   Occasional   Social   Recreational   Heavy   Problem   Dependent

2.3 Temptations and Threats

Aim: To explain the extinction burst that the concerned other may experience as they implement changes in their established relationship with their loved one. This is in order to anticipate attempts by the loved one to undermine the concerned other's commitment to the programme.

Rationale: Implementing changes in the relationship can cause the loved one to react. This can occur even when the loved one is told that the concerned other is seeking professional help. The loved one may anticipate that the concerned other will force them to change or cease to support them in ways that has inadvertently enabled their use. In response to these changes, imagined or real, the loved one will resist them. This may cause a burst of antagonistic behaviour that is an attempt to restore the previous status quo where the use was either tolerated, permitted or assisted. This can range from dismissing the help that the concerned other is receiving to threatening, sulking or even tantrum-like behaviour. Alternatively, the loved one may attempt a charm offensive in order to mollify the concerned other into believing that such help is unnecessary. However, this will only be sustained for the short period of time necessary for the concerned other to drop out of the programme and the previous status quo will be resumed. This behaviour is referred to as an 'extinction burst' and occurs when any anticipated reward is withheld. As this is a highly predictable response, it is likely to occur when the concerned other makes changes that disrupt the loved one's pattern of use. However, the extinction burst occurs prior to the cessation of a behaviour. As such, it is a signal that the concerned other's strategies are working.

Preparing the concerned other for this response at the outset is important. As the concerned other implements changes it may trigger an apparent worsening of behaviour in the loved one. This is especially important if the loved one has a history of domestic abuse and will need careful management. Where domestic abuse or violence is occurring it is essential that the concerned other identifies this at the outset of the programme. Where it is occurring, the management of domestic violence is a priority regardless of any other competing priorities. Even where there is no domestic violence, it is important the concerned other understands the extinction burst. At the start of the programme their confidence may be low and so they may be vulnerable to being undermined in their application of the programme by a loved one. Describing the extinction burst can help them reframe the response in the loved one as a signal of effectiveness rather than the situation worsening. The concerned other should be reminded that any increase in the frequency of antagonistic behaviours tends to be short lived and occur because the changes are affecting the loved one's using patterns. Furthermore, the practitioner's ability to predict these responses can reinforce the concerned other's belief in the programme. Hence rather than the extinction burst undermining the concerned other's confidence, it can increase it.

Step 1: The practitioner should explain to the concerned other that the role of the worksheet is to identify reactions in the loved one's behaviour that might be caused by the changes the concerned other is trying to make. An understanding of these reactions is important because the loved one may try to undermine the concerned other's resolve to make positive changes in their life. These attempts to undermine their efforts are referred to as 'extinction bursts' and always occur when an expected reward is withheld. As such, the concerned other may occasionally experience a burst in antagonistic behaviour in their loved one as the programme unfolds. However, this burst occurs because the programme interferes with the loved one's expected reward: using drug or alcohol.

Step 2: Considering the following list of typical responses, has the love one ever responded in these ways when they have been unable to get you to do something that they wanted you to? Run through the list to identify as many as possible.

Step 3: For each example that the concerned other identifies, explore whether the loved one ever appeared to follow through on any of their threats or promises. This may indicate domestic violence and abuse. Wherever domestic violence is an issue the concerned other should be advised that in the face of personal threat they should give the loved one what they want and escape the situation as quickly as possible. It is also important to review how the concerned other responds to these threats and how helpful these responses are in addressing the issues of substance misuse.

Step 4: Based on this assessment the practitioner can ask how the loved one might respond to knowing that the concerned other is seeking professional help? This is an opportunity to explain that the extinction burst is often a sign that the approach is working or threatens the loved one use. Asking the concerned other what has been helpful in reducing these behaviours in the loved one in the past can help them prepare for any reactions in the loved one.

Treatment goal:	Induction
Associated worksheets:	2.1 What Have You Tried so Far? 2.2 How PACT Changes Your Loved One's Use **2.3 Temptations and Threats**
Further context:	1.20 Extinction Burst

2.3 Temptations and Threats

Threats	Have they followed through on these statements?	How have you responded to this?
They will hurt you		
They will hurt themselves		
They will divulge personal information about you		
They will leave you		
Blame a hurtful past		
Infer you do not love them		
Blame you for the problems		
Belittle you		
Other:		
Other:		
Temptations		
Remind you of how much they love you		
Promise it will be different		
Become distressed or vulnerable		
Remind you of how good things were between you		
Remind you that you are special		
Tell you that they are changing now		
Other:		
Other:		

Assessment

2.4 Comprehensive Assessment

Overview of Assessment: This section describes the comprehensive assessment, baseline measures and comprehensive care planning stages of the programme. Once the concerned other has been inducted into the programme, understands the demands that the programme requires and is committed to the process, there should be a comprehensive assessment of their needs. The comprehensive assessment has multiple functions. It allows the concerned other to ventilate emotion by organising their understanding and experiences into a coherent narrative. This should offer insight into the exact nature of the loved one's problems as well as the hardships that they face in their own lives. It will also offer the concerned other the opportunity to prioritise their treatment goals. It is important to recognise that not all elements of the programme are to be deployed. The corresponding case management (My Better Life) harmonises with the life domains set out in the comprehensive assessment tool. This is to ensure that there is a good fit between the treatment programme and the issues raised at assessment. Finally, whilst some outcome data is included within the comprehensive assessment in order to limit duplication, additional outcome tools are employed to take objective readings of the concerned other's current functioning at the outset of treatment. All this information can be used to offer feedback to the concerned other regarding their current situation, the severity of the loved one's use and can also be used at follow-up or treatment completion to quantify their treatment gains and the programme as a whole.

Aim: The aim of the assessment is to establish mutual understanding of the loved one's use and its impact on the concerned other to enable effective treatment planning.

Rationale: Assessments of concerned other needs to be comprehensive for several reasons. First, it must be remembered that two people are being assessed; the severity of the loved one's substance use and the impact of this on the concerned other's life. These issues can be difficult to separate at assessment. Concerned others tend to see the needs of their loved one as paramount. Calibrating the severity of the loved one's use is important in identifying appropriate treatment responses. However, the assessment can be biased towards the loved one with the concerned other presenting their current situation exclusively in relation to their loved one's use. This may detract from the concerned other's needs which are often pressing and intolerable. Assessing both sets of needs is important in order to negotiate a meaningful care plan to assist the concerned other as well as provide a clear understanding of the loved one's difficulties. This information can also offer the concerned other a perspective on the loved one's use and increase their trust in the skills of the practitioner.

There is also another important sub-goal in the assessment process. Concerned others have battled with the problem for some time prior to seeking professional help. The comprehensive assessment should allow them to ventilate their feelings of frustration in a systematic and focused way. Allowing the concerned other to not only voice their feelings but also have their stresses acknowledged at assessment can help discharge these historic frustrations. This can allow for greater focus on the skills element of the programme that follows.

Personal details: This records the personal details of the concerned other and the problematic user. It must be remembered that many concerned others do not want their loved one or places of work to know that they are seeking professional help. Arranging appropriate contact points and times respects the concerned other's privacy and sets a respectful tone at the outset of the programme. The concerned other does not have to disclose the full name or address of the loved one. Having a first name can be helpful in referring to the loved one in more personable terms. The type and length of relationship between the concerned other and loved one can help with the prognosis of the PACT intervention. Long term kinship relationships or outstanding partnerships are more likely to influence the problem user. Collecting this data can also be invaluable in assessing the effectiveness of the programme across different treatment groups.

The loved one's drug and alcohol use: This looks to assess the range of substances currently used by the loved one. Increasingly people are combining drugs and alcohol. The substance that causes the concerned other the most worry should be considered the primary substance. Exploring the concerned other's knowledge of each substance used or any evidence that supports the belief that their loved one is using can also be helpful. The concerned other may not always be sure what drugs are being taken but may offer descriptions of substances or paraphernalia. Clarifying evidence of the loved one's consumption can eliminate misunderstandings or address fears at the outset of treatment. The concerned other may or may not have a clear idea of how much and how frequently the loved one uses substance(s). This information can be useful for building a picture of the current drug/alcohol problem but is not mandatory. Guesstimates can suffice here, and can be marked with a (g).

The evolution of problem use: Here the concerned other is given the opportunity to tell their story of events and allow for ventilation of feeling and can then be cross referenced to the symptoms of 'physical dependence' in order to identify any discrepancies. This is not designed to catch the concerned other out. It does allow for the practitioner to develop a clearer sense of the loved one's use where there is strong agreement. The concerned other may not know when the use was initiated in the first instance but they will have a clear sense of when the loved one's behaviour or personality began to change. Exploring the moment when they found out or realised their loved one was experiencing problems with drugs or alcohol can illuminate the family responses and their coping. This is a considerable shock for parents and can often lead to confrontation and conflict. Concerned others will usually suppose that their initial response was wrong. Reminding the concerned other that there is no correct response to this realisation or normalising their response can help foster a climate of non-judgmental support. Establishing when drug or alcohol use began to interfere with their loved one's life may give a guide to whether the loved one has experienced social exclusion and for what period of time. Descriptions of the loved one's life prior to the onset of the problem can give some indication of the treatment prognosis. Individuals who have had extensive periods of managing pro-social roles and remain connected to institutions of family, partners, work and non-using social groups may benefit from briefer interventions.

Using pattern: Inviting the concerned other to offer more detail about use is necessary to establish the pattern and intensity of consumption. There are three possible patterns to be considered. The first is a regular pattern characterised by daily use which is often seen in depressant drugs like alcohol, benzodiazepines, valium and opiates. If these drugs are identified in a daily pattern then there may be indications of physical dependence. Other drugs like cannabis can also be used in this way but will not cause physical dependence. The second pattern is episodic use. This is where the loved one binges on the drug for short periods of time. This often makes the loved one unpredictable, volatile or prone to long abscences. Stimulants like cocaine, crack, methamphetamine or amphetamine tend to be used in binge cycles of use with up to two weeks recovery periods. Alcohol and other drugs can also be used in this fashion too but the greater the daily drinking then the more likely physical dependence will develop. Finally it is a possibility that the loved one is currently drug or alcohol free. Establishing the period of time that the loved one has sustained sobriety is important, especially in the case of stimulant 'binge' drugs where the user may sustain short periods of abstinence for up to two weeks before succumbing to use again.

The concerned other should be asked what they believe is the loved one's current using patterns and a weekly use table completed. Whilst some concerned others are very familiar with the exact amounts that the loved one uses, many find this a more difficult area. Instead of looking at consumption, the concerned other should identify the levels of intoxication of their loved one to the best of their knowledge. The concerned other should reflect on the last week and gauge how intoxicated that their loved one appeared to them on the scales provided. If the concerned other had no contact with the loved one on any given day then they should complete the 'N/C' option instead of scoring the loved one. This information gathered will identify a base line measurement of their loved one's use. As such, as long as the concerned other remains consistent in their evaluations the differential between pre- and post-treatment consumption can be established. Consistently high daily use which corresponds with recognised symptoms of profound tolerance and withdrawal provides substantial evidence of physical dependence. This must be accounted for in any subsequent treatment plan for the loved one. If the concerned other does have more information regarding the amount the loved one uses, spends or the amount of time they spend intoxicated each day, this can also be recorded here for future comparison.

Physical dependence: The record of physical dependence is based upon the World Health Organisation's ICD-10 which describes the critical elements of physical dependence. As a general rule, this section will only apply to depressant drugs and alcohol that cause increased tolerance *and* profound withdrawal as opposed to stimulants. However, psychiatric drugs may have a more complex action. Many prescribed drugs do not necessarily increase tolerance but can induce withdrawal. The practitioner should check if any prescribed drugs being used are associated with dependence or withdrawal. This observation is not to suggest that certain drugs are 'non-problematic' because they do not induce dependence. It is to suggest that drugs and alcohol can cause physical and/or social problems. It is important to remember that the social problems of the loved are often more intractable than the dependence.

The practitioner need not read aloud the names of each descriptor of physical dependence highlighted in bold, which may be off-putting for some concerned others. These headers are primary an *aide-memoire* to remind the practitioner of the elements of dependence but they need to be managed very carefully. The concerned other must not be led with these questions regarding symptoms of physical dependence. They should be pitched with the context of 'Have you ever noticed that . . .' At the same time we do need to establish whether their loved one is experiencing more profound physical problems from their consumption. Exploring each item with the concerned other in an open way may allow them to identify any of the cluster symptoms of physical dependence. These symptoms can exist on a spectrum from mild to severe. They must be able to identify at least three symptoms which should include abnormal levels of tolerance and withdrawal symptoms that go beyond 'hangovers.' Loved ones who report engaging in consumption solely to relieve withdrawal symptoms indicate the severest levels of dependence.

Should the concerned other identify the positive symptoms of dependence, this should always be cross referenced against other information in the assessment before arriving at a conclusion. For example, does the use occur on a regular basis that involves substantial volumes of alcohol or the drug? People with physical dependence are very unlikely to show an episodic pattern of use because of the physical discomfort they experience without the substance. Secondly, the symptoms of dependence tend to be proportionate to each other. So, the problem drinker who experiences profound withdrawal begins to organise their life around consumption, making it ritualistic (narrowing of repertoire) and a priority over other activities (salient). This level of withdrawal can only be achieved with high consumption that would incapacitate others (tolerance). These symptoms do not always agree in this way but this should always be considered. Finally, the depiction of present consumption should relate to the concerned other's description of the evolution of the problem and relate to the social complications that the problem user is experiencing. The more profound the physical dependence then the more likely it is to impede the individual's social functioning. Working with the concerned other to achieve a mutual and consistent understanding of the loved one's problems is important. Where discrepancies arise, the practitioner should discuss this with the concerned other in order to clarify the situation. Finally, the last question the concerned other is asked is whether they feel that the loved one is at risk or experiencing direct harm from the use and may be more appropriate for clients who are not yet experiencing dependence or binge drinking.

Treatment planning for the loved one: The concerned other may not be the only person offering the loved one help. Other family members, friends or work colleagues may also be attempting to support the loved one in a multitude of ways, some of which may be helpful or unhelpful to the delivery of this programme. Obvious candidates are the immediate family but extended acquaintances can also be involved and sometimes these well-meaning gestures are kept secret from others. Identifying involved others is important, especially if the support they are offering is incompatible with the effective delivery of the programme. Consistency across a range of supportive relationships will help change the loved one more quickly.

Readiness to change: It is helpful to establish whether the loved one has sought any treatment before. This can offer insight into a number of areas. Firstly, treatment gains tend to be accumulative. Therefore, prior change attempts that supported increasingly protracted periods of abstinence may be a strong indicator of future success. Secondly, it may indicate what the loved one found helpful and unhelpful in previous treatment. This offers guidance regarding what future treatment the loved one may respond to or reject. Thirdly, the duration that they remained in treatment previously may give us a base indication of whether the concerned other's adoption of the PACT programme has helped their loved one stay in treatment. Asking how the loved one would respond at the present time to the suggestion to seek treatment will give some indication of their current state of readiness to change. If they were to reject the offer out of hand, it will indicate that they are in pre-contemplation. This can be explored further to gain insight into the nature of their reticence. This might be because of shame, pessimism that they can be helped, denial that they have a problem or because they are prone to explaining away their problems. Again this kind of detail can be helpful later in treatment when exploring prompts into treatment and what possible resistance might occur. This will help prepare for the possibility of rebuttal and offer guidance on managing these refusals.

It may also highlight that the problem user is currently displaying some motivation to change. If the concerned other believes that the loved one might consider the option of seeking professional help, in the light of some recent event that has troubled them both, the Rapid Entry sheet should be conducted immediately after the assessment to capitalise on any current internal motivation to change. This should only be done if there is very clear evidence of current motivation. This can be completed in combination with a problems-solving worksheet in order to establish the best time to make a rapid approach to treatment entry. If this is the case, this opportunity should be exploited and may result in treatment entry without recourse to the full programme. However, it must be remembered that treatment entry does not automatically reduce the concerned other's stresses or improve their life. Therefore, even in the light of rapid treatment entry, concerned others should be advised to work through this section of the programme.

The concerned other's social functioning: This explores the impact of the loved one's drug and alcohol use on the concerned other's own life. When interviewing the concerned other there is always a tendency for them to speak in terms of the loved one's hardships. This distracts from the struggles the concerned other may experience and the effects which the loved one's use can have on their physical and mental health and social functioning. This can be a difficult process for concerned others as it may be the first time that they have systematically reviewed the impact on their life or voiced their own anxieties. Despite the possibility of this feeling emotionally difficult, it is important to remind the concerned other that they have entered into a programme that will help them to overcome these problems.

In examining the wider social complications for the concerned other, we should be careful not to get too much historical detail. Assessment of social functioning is always about relevance. It is important to identify specific issues that are currently impeding the concerned other's life in each domain. The domains on the assessment tool can be changed, but if this is done it is imperative to include these changes on the corresponding Life Satisfaction Audit. This is to ensure that what is assessed is directly related to the treatment provided.

Mental health is an especially important domain for the concerned other. The pressures of living with a problem user can invoke depression and even suicidal feelings as the concerned other reaches a point of complete emotional exhaustion. If the assessment of mental health indicates severe mental distress in the concerned other, it is important to address these issues. The Mood Screener and CES-D Depression Scale should be used routinely even if any profound level of depression is not identified at the assessment stage. Where profound levels of mental illness are experienced, this should be addressed as a priority. Where the practitioner does not feel competent in this area, appropriate referrals should be made in negotiation with the concerned other.

Treatment planning: The ultimate happiness for the concerned other should be as open and optimistic as possible. We should invite the concerned other to let themselves go and really consider what they truly desire in terms of the relationship with their loved one. This goal is an important reinforcer for the concerned other. In times of doubt or uncertainty during the programme the concerned other can focus on this desire as their motivation for continuing. Checking progress in subsequent treatment that indicates that they are moving towards this goal can reinforce their motivation and commitment to the programme. The practitioner and the concerned other should also review which aspects of treatment are a priority for them. Evaluating the importance of each of the components of treatment on a scale of one to ten and their reasons for these evaluations can help the concerned other priorities target their current needs. This is to ensure that the concerned other experiences early subjective improvement in areas important to them which will have a beneficial effect on their commitment and engagement to the subsequent sessions. The exception to this rule is where domestic violence is indicated. Where the concerned other has experienced domestic violence of any kind, then the sub-sections of the programme dedicated to reducing these incidents should always be a priority regardless. The concerned other should be informed that their welfare and safety is the priority during this programme.

Other considerations: This core assessment should be supported with other relevant agency assessment tools. This should include risk assessment, child protection and any information regarding children who may be affected as directed by hidden harm. These assessments are not included in this manual as agencies should have their own policies in these areas.

Treatment goal:	Assessment
Associated worksheets:	**2.4 Comprehensive Assessment** 2.5 Mood Screener 2.6 (CES-D) Depression Scale 2.7 Life Satisfaction Audit 2.8 My Better Life
Further context:	1.1 What is Problematic Use? 1.2 Social Consequences of Use 1.14 PACT: Assessment

2.4 Comprehensive Assessment

1. Concerned other personal details

Client's name (concerned other):

Address:

Home telephone number:	Work telephone number:

Can we contact you by post? Yes/No

Can we contact you by phone? Yes/No

Preferred contact number:	Preferred times:

2. Loved one's details

Loved one's name:

Age:

Loved one's relationship to concerned other:

If, non-kinship relationship:
How long have you known the loved one: Years:
To the best of your knowledge, did your relationship begin before the alcohol or drug problem was established or after?

Do you live with the loved one?

If no, how much weekly contact do you have with the loved one? (Hours approx)

What kind of contact do you have? (Face-to-face, telephone etc.)

3. Loved one's alcohol or drug use

To the best of your knowledge, what substance is the loved one currently using?

Substance	Prescribed	Amount (volume or cost)	How often in last 30 days	Administration route
	Y/N		/30	
	Y/N		/30	
	Y/N		/30	

4. The evolution of problem use

To the best of your knowledge, when did your loved one begin taking this substance?

When did you feel that their use became a problem?

How did you find out your loved one had a problem?

How you see your loved one's drinking or drug use at this present time?

5. Loved one's social functioning

Domain	Prior to alcohol or drug problem, how well did your loved one function in the following areas?	What impact is their use now having in these areas?
Individually (mental health, emotional stability, self-control, physical health)		
Self-management (self-care, financial management, general life-skills, independence, crime)		
Relationships (family, intimate relationships, partnering)		
Social life (friends, hobbies, interests, community attachments or activities)		

Employment and training (work, training, finances)		

6. Which of the following statements best describes the pattern of your loved one's current use?

(a) their drinking or drug use follows a steady or regular pattern

(b) their drinking or drug use follows an episodic or binge pattern

(c) they are currently abstinent

Pattern table: Considering your loved one's use over the last seven days, how would you rate their level of intoxication at its highest?

Day	No contact	Certain they did not use	Not sure whether they had used but suspected	They showed signs of mild intoxication	They showed signs of obvious intoxication effecting mood or behaviour	Intoxicated to a point of incapacitation
Mon	N/C	1	2	3	4	5
Tues	N/C	1	2	3	4	5
Weds	N/C	1	2	3	4	5
Thurs	N/C	1	2	3	4	5
Fri	N/C	1	2	3	4	5
Sat	N/C	1	2	3	4	5
Sun	N/C	1	2	3	4	5

Would you say this was a typical week?

Is it better or worse at other times?

7. If your loved one is currently abstinent, to the best of your knowledge, when did they last use alcohol or drugs?

Date of last use:

Reason for loved one stopping?

8. Physical dependence

It is important for us to gain an understanding of the *physical* impact of use on your loved one, especially in regards to depressant drugs or alcohol. To the best of your knowledge, have you noticed any of the following behaviours or reactions in your loved one relating to their use?

Indicators	Yes/No	If Yes, what have you observed . . .
(A) Repertoire: Have you noticed that the pattern of your loved one's use has become increasingly routine regardless of the time of week?	Yes/No	
(B) Salience: Have you noticed that your loved one has neglected other interests, commitments or important relationships, preferring to use alcohol or drugs?	Yes/No	
(C) Tolerance: Have you noticed whether your loved one is taking increasingly large doses of alcohol or the drug without it appearing to affect them?	Yes/No	
(D) Withdrawal: Have you noticed your loved one experiencing physical reactions or withdrawal when they do not have alcohol or the drug?	Yes/No	
(E) Relief of withdrawal: Have you noticed your loved one ever use alcohol or a drug simply to alleviate the symptoms of withdrawal? Do they report that this use just makes them feel 'normal'?	Yes/No	
(F) Subjective compulsion: Have you ever noticed your loved one dwelling, obsessing or become anxious and irritable if drugs or alcohol are not available?	Yes/No	
(G) Reinstatement of use: Have you ever noticed that your loved one has rapidly returned to previous levels of use after attempts to stop despite knowing the harm it causes them?	Yes/No	
(H) Harmful or hazardous use: Is the drug or alcohol use presently causing harm to the loved one either physically or mentally or do you feel that they are at risk of harm?	Yes/No	

Note: This is relevant to alcohol, benzodiazepines and opiate use. It may also apply to psychiatric drugs. Three positive answers, with the presence of abnormal tolerance and withdrawal, may indicate dependence. Use of alcohol or drugs to alleviate withdrawal symptoms may indicate severe physical dependence.

9. Loved one's readiness to change

Has your loved one previously sought treatment for their alcohol or drug use?

Yes/No If yes, please complete the items below:

What treatment did they receive?

What did they value about the treatment experience (if known)?

What did they dislike about the treatment experience (if known)?

How long did they remain in treatment to the best of your knowledge?

What reason did they give for leaving treatment (if known)?

10. Has your loved one expressed any desire to change their drug or alcohol use in the past 14 days?

Yes/No. If yes, what triggered their current interest in seeking help?

What did they say regarding seeking help for their drug or alcohol use?

11. How do you think your loved one would respond if you suggest that they enter into treatment right now?

Positively or Negatively

If Positively, what makes you think that they would respond positively to this suggestion?

A 'yes' or 'positive' response in 10 and 11 may indicate existing motivation in the loved one. The rapid treatment entry procedures should be considered.

12. To the best of your knowledge, are any other people supporting your loved one at present?

Who are they?

Relationship to the loved one

What support do they offer?

_____

13. Social complications for the concerned other

What hardships are you experiencing as a result of your loved one's use in the following area?

Domain	Key problems
Marriage (partnering)	
Family	
Finances	
Social life	
Housing	
Employment and training	
Physical health	
Mental health	
Your own drug or alcohol use	
Hopes, future plans or aspirations	
Other:	

14. Child protection and hidden harm: Are any children (under 16s) or vulnerable adults being affected by the loved one's use?

(Explain the agency's 'child protection', 'confidentiality' and 'hidden harm policy' prior to asking the following questions.)

Who are they?

What support are they receiving?

What support do you feel would be helpful for them right now?

15. Have you or other members of the family experienced any kind of domestic abuse from your loved one?

Yes/No. If yes, what kind of abuse has occurred?

Does it occur when they are intoxicated or withdrawing from a substance?

How many times does this occur in a month?

Has any abuse intensified over the last six months (intensity or frequency)?

16. Considering the information we have just assessed, please indicate on a scale of one-ten, what you feel is a priority for you right now in terms of the support you need?

Treatment priorities	Importance Low High	Comments
Getting your loved one into treatment?	1 2 3 4 5 6 7 8 9 10	
Reducing the pressures you are currently under?	1 2 3 4 5 6 7 8 9 10	
Improving the quality of your life?	1 2 3 4 5 6 7 8 9 10	
Supporting your loved one in treatment?	1 2 3 4 5 6 7 8 9 10	
Obtaining support from others in a similar position.	1 2 3 4 5 6 7 8 9 10	
Other:	1 2 3 4 5 6 7 8 9 10	

17. If this programme was 100% successful for you, what would be different . . .

. . . in your relationship with your loved one?

. . . in your own life?

18. Is there anything that you feel is relevant that we have not covered?

(Use separate sheet if necessary)

2.5 Mood Screener

Aim: The Mood Screener is an assessment tool designed to detect the past or present symptoms of major depression.

Guidance: This screening instrument is designed to detect the presence of depression in relation to the nine major symptoms of the disorder. The screener asks the client to report whether they have ever, or are currently, experiencing any of these symptoms. These tools do not represent a certifiable diagnosis. They detect only whether the common symptoms have been or are present. Conversely, if the screener does not detect depression, it does not imply that another condition may not be present. This tool can be useful to assess the current baseline mood of the concerned other at treatment entry. It should be considered an indicator of whether the concerned other currently needs to seek more help if depression exists. The concerned other who reports current levels of depression which are not currently being treated should always be advised to seek further assistance from their GP or medical practitioner.

Scoring: The concerned other should read the questions in column A and tick Yes or No as appropriate to their own life history. If they answer Yes in the Lifetime column A, they should place a tick in the adjacent column. When they have answered all questions in column A, the number of ticks should be added together and recorded in the bottom row. Once completed the client should repeat the process for the Current column B which asks them whether they have experienced any of these symptoms in the last two weeks. Where they tick any box, Yes, the second column should be completed. The total number of Yes answers can be added up and recorded at the bottom of the column once all questions are completed.

If the client has answered Yes to five or more questions in the Lifetime column A, along with ticking that these symptoms 'interfered with their life', it may suggest that they have suffered from depression. If the concerned other has answered Yes to five out of nine boxes in the Current column B, including answering Yes to Question 1 (feeling depressed) and 2 (loss of pleasure) and marked that these problems did interfere with their lives a lot, this could indicate that they are currently suffering from depression. Any concerned other currently experiencing clinical depression should be advised to see their GP and report their symptoms to assess whether further treatment is necessary. When the concerned other does not indicate symptoms of depression then treatment may progress.

Considerations: Indications of depression need to be considered in treatment planning. Clients who are depressed may experience greater doubt, demoralisation or fail to recognise any treatment gains. As such they may be more prone to not applying the intervention or lose the motivation to continue. This needs to be considered as treatment progresses. Baseline measures and objective feedback may be used more regularly to reinforce changes made.

Broader applications: The Mood Screener may be repeated when the client doubts the effectiveness of the approach or is considering terminating their relationships with the problem loved one. Initial scores at intake will offer a baseline measurement which can be compared to future scores to measure reductions in the negative emotions of the concerned other.

Treatment goal:	Assessment
Associated worksheets:	2.4 Comprehensive Assessment **2.5 Mood Screener** 2.6 (CES-D) Depression Scale 2.7 Life Satisfaction Audit 2.8. My Better Life
Further context:	1.3 Family Hardships

2.5 Mood Screener

Name: **Date:**

	A. Lifetime		B. Current	
	Have you ever had two weeks or more when nearly every day . . .	Tick if any answer was 'yes'	Have you had this problem nearly every day in the last two weeks?	Tick if any answer was 'yes'
1. Felt sad, blue or depressed most of the day every day?	Yes No	1.	Yes No	1.
2. Lost all interest or pleasure in things you usually cared about?	Yes No	2.	Yes No	2.
3a. Lost or increased your appetite every day? 3b. Lost weight without trying to? 3c. Gained weight without trying to?	Yes No	3.	Yes No	3.
4a. Had trouble falling asleep or waking early? 4b. Been sleeping too much every day?	Yes No	4.	Yes No	4.
5a. Talked or moved more slowly than is normal for you? 5b. Had to be moving, pacing or unable to sit still?	Yes No	5.	Yes No	5.
6. Felt tired all the time?	Yes No	6.	Yes No	6.
7. Felt worthless or guilty every day?	Yes No	7.	Yes No	7.
8a. Had a lot of trouble concentrating or making decisions? 8b. Noticed your thoughts came much slower or seemed mixed-up every day?	Yes No	8.	Yes No	8.
9a. Thought a lot about death: your own, someone else's or just in general? 9b. Wanted to die? 9c. Felt so low that you thought about suicide? 9d. Attempted suicide?	Yes No	9.	Yes No	9.
	No of ticks =		No of ticks =	
Did these problems interfere with your life or activities a lot?	Yes No		Yes No	

The Mood Screener can be reproduced without permission from the author (Robins et al., 1981)

2.6 (CES-D) Depression Scale

Aim; The CES-D is an assessment designed to measure negative moods that can occur in non-depressed people.

Rationale: The CES-D is an assessment tool that has been tested on large populations of people. It does not detect depression. Instead it offers a comparative rating of mood in non-depressed individuals. It can offer detailed information regarding the intensity of non-depressive moods. A high score indicates more depressing mood states.

Scoring: To score the CES-D, the concerned other should answer all 20 questions listed without missing any items. All the numbers circled are then added up to a total score which can range from 0–60. The norms for these scores are described in the table below.

Norms	CES-D
Average CES-D score for people aged 25–74 (women may score slightly higher)	8.7
Men living alone	8.5
Women living alone	10.8
Men living with partners	6.8
Women living with partners	9.3
Women head of household	12.5
Lower income and less educated people may score slightly higher	

Interpretation

Score	Indication	Consideration
16 or less	Within an average range	No depressive mood indicated.
16–24	High incidence of depression compared to other adults	Depressive mood could be a concern for you. Monitoring may be important.
24 or higher	Significant depressed symptoms when compared to other adults	Depressive mood is significant here. If the client has not scored highly on the Mood Screener but scores highly here they may be under temporary but considerable strain. Monitoring mood is essential to screen for increased risk of depression.

Broader applications: The CES-D may be repeated where the concerned other doubts the effectiveness of the approach or are considering terminating their relationship with the problem loved one. Initial scores at intake will offer a baseline measurement which can be compared to future scores to measure reductions in the negative emotions of the concerned other.

Treatment goal:	Assessment
Related worksheets:	2.4 Comprehensive Assessment 2.5 Mood Screener **2.6 (CES-D) Depression Scale** 2.7 Life Satisfaction Audit 2.8. My Better Life
Further context:	1.4 Family Coping

2.6 (CES-D) Depression Scale

Name   **Date**

Below is a list of ways you may have felt. Please indicate how often you have felt this way during the last week.

During the last week until today . . .	Rarely or none of the time (less than 1 day)	Some or a little time (1–2 days)	Occasionally or a moderate amount of time (3–4 days)	Most or all of the time (5–7 days)
1. I was bothered by things that do not normally bother me.	0	1	2	3
2. I did not feel like eating as my appetite was poor.	0	1	2	3
3. I felt that I could not shake off the blues even with help from my family and friends.	0	1	2	3
4. I felt that I was just as good as other people.	0	1	2	3
5. I had trouble keeping my mind on what I was doing.	3	2	1	0
6. I felt depressed.	0	1	2	3
7. I felt that everything I did was an effort.	0	1	2	3
8. I felt hopeful about the future.	3	2	1	0
9. I felt my life had been a failure.	0	1	2	3
10. I felt fearful.	0	1	2	3
11. My sleep was restless.	0	1	2	3
12. I was happy.	3	2	1	0
13. I talked less than usual.	0	1	2	3
14. I felt lonely.	0	1	2	3
15. People were unfriendly.	0	1	2	3
16. I enjoyed life.	3	2	1	0

17. I had crying spells.	0	1	2	3
18. I felt sad.	0	1	2	3
19. I felt that people dislike me.	0	1	2	3
20. I could not get going.	0	1	2	3

This scale is in the public domain (Radloff, 1977)

2.7 Life Satisfaction Audit

Aim; The aim of the Life Satisfaction Audit is to assess the concerned other's life in a systematic approach in order to generate ideas and suggestions that could improve every aspect of their life.

Rationale: The Life Satisfaction Audit is introduced to the concerned other as a means of assessing their current quality of life. The pressures of living with and managing the needs of a problem user will inflict profound social isolation on the concerned other as their own needs are sacrificed for their loved one. This can lead to the chronic neglect of many aspects of their own lives and the abandonment of their personal aspirations. The social deprivation that ensues can drain the concerned other of the emotional resources to invest in their own well-being prompting depression and even further self-neglect. This depression can make it even more difficult for concerned others to recognise their own needs and muster the energy to respond to them.

Long term isolation and depression can interfere with the ability of some concerned others to readily identify areas of improvement in their lives. Pessimism, emotional exhaustion and an over-emphasis on the loved one can make the review of their own wants feel novel, irreverent or even pointless. The role of the Life Satisfaction Audit is to provide a bridge between the comprehensive assessment that identifies the ruptures and a personal care plan. The Life Satisfaction Audit is designed to generate leads, ideas and suggestions that can improve the concerned other's life. It invites the concerned other to scale their satisfaction in each area of their life on a scale of one to ten. The tool is then used to evaluate what factors are contributing to the current score, and more importantly, what would need to happen to increase these scores. The Life Satisfaction Audit is designed to target every aspect of the concerned other's life to ensure a systematic care plan is adopted to meet this wider range of needs. Each domain of the Audit corresponds with the comprehensive assessment to ensure that subsequent treatment is relevant to the presenting concerns of the client.

The 'Frequency' column refers to how many times they have experienced problems in this area in the last month. It may not be relevant in every domain but it may offer guidance in prioritising goals where particular stresses or difficulties persist. The 'What makes an . . . (x)' column refers to the actual score the client circles in each domain in order to gain a clearer understanding of the concerned other's evaluation. Whilst the 'What is it like when it is better than . . . x?' column offers an indication of what might need to happen in order to increase their satisfaction in that particular domain. This may provide important hints and ideas for the goal setting and action planning that will follow in the 'My Better Life' care plan which is completed after the Life Audit.

Step 1: The purpose of the Life Satisfaction Audit should be explained to the concerned other clearly and it should be emphasised that they are to rate the current levels of satisfaction in each domain. These ratings are relative and not absolute. They will provide a means to simply evaluate rather than diagnose their situation. This information will be used to help the practitioner and the concerned other to develop a care plan that addresses their own unique needs in every area of the concerned other's life.

Step 2: Once the client has rated a domain, they should be asked about the frequency of problems in this area in the last 30 days, if relevant. This may help with subsequent prioritising of goals within the subsequent care plan.

Step 3: The concerned other is then invited to explain what made them rate this domain as . . . (x). This will offer insight into current strengths and issues that are present for the concerned other. This discussion should include what is good in the concerned other's life. Asking them what is stopping their score from being higher than (x) will also reveal the pressures and stresses that they are currently under.

Step 4: The concerned other should then be asked what their life is like in this specific domain when it is better than their current rating. This offers insight into improvements in the quality of their life. This should be recorded in the final column. Concerned others may find it difficult to articulate improvements at first. Under constant life pressures, many concerned others may be tempted to describe better times either in *negative* or in *nominative* ways.

Negative responses: This is where the concerned other describes any improvement as being the absence of current pressures. They may report that they are 'not as depressed,' 'feeling less stressed', or 'not as anxious' at these times. However, the practitioner must also gain insight into what will improve the concerned other's life. This demands that the practitioners be vigilant to the concerned other presenting negative goals and then responding with understanding and empathy before asking questions that can identify positive responses. This can be achieved by asking the concerned other who answers in the negative:

- So what would you be doing *instead* of feeling anxious . . .?

- So what would you be doing *instead* of sorting out your loved one's problems?

Nominative responses: Nominative goals are so broad that their meaning would not be commonly agreed upon. For example, the concerned other might suggest that their life would be improved if they 'felt better about work,' 'felt closer to their partner' or that they just did 'normal things.' However, what feeling better about work, closer to partners or doing normal things entails would be very different from individual to individual. Therefore it is important to explore these in more detail in order to get more concrete responses that the practitioner and the concerned other can agree upon. The practitioner should use the following questions, which ask the concerned other for the evidence that they had achieved this:

- *How would you know that you were feeling better about work?*

- *What would be different?*

121

- *If you did feel closer to your partner, what would you be doing differently?*

- *How would they know you were closer?*

- *What would they notice that was different?'*

- *What kind of things would you be doing that would feel normal to you?*

These areas can be explored further by asking for more detail or by using prompts such as:

- *What else would be different?*

- *Is there any more to this?*

- *In what way would it be even better?*

- *Can you give me an example?*

The Life Audit can be repeated with clients across the course of the programme to ensure that the quality of life is improving. This can be particularly compelling because the concerned other will trust any gains more deeply when they are part of an overall pattern of improvement.

Treatment goal:	Assessment
Associated worksheets:	2.4 Comprehensive Assessment 2.5 Mood Screener 2.6 (CES-D) Depression Scale **2.7 Life Satisfaction Audit** 2.8. My Better Life
Further context:	1.26 Improving the Concerned Other's Life

2.7 Life Satisfaction Audit

C.O. Name _____ DoB _____ Client ID _____ Assessor _____

Domain	Satisfaction Not at all Very	Freq/ Mth	What makes you score this (x)?	What is it like when it is better than (x)?
Partnering	1 2 3 4 5 6 7 8 9 10			
Family	1 2 3 4 5 6 7 8 9 10			
Finances	1 2 3 4 5 6 7 8 9 10			
Social life	1 2 3 4 5 6 7 8 9 10			
Housing	1 2 3 4 5 6 7 8 9 10			
Employment and training	1 2 3 4 5 6 7 8 9 10			
Physical health	1 2 3 4 5 6 7 8 9 10			
Mental health	1 2 3 4 5 6 7 8 9 10			
Your own drug or alcohol use	1 2 3 4 5 6 7 8 9 10			
Hopes, future plans or aspirations	1 2 3 4 5 6 7 8 9 10			
Other: Please state	1 2 3 4 5 6 7 8 9 10			

2.8 My Better Life

Aim; To create a comprehensive care plan which is tailored to improving the quality of life of the concerned other, regardless of the loved one's use.

Rationale: The care plan can be completed at different stages of the programme. For individuals reporting that they are under immense pressure with pressing mental health needs, it may be important to prioritise their care plan first. For other clients, who are otherwise relatively stable but deeply anxious about their loved one's use, the care plan may be set aside until the treatment entry section is mastered. Alternatively, the sessions can be split between the need to teach the skills to effect change in the loved one and the focus on the concerned other's needs. The care plan should be completed in conjunction with the Life Audit and is designed to cater for the specific needs of the concerned other in each domain of their life. Information gathered in the Life Audit can be useful in informing the goal setting in each domain. Use the general principles of reinforcement. Remember reinforcers are always specific. If the concerned other suggests 'going out more', explore the specific of where they would like to go and with whom. The follow up question, 'what would make this even better for you?' can enhance any positive goals that they have set. Check the concerned other's body language and response for genuine enthusiasm. If it is not apparent, explore other options.

Step 1: Explain the purpose of the care plan and its relationship to the Life Audit.

Step 2: For each domain, ask the concerned other to consider what might improve their life in this particular area. Where the concerned other is not clear, refer to the areas identified in the Life Audit as the basis for discussion about possible current goals.

Step 3: Review the goals suggested by the concerned other. Ensure that there is a balance between goals that alleviate the negative pressures they are under as well as positively increasing areas of satisfaction.

Step 4: Record the goal. The general rule for recording goals is that they are written as briefly as possible. This ensures that they are specific and that there is no room for ambiguity. The second general principle is that goals are recorded in the positive, clearly stating what the client will do as opposed to what they will refrain from. The 'instead' prompt can be useful here. This will convert this negative response into a positive one. By setting goals in the positive in this way will ensure that we devise an 'action' plan rather than an 'inaction' plan. By offering the concerned other concrete things to do we will also have a general effect on their well being, as taking action in itself tends to reduce anxiety.

Step 5: For each goal stated within the domain, it is important to consider how the goal will be achieved. For the confident concerned other with lot of skills and experience, this is a very straightforward process. They may automatically suggest the steps they should take, and each one is recorded in the second column. For concerned others who have experienced an erosion in confidence, a solution focus can be utilised. This is where we ask the concerned other whether they have tried such a goal or similar before. We then explore how they did this and what helped it along. This will give insight into their current mastery levels and talk up their own self-belief. Should the concerned other not have any suggestions for achieving their goal, we can use the general problem-solving sheet or even provide direct advice to identify how they might achieve their goal and assist them in deploying it.

Step 6: For each agreed goal and tasks, it should be recorded who is responsible for what elements of the care plan delivery.

Step 7: Finally, once the care plan is completed, the priority of goals can be agreed with the concerned other. Goals can be prioritised in many different ways. The most obvious way is to focus on the most immediate and pressing need. The 'Frequency of Problem' in the Life Audit may give some insight into the most pressing need. However, it may be more useful to prioritise goals that the concerned other feels most confident in addressing. This will build their self-belief in order to address more challenging elements of the care plan later. For concerned others who feel depressed and isolated, their social life may be a more relevant target to address first. Each case can differ in these respects and negotiation is important in getting the best approach for each particular person.

Step 8: Depending on the priorities set in each domain, a date should be recorded when these goals will be reviewed. At this review, any strengths, progress and achievements should be validated and recognised and any necessary further action recorded in the final column.

Treatment goal:	Assessment
Associated worksheets:	2.4 Comprehensive Assessment 2.5 Mood Screener 2.6 (CES-D) Depression Scale 2.7 Life Satisfaction Audit **2.8. My Better Life**
Further context:	1.26 Improving the Concerned Other's Life

2.8 My Better Life

Name:	Client ID:	Case worker:	Care plan created:	Review date:
Partnering			Agency CSO Other	
			Review date:	
Family			Agency CSO Other	
			Review date:	
Finances			Agency CSO Other	
			Review date:	
Social life			Agency CSO Other	
			Review date:	
Housing			Agency CSO Other	
			Review date:	

	Agency CSO Other		Review date:
Employment and training			
Physical health			
Mental health:			
Your own drug or alcohol use			
Hopes, future plans or aspirations			
Other: Please state			

How to Get the Loved One Into Treatment

Rapid Entry Procedure

2.9 Readiness Assessment

Aim; To provide a brief intervention to assist loved ones into treatment where they currently demonstrate motivation to change.

Rationale: During the comprehensive assessment the concerned other may identify that their loved one would be receptive to the idea of professional help. This should be explored fully to identify whether there is sufficient motivation in the loved one to enter into treatment. Where motivation currently exists, it is important to take advantage of the situation and act quickly before the impetus for change is lost. Motivation is likely to occur when the loved one feels a dissonance in their use. This occurs when they perceive a conflict between their priorities, values or aspirations and their actual behaviour. When they experience this conflict, the psychological discomfort generated tends to elicit a motivational response to act in greater accordance with one's values. However, research demonstrates that whilst this effect has a swift onset it demonstrates a decay line over a two week period. Therefore, if the readiness for change section in the initial assessment does indicate that the loved one might consider treatment and has voiced this opinion within the last two weeks, this intervention can be deployed to effect rapid treatment entry. Beyond this timeframe the process may be less likely to work as motivation will naturally subside.

For the rapid entry process to have the best chance of success it is important that the request is presented in a manner that is likely to limit or reduce any natural resistance to the idea of treatment. This resistance can be diminished by observing some general principles. Firstly, the request needs to be grounded in the loved one's own concerns as they themselves present them. Using their exact phrases, words and thoughts will diminish resistance as it is hard for people to contradict their own statements. Secondly, the loved one is liable to have mixed feelings regarding seeking treatment. This does not mean that they do not want to enter treatment. Experiencing mixed feelings about committing to change is the natural order of change, not the exception. Coaching the concerned other to explore the loved one's pros and cons for change is important in opening up the discussion. Any pressure at this point will only make the loved one retreat from the idea. Finally, any request to enter into treatment should be couched in a sincere tone of concern for them. The most well-crafted and sensitively composed statement can easily be tarnished by a deadpan or sarcastic delivery. Therefore the assessment for readiness gathers specific details regarding the signs of the loved one's readiness and explores any ambivalence that may surface in the loved one when the request is made. This information will then be used to form the basis of a planned request.

Step 1: The practitioner should explain that the Assessing Readiness questionnaire is used to gather important information regarding the loved one's current readiness to engage in treatment. It is important that the concerned other is as specific as possible in describing the events surrounding the loved one's own admission of the need for treatment and elements of the loved one's readiness in order to devise an effective plan to move them into treatment quickly.

Step 2: Begin the Readiness Assessment questionnaire by establishing when, where and to whom the loved one raised their current concerns. This may give some indication of the best time and situation to revisit the subject of change with them. It is also important to check that this admission of the need for change has occurred within the important two-week timeframe.

Step 3: Invite the concerned other to describe the events that lead up to the loved one voicing their concern. Pay particular attention to the loved one's specific triggers for change. What did they find discomforting about these events? Even if the rapid treatment entry is not successful, knowledge of these triggers for change will be useful later in the intervention.

Step 4: How was the loved feeling emotionally when they raised the subject of change? The contemplation stage of change is often characterised by emotional release, deep introspection and ambivalence about change. This is an emotionally charged event that is often precipitated by crises. Did the loved one's demeanour fit this criteria at the time they expressed concerns about their own use? Were they very rational in their discussion? Did the loved one seem sincere in these discussions? What, if anything, stuck the concerned other about the loved one's thoughts or demeanour at this time, which made them feel that this was a genuine plea for change?

Step 5: Capturing the loved one's phrases and words regarding the need for change is important. When we raise the subject of change with them it is important that the concerned other does not present their own reasons for change. Instead, it is more powerful to present the loved one with the loved one's reasons. Whilst it is easy to contradict another person, it is hard to contradict yourself. Identifying the exact phrases they used regarding their dissatisfaction with their use and their own reasons for change can be much more powerful, less threatening and feels less judgemental. This means that the loved one is less likely to react against the concerned other. This can be focused further by considering whether the loved one's use is interfering with other things in their life that they value highly, such as children, work, relationships or even faith and spiritual beliefs. Whereever a tension exists between their use and these other prized aspects in the loved one's life, leverage for change is created.

Step 6: Considering what action the loved one might make can provide some important clues as to what treatment or support should be offered. Capturing the exact phrase as closely as possible is important again, as it means the concerned other will present the loved one's own treatment options. The loved one might not have voiced a desire to see a professional. It should be remembered that not all treatment needs to be formal. Whatever people believe to be helpful in overcoming drug and alcohol problems invariably is helpful. It is possible for those loved ones with reasonable social functioning and lower levels of physical dependency to implement their own process of change. If people should fail at this first option, treatment can be increased with intensive approaches later. Therefore, establishing what course of action the loved one might take can inform the treatment process. Loved ones often suggest talking to someone they respect and trust in their community who is not using in the first instance. This may not seem enough to the concerned other, but it is a major step to have their loved one talking about their situation as a problem to someone else. It will augment their awareness of the current problems that they are experiencing. The person the loved one freely chooses to speak to may be able to offer more leverage on change. They are in a more neutral position, outside the increasingly charged relationship between the loved one and the concerned other. So this can be a very important first step, even if it does not prove to be the last.

Step 7: Loved ones often have very mixed feelings about change. This should not be construed as the loved one proving difficult but as an inevitable product of the change process. Reviewing the mixed feelings that the loved one might present can help the concerned other empathise with them. Furthermore, an open exploration of the pros and cons of seeking help with the loved one is often the best strategy to overcome the mixed feelings. Anticipating these contradictory feelings can inform the concerned other of the block to their loved one changing and help them evaluate the need for change with the loved one more openly. If there are any specific objections to treatment the concerned other can anticipate, they might also consider how they can address these objections. For example, worries that the practicalities of seeking treatment could demand time off work that the loved one may feel they cannot take, can be nullified if the concerned other knows of weekend and evening appointments. It is important though that the concerned other understands the importance of being even-handed with the pros and cons of change.

Step 8: For the concerned other to demonstrate explicit understanding of the loved one's current pressures, stresses and tensions can also assist in overcoming resistance to change. Addictions do not occur in a vacuum. They occur at points of high stress, depression or conflict. Recognising the exact pressures the loved one currently experiences can have a profound effect on their sense of themselves and the value of the relationship they have with the concerned other. It is also mitigates against the sense of attack that the loved one may feel from the request to enter treatment.

Step 9: Loved ones may or may not be sensitive to the risks of use in terms of health or wider social complications. Appealing to these wider factors may not influence the decision to change, especially in younger people who often consider themselves invincible. Therefore considering how the drug and alcohol use diminishes the relationship with the concerned other specifically may offer more leverage for change. Presenting any evidence of how they once were in their affections compared to recently may highlight this deterioration in a concrete and irrefutable manner. This can be softened with the concerned other taking some responsibility for this change too. Stating that they have not always been helpful, that any previous conflict has made it worse or their well-meaning efforts were misguided, can redress an imbalance that suggests the current situation is all the loved one's fault. This can be especially powerful when this is phrased in terms of the loss of intimacy, affection and closeness.

Step 10: The diminishment of the relationship between the concerned other and the loved one can be extended further. Alongside the fear of the deterioration of the relationship, comes the stated desire of the concerned other. Spelling out what it would mean to them if the loved one did seek help can increase the compliance of the loved one. Again, even suggesting the loved one might just sample the treatment and give it a go without commitment, this may assist the reluctant user over the threshold for the first time.

Step 11: The offer of assistance and support in this process can be essential. This can occur on several levels. It should never be assumed that the loved one will now initiate treatment entry alone. The offer of assistance to go with them to the treatment provider is important. Some loved ones may prefer to have their concerned other attend the session with them. Others prefer to go in alone. Some loved ones may be inclined to meet with the concerned other's current worker. However, others may be suspicious that the worker has been co-opted by their family member and may wish to see someone else. These options should be given consideration prior to treatment entry, and where possible, the loved one given a choice. The offer of support can also be extended beyond treatment entry. Offering to stand by the loved one and helping them deal with any pressures that may be sustaining use can underline the concerned other's commitment to change. Offers to help with the wider social pressures should remain contingent on their commitment to treatment. Identifying what kind of support the loved one could be offered in terms of entering treatment and what help might be given to support them address these wider social complications should be described in concrete and clear terms.

Treatment goal:	Rapid Entry Procedure
Associated worksheets:	**2.9 Readiness Assessment** 2.10 Readiness Approach
Further context:	1.17 Reinforcement and Change

2.9 Readiness Assessment

(1) When did they raise the subject of changing or seeking help?

Date:

Where:

When:

Anyone else present?

(2) What recent incident prompted your loved one to consider change?

(3) How were they feeling emotionally when they were considering change?

(4) What were their exact words to the best of your recollection?

**(5) What do you think concerned them the most about their use at this time?
Is use interfering with anything important to them?**

(6) Did they mention any specific actions that they might make regarding their use?

(7) Do you think that they may have any mixed feeling about seeking help?

For:	Against:

(8) How could you show understanding for their current situation?

(9) How is their use affecting your relationship with them?

(10) What would it mean to you if they did seek help?

(11) How could you support them if they did seek out help?

2.10 Readiness Approach

Aim: To formulate a request for the loved one with high motivation to enter into treatment using the information gathered on Rapid Treatment Entry: Readiness Assessment.

Rationale: Using the specific and detailed information gathered from the exploration of the loved one's expression of interest in change, the concerned other should be supported to formulate a naturalistic intervention based on the loved one's own stated dissatisfaction with use and necessity for change. In order to maximise the opportunity, it is important to assess the most appropriate time and place to deliver this request. Consideration of the circumstances where the loved one last readily discussed the issue can give important clues as to the optimal moment to re-visit the subject.

In formulating the request, the concerned other should draw upon the material identified in the Readiness Assessment and begin to organise this information into a request to enter treatment. This Readiness approach offers a proforma in which to organise this information. It does not have to be followed verbatim but offers guidance. In formulating the response the practitioner should check-in frequently with the concerned other with regards to how they think their loved one might respond to the request as it is developed. Wherever possible, the loved one's own words and presentations should be included in the first section in order to reduce the potential for resistance.

Raising the issue of treatment is likely to elicit mixed feelings in the loved one, which will need some exploration by the concerned other. The Readiness Assessment may indicate what pros and cons the loved one is likely to raise. The concerned other should be advised to explore these with the loved one without over-ruling them – tempting as it can be – to emphasise the benefits and reasons for change. Explain to the concerned other that at this stage of change, mixed feelings are normal. Pressure will only entrench them in the opposite direction. Instead, the concerned other should expect and invite the loved one to consider the pros and cons of seeking help. By doing so they will allow the loved one to think the issue through for themselves. Role-playing this with the concerned other can be helpful, ensuring they remain neutral in this discussion.

After exploring the blocks to change the concerned other can state their position, regarding their fears and what it would mean to them if the loved one did enter treatment. Again, the most polished and sensitive request for treatment on paper will mean nothing if it is not delivered with sincerity and concern. Role play may help soften any underlying frustration or fear in the concerned other that may make their approach appear sharp. Should the loved one agree to try treatment, the concerned other should make an appointment as quickly as possible to build on this motivation. As internal motivation is unlikely to endure for a long period of time, it can be a good guarantee to work with the practitioner about local treatment options, availability and waiting lists from the outset. Should the loved one refuse, this should be met with understanding and acceptance. The concerned other can inform the loved one that they are seeking help for themselves as they are finding the current situation difficult. And as they are respecting the loved one's decision to not seek help, they would ask the loved one to respect their decision to continue with their own support.

Step 1: The rationale of the Readiness Approach should be explained to the concerned other. Using the information from the Readiness Questionnaire the practitioner will assist the concerned other to formulate a request to the loved one to enter treatment. Emphasis should be given to incorporating all the words, phrases and concerns of the loved one rather than the concerned other in formulating this response.

Step 2: The process should begin by considering the best time to approach the loved one. Section A of the request invites the concerned other to identify when would be the best time to raise the subject. Considering the last time that the issue was raised and the loved one was receptive can give important clues. For example, was it after an argument? Did the concerned other and loved one go somewhere special? Did it occur whilst they were doing some other chore together? Identifying the most apposite time and place means the concerned other can re-engineer these events or if not, wait for when it would be a good time to broach the subject.

Step 3: Information from the Readiness Assessment can be slotted into the appropriate areas in Section B marked on the pro forma. The first section focuses on the loved one's stated reasons and motivation to change. The concerned other's hopes should be stated in the third section. Using language or phrases that the loved one will respond to is important. Careful attention should be given to the wording and style and the practitioner should check in with the concerned other whether the statements will resonate with the loved one. Too much jargon or technical terms may allow the loved one to dismiss the concerned other's request. Short, clear interjections are better than long or indirect statements.

Step 4: The concerned other should be coached in dealing with any ambivalence that the loved one might have about seeking help as described in Section C. Should the loved one respond with 'yes, but . . .' the concerned other will need to explore the advantages and disadvantages of treatment without pressurising the loved one on either side of the debate. This should begin by exploring the loved one's objections to entering treatment. The concerned other should elicit as many reasons as possible and listen respectfully. Once they have listened to these, they should explore what might be the benefits of seeking help. Again, this should be done respectfully.

Step 5: Once the loved one has explored the disadvantages and benefits of seeking help thoroughly, the concerned other can then present their hopes in Section D. This is important, because if the loved one has not expressed their own opinion fully in the first instance, they are likely to retreat into the disadvantages of change when the concerned other presents their feelings. Allowing the loved one to talk out their opinion and have their reasons acknowledged prevents this retreat and gently manoeuvres them into having to listen to the concerned other without interruption. This is because it is difficult to restate an opinion that has already been accepted. It is essential that the concerned other's view is phrased in affection and respect. It should focus on the behaviour that the concerned other hopes for, rather than judgments on the poor behaviour that needs to change. Emphasising what the concerned other wants in their future relationship with the loved one is also a powerful motivator.

Step 6: The practitioner and concerned other should also consider the response should the loved one choose not to seek help at this time. It is vital that this does not result in conflict. The concerned other should prepare a response in case of this eventuality that is understanding and respectful for the loved one's choice. This is also an good time for the concerned other to inform the loved one that they are seeking help if they have not done so and, in return, ask the loved one to respect this choice too. An example might include:

> *Well, I can see this is not what you want right now and I am not going to fight with you anymore. I accept that. But I am seeking the help I feel I need at the moment. I hope that you can respect this as I respect your decision.*

> *Well I did hope that you would get some help as I am worried about what is happening and how it affects us. But I can see you do not feel the same as me and that is fine. I do feel that I need to make some changes for myself though.*

Step 7: Once the concerned other has prepared their approach, it should be practiced with the practitioner. This can be broken down into the three smaller sections:

- the loved one's concern

- dealing with mixed feelings

- presenting their case

The intervention should be delivered in a considered but warm manner. Genuine concern must replace anger or frustration, even in the face of objections from the loved one. The practitioner must place themselves in the shoes of the loved one to ensure that no phrase appears too aggressive or threatening. Short role-plays of a couple of lines are better than long re-enactments. Gentle feedback on the strengths and shortcomings of the presentation can help refine the detail and increase the concerned other's confidence. Provisional appointments can be scheduled in advance should the loved one respond.

Treatment goal:	Rapid Entry Procedure
Associated worksheets:	2.9 Readiness Assessment **2.10 Readiness Approach**
Further context:	1.17 Reinforcement and Change

2.10 Readiness Approach

Section A: The setting
When would be a good time to revisit the subject of change with your loved one?

Where would be a good place to revisit the subject of change with your loved one?

When would be a good time for your loved one to attend an appointment?

Would your loved one like you to go with them?

Section B: Talking to your loved one about change

Remember last (1) _____, after _____ (2) happened?

You seemed very (3) _____ (Feelings/concern) about your use.

I was struck when said you that you were thinking about change because (4)

_____

You seemed very (5) _____ about your use then

and said you might consider doing (6) _____

I wondered whether you have thought any more about doing anything about this?

Section C: Explore mixed feelings about change

What holds you back from entering treatment? (7)

What might be helpful?

Section D: What the loved one's change would mean to you.

I know this is not easy for you because (8) _____

_____

But I am worried that your use is affecting us in (9) _____

_____

It would really mean (10) _____ to me if we could go to
see someone just to check it out.

I know I have not always been helpful to you in this, but I will try to support in any way I can. I will help in any way,

such as (11) _____

Make the offer to just see what it is like. If it is not useful you can consider other options.

Section E: If your loved one refuses the idea of treatment

What can you say to explicitly accept their decision without conflict?

What can you say to your loved one about the help that you are seeking for yourself?

**Remember: If they do not take up the offer to enter into treatment, do not pressurise them.
Accept their current decision by taking a longer term view of the programme.**

Treatment Entry

2.11 Rewards for the Loved One

Overview: This section provides the assessment and planning tools to facilitate change in the unmotivated loved one. It covers the four core elements of treatment entry:

1. providing competing rewards at times of use
2. reducing conflict between the concerned other and the loved one
3. disabling enabling
4. withdrawing without conflict when the loved one uses drugs or alcohol

The assessment and development of these skills takes time and the concerned other should be advised to work slowly and methodically through the programme. The concerned other should be encouraged to trial each element of the treatment entry skills as they progress though the programme and assess progress in subsequent sessions. This section also includes Functional Analysis Logs and Intervention Planning tools. These can be used to orchestrate comprehensive responses once the concerned other has begun to master each of the independent elements. This will provide the framework for a powerful response that utilises each element in a systematic and focused manner. In addition, at the end of this section is a generic Problem Solving worksheet. This can be called upon at any time in the process in order to troubleshoot the application of the skills, the timing of interventions, or planning any approach should it be necessary.

Aim: To identify and evaluate possible rewards that might challenge or interfere with the loved one's use.

Rationale: Selecting the rewards that can be deployed at times of use can be difficult. Rewards need to be compelling for the loved one if they are to compete with the powerful effects of drugs or alcohol. Rewards can span a number of domains including activities, people, material items, favours and affection. Within this, it must always be remembered that reinforcers are specific and unique to each individual. Generating as many options as possible, and considering how they can be enhanced for maximum effect, is necessary to ensure that they can compromise use. Furthermore, there are other constraints that need to be considered. The concerned other will have to participate and engage in the activity with the loved one and there may be cost implications. Therefore, competing rewards need to be enjoyable for the concerned other and they must feel comfortable in engaging in the activity. The cost of the reward should be financially manageable and relatively cheap. The concerned other should be reminded that if their loved one is intoxicated at the time of the reward or uses drugs or alcohol then the reward will be withdrawn without conflict. This worksheet is designed to cover these specific areas in order to evaluate whether any possible suggestions are appropriate for both the concerned other and the loved one.

Step 1: The rationale for the Rewards for the Loved One assessment should be explained to the concerned other. The function of this worksheet is to identify the first element of facilitating treatment entry by identifying what rewards might compete with the loved one's use. Identifying as many rewards as possible is important in ensuring that a variety of responses can be used and that the loved one does not tire of being exposed to the same approach. Besides mapping as many rewards as possible the concerned other and the practitioner will work together to identify how these rewards could be enhanced for maximum effect. It must be stressed that these rewards must be suitable for the concerned other as well as their loved one. Again the concerned other must be informed that they will not be asked to do anything that they are not comfortable with. This worksheet will help generate options in the first instance. This will be combined with a problem-solving approach later to plan the best time to intervene in the loved one's use.

Step 2: Exploring the Type of Reward column and consider the first sub-heading of Treats, where the concerned other should identify as many rewards as possible that their loved one would enjoy in this domain. If some of their suggestions fall outside of this remit, they can be added to the other categories listed below. However, the generation of ideas is the most important aspect of the process and so where they are recorded is not as significant. The concerned other may readily know what interests the loved one has in this area. Alternatively the practitioner can support the concerned other who struggles to answer by asking the following questions:

- What did they once enjoy doing but no longer do?

- What have they always wanted to try?

- Who does the loved one respect and what do they do?

- What rewards may be done in a few minutes?

- What rewards take a few hours?

- What may take a few days?

- What do they like to do in the city?

- What do they like to do in the country?

- What things go on in your area that the loved one might like?

It is important to be as specific as possible regarding any reward. For example, if the loved one enjoys films, what kind of films do they like to watch? If the loved one enjoys food, what kind of food? If the loved one likes spending time with a family member, which family member is it? If they enjoy doing activities with their children, what activities in particular do they enjoy? These questions are designed to firm up the response to be as concrete as possible.

Step 3: As drug and alcohol use has a powerful effect on the loved one, it is important that we increase the value of these rewards. For each item listed as a possible reward, the concerned other should rate how desirable it would be for the loved one. Exploring what makes science fiction films an 8 may offer further clues as to the reinforcers of the loved one. For example, the fact that they always watched these TV shows with their brother, offers further indications of what might enhance the reward.

Step 4: The reinforcing qualities of the reward can be further enhanced by the question, 'What would make this even better for your loved one?' This can bring more out of the situation. This may identify additional treats, such as the place where the reward is delivered or the involvement of important others.

Step 5: The identified reward can then be evaluated against a clear criteria to ensure that it feels appropriate and comfortable for the concerned other too. Whenever possible the reward should be engaging for both parties. The following checklist is used to ensure that the concerned other would find any identified reward pleasurable too; that it is not a financial burden to deliver and that the concerned other feels comfortable in delivering the reward. As important, is that such an intervention will only be delivered to the loved one whilst they are sober.

Step 6: Repeat the above process on the other sub-headings of Activities and People and affection to generate other possible rewards for the loved one.

Step 7: Once a list of alternative rewards are identified and evaluated as suitable, it should be possible to select the option which the concerned other feels has greatest potential and should then be scheduled in for a time when the loved one is liable to drink. In this way the loved one should be invited to participate and the planned reward should go ahead at the agreed time. If any difficulties present in the application of the reward, consider problem-solving to identify ways to best implement the intervention.

Step 8: Should the concerned other find it exceptionally difficult to identify any rewards, then the Rewards for the Loved One worksheet can also be used to generate leads, but from the loved ones perspective.

Treatment goal:	Treatment Entry: Competing Rewards
Associated worksheets:	**2.11 Rewards for the Loved One** 2.12 Problem Solving
Further context:	1.16 Reinforcement and Substance Misuse 1.18 Principles of Treatment Entry

2.11 Rewards for the Loved One

Type	Loved one's rating	What would make this even better for your loved one?	Pleasurable for you too?	Is it cheap?	Available sober?	Comfortable for you?

Treats: What did your loved one once consider a real treat? This might be favourite foods, films or 'girls nights in'?

Type	Loved one's rating					
1.	1 2 3 4 5 6 7 8 9 10					
2.	1 2 3 4 5 6 7 8 9 10					
3.	1 2 3 4 5 6 7 8 9 10					
4.	1 2 3 4 5 6 7 8 9 10					
5.	1 2 3 4 5 6 7 8 9 10					

Activities: What did your loved one like to do before the drug or alcohol use become a problem? What things did they always want to try? Do they like sporting activities? Artistic ones? Films? Music? Gardening? Walks? Solving problems?

Type	Loved one's rating					
1.	1 2 3 4 5 6 7 8 9 10					
2.	1 2 3 4 5 6 7 8 9 10					
3.	1 2 3 4 5 6 7 8 9 10					
4.	1 2 3 4 5 6 7 8 9 10					
5.	1 2 3 4 5 6 7 8 9 10					

People and affection: Who is really important to the loved one? What did they do together? Who have they not seen in a long time? What signs of affection do they respond to -praise, attention, recognition or physical contact?

1.	1 2 3 4 5 6 7 8 9 10			
2.	1 2 3 4 5 6 7 8 9 10			
3.	1 2 3 4 5 6 7 8 9 10			
4.	1 2 3 4 5 6 7 8 9 10			
5.	1 2 3 4 5 6 7 8 9 10			

2.12 Problem Solving

Aim: Problem solving is a generic skill to assist the concerned other to develop a range of interventions in implementing the programme and overcoming obstacles to change. It can also be useful in considering the implementation of planned rewards for the loved one.

Rationale: The application of the programme needs to be tailored to the particular situation that each concerned other finds themselves in. Therefore it is important to adapt any interventions to the specific circumstances of their loved one's use. The Problem Solving sheet can provide an opportunity to translate any intervention or strategy into the unique reality of the concerned other and the loved one's relationship. This can be helpful in identifying and applying alternative rewards to compromise their loved one's use. It can also be used to deal with wider issues such as problem solving improvements in the concerned other's life, dealing with domestic violence, planning to raise the subject of treatment and when the loved one is in danger of dropping out of treatment. Whenever the concerned other is uncertain about any course of action that they should take, the Problem Solving sheet can be used to assist them to develop and evaluate the best course of action. Once the concerned other has mastered the process, they should be encouraged to use it themselves whenever the need arises.

Step 1: The concerned other should state the problem as simply as possible. Phrasing the problem simply will help identify the specific problem that needs to be addressed and may clarify complex situations that might be characterised by multiple issues. Any sub-goals that are identified can be addressed separately.

Step 2: The concerned other should identify as many possible options to the problems as possible. Nothing should be discounted at this stage, with every possible strategy written down regardless of how outlandish or impractical it may appear at this stage. The practitioner should feel free to make suggestions in the first attempts at problem solving but as the client begins to master the process they should encourage the concerned other to identify their own solutions.

Step 3: The identified options should be reviewed and suggestions that the concerned other does not feel comfortable with should be eliminated. There is no need to debate this winnowing process. If the concerned other believes them to be unviable, then they are deleted.

Step 4: The remaining options are then evaluated in more detail. This involves reviewing two important facets of each option. This begins with an examination of the possible benefits and consequences of applying this approach. This should be reviewed equitably and in detail so that the concerned other can anticipate any probable reactions to taking this course of action. Once these consequences are identified, we ask the concerned other to rate their confidence in applying the strategy. This is rated on a scale of 1–10, with 10 representing the highest degree of confidence. This scale may also be used to identify refinements that might improve the concerned other's confidence in applying the strategy. For example, asking them what might raise this confidence by one point may assist them to identify additional support or tactics that would improve their ability to apply this approach. Once the evaluation is completed the concerned other can select the option with the least negative consequences and the highest confidence rating.

Step 5: The concerned other then reviews whether any wider factors may interfere with the application of the skill. For example, does it depend on the involvement of others? Are there times which are less conducive to applying the approach or is it dependant on a more unpredictable aspect of the loved one's behaviour? Will they need to practice or rehearse any statements or conversations with the loved one? This possibility of wider interference will need to be considered in order to hone the approach.

Step 6: The action plan is agreed. Writing down the exact solution can help serve as a reminder for the concerned other. This should also include when the solution will be deployed in order to encourage the concerned other to apply this skill in their life. Practitioners should stress at this stage that the approach does not have to be successful. This can reduce performance anxiety. It allows the concerned other to implement the strategy and then evaluate its success with the practitioner. Evaluation should always be encouraging and supportive of the concerned other's efforts. Alongside this affirmation for applying the approach, it can also serve as a chance to refine what worked well and what was not useful in refining the strategy and improving it. Strategies may not work perfectly at the first attempt. However, building on the aspects that were successful and addressing any elements that were not as useful, will allow for revision and increasing the effectiveness of the strategy.

Treatment goal:	Treatment Entry: Competing Rewards
Associated worksheets:	2.11 Rewards for the Loved One **2.12 Problem Solving**
Further context:	

2.12 Problem Solving

1. State the problem as simply as possible

My problem is . . .

Secondary problems (if any):

2. Generate as many options as possible

My options are . . .

Now eliminate any options that are not viable without discussion.

3. Evaluate the remaining options

Options	+/− Consequences of applying	Confidence
A.		1 2 3 4 5 6 7 8 9 10
B.		1 2 3 4 5 6 7 8 9 10
C.		1 2 3 4 5 6 7 8 9 10

4. Any foreseeable problem in applying?

How can these be eliminated?

5. My plan is . . .

6. I will try this on (date) . . .

2.13 Flashpoints

Aim: To identify and implement the second element of treatment entry by identifying and practicing key communication skills that reduce conflict.

Rationale: Relationships with problem users and the family are characterised by conflicts. These conflicts extend beyond drug and alcohol use and into many facets of the relationship between the loved one and the concerned other. These tensions can make a substantial contribution to the loved one's use. Negative moods and conflict are very powerful determinants of use and relapse in particular. Therefore, by mapping and reducing the conflict, the concerned other can have a profound effect on the loved one's consumption.

This process begins with the identification of the flashpoints of conflict. These flashpoints refer to typical areas of conflict between the concerned other and the loved one that are consistent, repetitive and predictable. Learning and then deploying communication skills is difficult, especially in the moment or when under emotional pressure or psychological stress. Identifying the nature, timing and rhythm of typical conflicts will allow the concerned other to plan for these specific events in advance and to ensure that they are as well rehearsed as possible. This will increase the confidence of the concerned other in dealing with more spontaneous conflicts later. Mapping typical conflict will also offer the concerned other a clear signal as to when they should apply the skills.

Further to this element of skills development, the Flashpoints worksheet is also designed to help the concerned other to recognise that conflict is draining and unproductive. This realisation is an important first step in heightening their awareness of the futility of conflict. Whilst the concerned other's desire to vent their frustrations out on the loved one is perfectly understandable considering the intolerable strain that they are placed under, it will not help them change the loved one in the longer term. Again, the practitioner must be careful not to blame concerned others for typical responses to hostile situations that they are placed in by the loved one. Within this though, they can influence these conflicts. By doing so, they improve their relationship, reduce the loved one's use and increase their own well-being.

It should also be remembered that conflicts are not restricted to the loved one and the concerned other. Problematic use in the family increases conflict among all the family members. This means that the communications sheets will be valid for exploring conflicts with other family members, not just the user.

Step 1: The practitioner should explain the rationale of the Flashpoints sheet to the concerned other. Conflict has a powerful effect on the loved one's use and the concerned other's own well-being. At the same time it is important in developing new communication skills so that the concerned other knows when to implement them. To assist in this, the following exercise is designed to map where flashpoints in the relationship typically occur. This can help planning in advance how we can respond to conflicts in different ways.

Step 2: The concerned other is asked to identify typical flashpoints in their relationship with the loved one. These might include perennial conflicts or tensions that repeat themselves. The list of domains at the top of the Flashpoints sheet offers prompts for the concerned other to consider. They do not have to be restricted to these. Invite the concerned other to describe these conflicts and make a note in the first column. Work through each example, one at a time.

Step 3: Based on the first Flashpoint identified, the concerned other should consider when this typically happens. This may be at a time during the week or weekends and it may occur at a specific time or place. Consideration should be given to the likelihood of it happening when the loved one is intoxicated or sober. This information can be important in order to understand the nature of some conflicts.

Step 4: Besides the point of conflict, the loved one may also employ a number of strategies to provoke the concerned other in these situations. This might be tone of voice, criticisms that antagonise or hurtful comments. These gestures often inflame the situation and make it difficult for the concerned other to remain calm. This may be particularly important if the loved one engages in these behaviours when sober. As such, there may be an extinction burst behaviour which is designed to elicit conflict with the concerned other which then justifies use. The responsibility for use can then be blamed on the concerned other's nagging and the loved one appears justified in their actions. This may not be a conscious process but a subconscious one. It is akin to massaging our own shoulders and neck when we experience tension. We may find ourselves doing this absentmindedly as we make deeper association that rethis behaviour leads to a desired consequence-relief. Likewise, the loved one may (un)knowingly engineer conflict because of a deeper mental association they have that conflict triggers use. Explaining this to the concerned other can help them understand the irrational antagonism of the loved one when sober and how conflict can feed their loved one's consumption.

Step 5: It is important to assess the impact conflict has on the loved one. The concerned other should consider what happens immediately after the conflict in terms of the loved one's consumption. Conflict and negative mood states negatively reinforce use. Establishing the relationship between conflict and consumption in the concerned other's own mind can be a powerful incentive for them to modify their communication. Research demonstrates that conflict fuels the loved one's consumption. As such, the concerned other should recognise that, whilst conflict it typical in these situations, it is counter-productive for both parties.

Step 6: The following column asks the concerned other to consider the impact of the conflict on the concerned other. This can be positive and negative. In the short term, conflict may allow them to vent their frustrations and tension. However, in the long term it becomes increasingly exhausting to battle with the loved one all the time. Considering how tiresome conflict becomes can help the concerned other revise their opinions regarding the need to reduce conflicts. Again, it is important to normalise the concerned other's responses to the intolerable pressure and hostile circumstances that they are often placed in by the loved one. Anger, desperation and sheer frustration are common responses to use but also self neglect and domestic neglect come with problem use. The focus should not concentrate on whether conflict is a natural response but on the toll it takes on the concerned other.

Step 7: This process can be repeated with other flashpoints that the concerned other has identified. This may establish some clear patterns in the conflict and how arguments in other areas often lead to the same conclusion: the loved one using more drugs and alcohol and the concerned other being left even more emotionally depleted.

Treatment goal:	Treatment Entry: Communication Skills
Associated worksheets:	**2.13 Flashpoints** 2.14 Reducing Conflict 2.15 The 'I' Message
Further context:	Principles of Treatment Entry

2.13 *Flashpoints*

Examples: substance use, money, work, college, school, affection, boundaries, household responsibilities, family

Flashpoints: What is the typical argument about?	When does it typically occur? (Time, day of the week etc.) Is the loved one sober?	What does the loved one do to provoke you?	What impact does the conflict have on the loved one's use?	What effect does the conflict have on you? (Short and long term)
Flashpoint 1:				
Flashpoint 2:				
Flashpoint 3:				
Flashpoint 4:				

2.14 Reducing Conflict

Aim: The role of this worksheet is to introduce the concerned other to positive communications skills. This will help them to identify positive components of good communication and negative components of poor communication.

Rationale: Mastering communication skills is vital in reducing the negative reinforcing consequences of drug and alcohol use. Constant conflict exhausts the concerned other, increases drug and alcohol use and erodes the relationship. At the same time, mastering a new style of communication is difficult, especially in emotionally charged situations. Any communication style must be simple in order to be delivered effectively in the pressure of the moment of conflict. It must also be naturalistic for the concerned other to deliver. Any communication which sounds too contrived can be easily attacked by the loved one as 'the counsellor talking.' The loved one can make the implicit assumption that the concerned other is insincere and therefore their position can be dismissed. This undermines the concerned other's composure, which is vital to implementing communication skills.

The first step in developing communication skills is to develop the concerned other's awareness of different communication styles and their impact. The Reducing Conflict worksheet allows the concerned other to consider the impact of two different communications styles on conflict. This can prompt discussion on what constitutes effective communication. This entails a shift from focusing on the other person's behaviour to expressing one's own feelings. When an individual begins a statement with 'You . . .' the listener automatically becomes defensive in anticipation of an imminent attack. Conversely, beginning a statement with 'I' simply expresses how the concerned other feels and is difficult to contradict. This allows the concerned other to transmit the same message but without the conflicts that inevitably lead to a stalemate at best and a battle at worst. Considering their own communication style and the influence this may have, will help the concerned other to recognise a need to adapt.

Step 1: Explain the rationale of the Reducung Conflict worksheet to the concerned other. This worksheet continues to explore the second element of treatment facilitation by examining the impact of different communication styles on conflict. This will help to develop more effective communication skills and an awareness of their importance.

Step 2: Invite the concerned other to read through the statements in each column of Section A. Once they have read them, they should be asked to identify what is different between these two different types of statements. They should observe the obvious difference between the sentences starting with 'You' versus those beginning with 'I.' Just looking at these statement on the page, the concerned other can be asked how they feel these lines are being said by different individuals. The 'You' messages should immediately come over as more aggressive than the 'I messages.' These observations can be recorded in the text boxes below. At the same time it is important that the concerned other recognises that the paired statements in Columns One and Two could be commenting on the same behaviour but are composed in a different way.

Step 3: The concerned other should then explore Section B. Considering the conflicts that they have identified in the Flashpoints worksheets, can they recall any examples of 'You' messages that they have used with the loved one at this time? Once examples are listed, they can then be asked to recall any 'I messages that they have used. If the concerned other finds this difficult they can be asked to recall a more recent conflict instead. Exploring how this escalated may offer examples of their communication style. This assessment will typically demonstrate a bias towards the use of 'You' messages. Again it is important to normalise this and acknowledge the pressure and stress that the concerned other is under at these times and that very often the loved one deserves to be told straight about their behaviour. Again, it is not an issue of whether this is the right or wrong approach, but whether it is an effective approach. This increases the concerned other's awareness of their communication style and creates capacity to reflect on modifying it.

Step 4: Considering the examples of 'You' and 'I' messages recorded, the practitioner can then explore what the concerned other feels the impact of these statements have on the loved one in Section C. This should explore the 'You' statements first and the impact that they have on the loved one. This can be reversed by asking the concerned other how they might respond to such messages. It usually elicits an equally powerful contrary reply coupled with counter-attacks. This can be followed by reviewing the 'I' messages. If the concerned other has no examples of 'I' messages, then the practitioner can ask them what they were feeling when they made their 'you' statements in order to develop the concerned other's insight into the process. Alternatively the concerned other can reflect on the 'I' message examples provided. Exploring how difficult it is to contradict 'I' messages can be useful in helping the concerned other recognise the power of these statements. A further angle to explore is considering what happens when any conflict identified in the Flashpoint stops and some reconciliation is achieved between the concerned other and their loved one. Reconciliation after conflict is characterised by a shift from accusation of the other to expression of personal feeling.

Treatment goal:	Treatment Entry: Communication Skills
Associated worksheets:	2.13 Flashpoints **2.14 Reducing Conflict** 2.15 The 'I' Message
Further context:	1.9 The Intervention 1.18 Principles of Treatment Entry

2.14 Reducing Conflict

Section A	
Column One	**Colum Two**
You always screw things up.	I find it really hard when you have been drinking.
You're so stupid.	I find it hard to understand why you take drugs.
You don't anything to help me around the house.	It really helps me when you give me a hand.
Go on, kill yourself, see if I care.	I really worry that your use is going to cause you serious problems.
You should be ashamed of yourself.	I like you so much more when you are sober.
You don't care about anybody but yourself.	I feel that you do not care about me sometimes.

What's different about these two styles of communication?

Section B	
Can you think of any examples when you have said something similar to your loved one?	**Can you think of any example when you have said something similar to your loved one?**

Section C
How would your loved one react to these approaches?

2.15: The 'I' Message

Aim: The purpose of the 'I' Message worksheet is to help the concerned other formulate positive communication statements to express their feelings to the loved one without conflict.

Rationale: Having assessed typical flashpoints of conflict and the concerned other's communication style under pressure, it is important to implement a communication style that can reduce these tensions. The central approach to reducing conflict is the use of 'I' messages. This demands that the concerned other switches their attention from describing the loved one's negative behaviour to conveying their own positive feelings about the situation. It is conducted in a non-blaming and non-judgmental atmosphere. This will allow the concerned other to focus on expressing their own feelings regardless of the loved one or their behaviour, even when the concerned other has justification to attack the loved one about their behaviour. In this way it is possible for the concerned other to express their worries, make requests or challenge their loved one without causing any conflict. These communication skills are akin to assertiveness skills. Assertiveness is often taught as the assertion of one's rights. However, assertiveness can be best understood as being able to say the right thing, to the right person at the right time. These communication skills will allow the concerned other to do this. They do not have to be used in conflict situations alone or just with the problem using other. They are helpful in communicating with a wide range of people in life and can be drawn upon to enhance many other components of the programme.

It should be recognised that breaking established patterns of communication is hard, especially when the concerned other is under enormous stress. Therefore, it is important to draw upon the specific flashpoints that are fairly typical in order for the concerned other to plan, practice and rehearse implementing these statements. Role-play with the practitioner can greatly assist in this preparation. This is because it is not simply the re-phrasing that is important, the concerned other must manage the emotional tone and pitch of their delivery and remain calm under duress from the loved one. The more prepared the concerned other feels in going into flashpoints with these skills to hand, the more effective they are.

Role play can be used in each column of the communication skills sheet. For example, when the concerned other expresses their feelings, when they show understanding or when they offer to help, the practitioner should adopt the role of the loved one and respond naturally. The practitioner's responses should be challenging but not impossible to respond to. The secret to effective role-play is to keep the conversations very short. It should be limited to one or two exchanges. Feedback should then be given on what the concerned other did well and what was not so good. The practitioner can do this through the eyes of the loved one. This might include whether the response sounded arched, insincere or half-hearted. Repeating the exact same scenario with the concerned other incorporating the feedback means that the role-play becomes a process of slow refinement until the concerned other feels that they have grasped the statements, tone and pitch.

The Flashpoints worksheet will also indicate common tactics that the loved one may use to provoke a response from the concerned other. This will indicate some of the ways in which the loved one may try to undermine the communication skills, especially if conflict has justified use. The concerned other must remember that if they are provoked, then the drugs and alcohol wins through. Conflict becomes the fuel for further consumption. Therefore it can be helpful to arm the concerned other with some techniques which can help them keep their own emotions under control, despite the provocation of the loved one. Whatever approaches the concerned other finds helpful in controlling their emotions in other aspects of their life experience can be called upon in these situations. However, some additional recommendations are described below:

- **Reiterate that you do not want to argue:** State explicitly that you do not want to argue with them as it does not help either of you, instead reiterate your own feelings.

- **The stuck record:** Repeat the 'I' Message calmly again to reiterate your point. This stuck record approach can be used up to three times before a different approach may be needed.

- **Show understanding:** Recognise the situation from the loved one's point of view. Offer empathy and recognise why the situation might be difficult for them, but reiterate your own feelings and why a situation is difficult for you.

- **Visualisation:** Visualise the addiction as a monster that has possession of your loved one. This monster is goading you, through your loved one, in order to deepen the hold it has on them. This monster grows weaker if you resist its attempts.

- **The hurt child:** When your loved one is angry envisage them as a hurt child. Imagine them younger than their age.

- **Offer to help:** Offer to help the loved one deal with the difficulty or suggest that you do this together. Suggest that between you, you can find a way to resolve the situation or you can support the loved one making change.

Step 1: Explain the rationale of 'The 'I' Message' worksheet. This worksheet will allow the concerned other to formulate 'I' messages in advance of any typical flashpoints. This will help them reduce conflict in these areas. The 'I' messages can be useful in a number of different areas as well, so this can be understood as a starting point in developing these skills.

Step 2: Refer to the completed Flashpoints worksheet and record the examples of typical conflict in the Flashpoints Identified columns. These will be the examples that the practitioner and the concerned other will work on first. Once they are recorded, the concerned other should be invited to identify the example that they feel most confident about as the starting point.

Step 3: Considering the example that the concerned other has chosen, the practitioner should explore what they feel, think, fear or want in this situation. Make notes in the column adjacent to the stated example.

Step 4: Based on these notes, consider how the concerned other can formulate an 'I' message regarding their feelings, wants or needs at this time. These can be rehearsed and practiced in order to develop a natural feel to the statements. The practitioner should offer feedback on whether the statements convey the concerned other's position clearly, but also on the pitch and tone of the delivery.

Step 5: Consider the tactics identified in the Flashpoints worksheets that the loved one may use in order to engineer conflict. Using this as a basis, the practitioner and the concerned other should discuss any probable response from the loved one that may undermine the concerned other. As many loved ones have set patterns of response it can be easy to identify their typical initial responses. These can be noted and used to discuss any follow-up response from the concerned other.

Step 6: The concerned other should consider how they can keep their focus at this time. Inviting them to consider how they could deal calmly with anyone who is difficult in their lives may offer insight into the skills that they have already developed in the workplace, managing children or any other area of their life. If they are not confident, they can be given the suggestions listed of tips to help them stay calm.

Treatment goal:	Treatment Entry: Communication Skills
Associated worksheets:	2.13 Flashpoints 2.14 Reducing Conflict **2.15 The 'I' Message**
Further context:	1.18 Principles of Treatment Entry

2.15 The 'I' Message

Flashpoints identified	What concerns, feelings, fears or wants *do you have* regarding this issue?	How can you express this using an 'I' statement?	How might the loved one respond to this statement?	What would help you to remain calm and focused in this situation?
1:		'I feel/want/need/. . .		
2:		'I feel/want/need/. . .		
3:		'I feel/want/need/. . .		
4:		'I feel/want/need/. . .		

2.16 Assessing Enabling

Aim: The aim of the Assessing Enabling worksheet is to identify the positive punishing consequences of the loved one's use and how the concerned other may inadvertently diminish their impact.

Rationale: In order for change to occur the loved one needs to experience a shift in balance of the consequences of use. As the negative consequences of use increase, they will challenge consumption. Punishing the user directly for using drugs or alcohol only serves to increase conflict and subsequent use. Instead, the concerned other must not become their loved one's enemy but simply allow their loved one to experience the consequences of their own actions. In this way, the loved one will experience increasingly hostile consequences from using without being able to attribute blame to anyone but themselves. It is very difficult for a concerned other to see their loved one in pain, distress or having to face profound consequences alone. It is a natural response to want to assist and either address or diminish these consequences on the loved one's behalf. This will inadvertently remove the very consequences that will prompt change.

In order to change the current status quo, the concerned other must understand what constitutes enabling. Enabling occurs when the concerned other reduces the negative consequences of their loved one's use *at a cost to themselves*. Enabling can be such a well-established pattern of response to the loved one that the concerned other does not recognise that they are doing this. Therefore systematically assessing the consequences for the loved one is important before considering how the concerned other might diminish these. Where it is apparent the concerned other does diminish these consequences, they should review whether it feels safe for them to stop doing so. This needs to be discussed carefully because enabling also serves a purpose for the concerned other. By removing the consequences from the loved one they may feel that they are saving them from being hurt, damaged or from suffering. This can make the concerned other feel less anxious. For example, a mother may quit her job in order to remain at home with an opiate-using son to protect him from overdose *and* alleviate her fear of it. Being close at hand may allow her to feel more able to respond if the son overdoses but it comes at a cost to herself: her career, her social life and her emotional well-being. Many concerned others will not be familiar with the term 'enabling' and it may confuse them, so the term 'helping' is used in this worksheet to begin with.

Besides the impact of nullifying the consequences that will change the loved one, the concerned other must recognise the cost of their behaviour on themselves physically, emotionally, socially and financially, and recognise that despite this sacrifice, the problem behaviour does not change. Not all enabling behaviours need to be disabled. If it feels too unsafe for the concerned to stop any given enabling behaviour, then their continuance should be respected. However, they must recognise that the greater the consequences of use, then the sooner the loved one will change. By only removing some enabling behaviours, the programme takes longer as the slow attrition of consequences will take longer to build.

Step 1: Explain that the Assessing Enabling worksheet is designed to assess the problems experienced by the loved one and the concerned other's response to them. This should include defining enabling to the concerned other, using examples if necessary. Remember to emphasise that not all responses to the loved one are enabling. 'Enabling' refers to the responses to the loved one's use, whether it is reducing the painful consequences of use or protecting them from other people's judgements or reactions and which comes at a cost to the concerned other. Normalise enabling as a typical and, at times, important response to the loved one's use in order to prevent the concerned other feeling judged. But if the loved one feels no consequences from using drugs or alcohol, they are unlikely to feel any necessity to actually stop taking the substance. Once the concerned other understands this, the practitioner can introduce the enabling assessment sheet. Alternatively, the word 'enabling' can be substituted with the word 'helping'.

Step 2: Invite the concerned other to consider the Problem Domains on the Assessing Enabling sheet. Reviewing the first column, the practitioner should ask the concerned other to identify what are the typical or frequent problems that their loved one experiences in each of these domains. This can be hard for the concerned other so additional prompts have been included for them to consider. These should be noted in the Loved One's Problems column. The practitioner may also refer to information gathered about the loved one's use during the Comprehensive Assessment if the concerned other still struggles to identify any specific issues. This information can be transferred across to the Assessing Enabling sheet.

Step 3: Once the loved one's problems are identified, the practitioner and the concerned other should work through each row, one at a time, repeating the same process. The practitioner should work with the concerned other to identify the ways in which they 'help' the loved one with each specific problem. This can be difficult as many of the enabling behaviours become so ingrained in the rhythm of the concerned other's life that they are not always immediately apparent. The phrase 'help' is used as this is often more meaningful to the concerned other who will not necessarily distinguish between 'help' and 'enabling' immediately. Whilst there can be some explicit enabling strategies like cooking them food or paying the loved one's rent, there can also be more implicit responses. These are often more subtle and can be more difficult to detect. These tend to take the form of protecting the loved one in anticipation of their behaviour. Examples include not going away for the weekend in case their loved one uses or defending their loved one's behaviour from other family members. The concerned other may be less aware of these strategies and may have simply embedded them in the routine of life without even thinking. For example, the concerned other who always declines social invites because of fear that the loved one will use or show them up. Identifying as many as possible is important if the programme is to have a clear impact on the loved one.

Step 4: Once the explicit or implicit behaviours are identified, each one should be examined one at time. Reviewing the enabling behaviours should be related to the demand that it makes on the concerned other. For example, concealing the loved one's use from wider family members may place intolerable strain on the concerned other and they may feel guilty for lying.

Paying off debts or repairing damage to the home after a loved one's drinking spree may cost time and money. Defending a loved one from another's criticism may alienate them from supportive relationships. Once complete, there can be wider reflections on the concerned other's well-being as a result of these constant sacrifices. It is the enabling of the loved one's use that tends to have the most corrosive effect on the concerned other's own life and mental health. And whether these continued efforts are sustainable can be reflected upon too. Most important is whether these demands are actually making any difference to their loved one's use right now? These broader questions can help concerned others come to terms with the necessity of making changes.

Step 5: The final column reviews the consequences of the concerned other stopping each of these enabling behaviours. Each should be examined carefully to consider the implications of withholding this enabling and the risk for the loved one or vulnerable others, such as children. It should be stressed that the enabling is done to protect both the loved one and the concerned other. Ceasing to respond to the loved one must feel safe for the concerned other. Therefore, evaluating the consequences thoroughly is important and will help increase the concerned other's motivation when they feel prepared for the implications. The practitioner and the concerned other should now agree which enabling behaviours they will cease. In some cases not all enabling needs to cease but can be diminished. For example, if the concerned other always cooks for a hungry loved one who has spent all their money on drugs or alcohol they do not have to cook a favoured or even a pleasant meal but put them on more basic rations.

Step 6: If the concerned other has not informed their loved one that they have sought professional help, they will need to do so prior to implementing radical changes in enabling. This can be done using 'I' messages. The concerned other should anticipate extinction burst behaviour as a result of dropping enabling behaviours. Again, this can be used as a useful indication that these enabling behaviours were actually facilitating drug or alcohol use as opposed to changing it.

Treatment goal:	Treatment Entry: Disable Enabling
Associated worksheets:	**2.16 Assessing Enabling** 2.17 Others Enabling
Further context:	1.4 Family Coping 1.18 Principles of Treatment Entry

2.16 Assessing Enabling

Problem domains	Loved one's problems	What do you do to help your loved one in this area?	What is the cost for you in doing this?	Does it feel safe to stop?
Family: Are their problems kept secret? Do others judge or criticise the loved one? Does the loved one contribute to the family?				
Parenting and child care: Are children looked after by others when they use? Do others pay for thier keep?				
Social relationships: Is the loved one shunned by others? Do others avoid them or make comments on their behaviour?				
Emotions and mental health: Does the loved one get depressed? Ask for reassurance? Persecute themselves? Feel remorseful or overwhelmed?				
Physical health: Does the loved one eat regularly? Suffer hangovers or withdrawal? Get into a poor physical state when using?				

Housing:
Can the loved one manage day-to-day demands?
Is their abode clean?
Can they pay their rent?

Work or college:
Do they get in on time?
Are they on disciplinary measure?
Have they been suspended or excluded?

Money and finances:
Are they in debt?
Do they ask for money?
Are dealers owed money?
Do they have any fines?

Legal:
Are they aggressive?
Do they damage your property or steal from you?
Are they in prison or on an order?

Other: Please state.

2.17 Others Enabling

Aim: The purpose of the Others Enabling sheet is to identify and address any others who are involved with the loved one who may be inadvertently enabling the loved one to use drugs or alcohol.

Rationale: The Others Enabling worksheet will not always be necessary if the concerned other is the only person trying to address the problematic use. But often the concerned other may not be the only person supporting the loved one. Numerous others may also be involved and trying to help them in the best way they can. This may become evident during the Comprehensive Assessment or emerge as the helping relationship unfolds. If these involved others are enabling use, it means that the best efforts of the concerned other to stop any enabling behaviour are negated. For example, if a father refuses to give his son money which he suspects will be spent on drugs, the son may then call upon the grandmother for money instead. In our experience this is more likely to happen when the concerned other who presents for help is male. They grasp the need to disable enabling but their efforts are often undone by other women who take on the vacated care-taking role. It may also occur between couples, separated or co-habiting, where one is 'softer' on the loved one than the other. In this situation it becomes easy for the loved one to play these individuals off at one another, causing conflicts that distract from their own use. This can be unhelpful as the loved one will remain immune to the consequences of their use.

Identifying these individuals and formulating an approach which will help them amend this behaviour without alienation is important. Care needs to be taken here, as it is easy to disturb more complex family dynamics. For example, the involved other may blame the concerned other for the problem, fail to recognise the severity of the issue or believe that the loved one needs a different approach. The concerned other needs to be able to increase their social support from others and not alienate them. Therefore careful preparation is needed to address another person's responses to the loved one, along with communications skills. Again, as many involved others do not know how to help, it can be useful to consider what they could do instead that would be helpful. This will offer them a clearer role and assist the concerned other's efforts at change.

Step 1: Introduce the rationale of the Others Enabling worksheet to the concerned other. This can be related directly to information that other people are trying to assist the loved one. The practitioner should express how important it is that everybody is consistent with the loved one. Therefore, evaluating the role of others and their impact on the delivery of the programme is important. Should other's efforts be counter-productive, then it will be necessary to develop a plan to address this unhelpful support and offer people guidance on a more effective role.

Step 2: List the names of each involved other in a separate column and their relationship to the loved one. Examine the roles these involved others are taking, one at a time.

Step 3: Ask the concerned other to identify specifically what each involved other does to reduce the consequences for the loved one. It is very important to be as specific as possible in this. Checking what concrete evidence the concerned other has for this person's involvement can avoid conflict or misunderstanding between them. Should the concerned other base their assessment on their suspicions, the approach to the involved other can be softened to incorporate this. If the concerned other is unsure, rather than making assumptions they can see this as an important check-in with the involved other to start with.

Step 4: It is important to identify concrete examples of where the involved others have intercepted consequences for the loved one. Again this should be as specific and detailed as possible. If the involved other should challenge the concerned other, they should always draw upon actual examples to illustrate their case. This is used as a fallback position only.

Step 5: The involved other's enabling will be frustrating for many concerned others. They may feel that the involved other is siding against them with the loved one or that they are trying to undermine their attempts at change. Whilst it is frustrating, the concerned other should try to understand the situation from the involved other's perspective. Considering how they think this behaviour assists the loved one can offer some important recognition of the involved one's efforts, which can, in turn, reduce conflict.

Step 6: Recognising that the involved other has acted in good faith to help the loved one can show appreciation of their input so far. Furthermore, it is the case that many people simply do not know what the best kind of help is in these situations. Valuing the attempts that they have made is important as a precursor to suggesting that other options can be more effective.

Step 7: The concerned other should consider what they want the involved other to do instead of enabling. If they just ask the involved other to stop, it may leave the involved other without the skills to follow through on this. Exploring what the alternatives are and why they are important can give them great impetus to follow through on the programme. This may be difficult for the concerned other to formulate. If this is the case, use a Problem Solving sheet with them to consider all the options available to the involved other, before deciding upon a couple of options to suggest.

Step 8: The concerned other can offer to support the involved other in changing the enabling. This can be done by having the concerned other coach them in what they have learned on the programme, deepening their own understanding in the process. Involved others who are close to the loved one may also attend specific sessions in the PACT programme to help the concerned other too.

Step 9: It is important to reinforce the role of the involved other. Appreciating their efforts, praising their willingness to implement the approach and seeking feedback, can augment their commitment and help establish a unified approach with a number of involved others.

Step 10: Once this information is collated, it can be used to inform a script for the concerned other to discuss the issues with the involved other in order to make changes.

Treatment goal:	Treatment Entry: Disable Enabling
Associated worksheets:	2.16 Assessing Enabling **2.17 Others Enabling**
Further context:	1.4 Family Coping 1.18 Principles of Treatment Entry

2.17 Others Enabling

	Name: Relationship:	Name: Relationship:
What are they doing *specifically* to enable the loved one's use?		
What evidence do you have for this?		
How does this reduce the consequences for the loved one?		
What does the programme say about this?		
In what way does this person think it helps the loved one?		
How could you show understanding to the involved member's responses.		
What would you like them to do instead?		
How could you offer to support them in this?		
What would it mean to you if they did this?		

2.18 Preparing to Withdraw

Aim: The purpose of the Preparing to Withdraw worksheet is to plan when the concerned other should withdraw themselves and any proposed rewards from the loved one if they have used drugs or alcohol.

Rationale: The use of rewards in order to facilitate change is only effective under certain conditions. Rewards only influence behaviour when they are contingent on the desired response. Therefore rewards should only be administered when the loved one has not, or is not, using drug or alcohol. If rewards are offered regardless of whether the loved one uses, they will not influence their behaviour at all. This demands that the concerned other is vigilant for signs of use in their loved one and has a clear strategy to withhold the reward and themselves without conflict should the loved one use.

The withholding of any reward is liable to elicit an extinction burst in the loved one, which can be intensified when they under the influence of alcohol in particular. This means that the withdrawal needs careful thought to eliminate any conflict. It is important to remember that the attention of the concerned other is a reward in itself. Therefore it is not always necessary to withdraw any given reward. Should the loved one use, any planned rewards can be delayed for another time or offered to the loved one but without the concerned other's participation. Modifying the reward and retracting participation can soften the extinction burst but still negatively punish use. For example, a mother might plan a 'girls night in' for their alcohol-using daughter. On the arranged evening the daughter arrives with obvious signs of intoxication. The mother would have the choice of continuing the evening as planned; withdrawing and cancelling the event entirely; deferring it to another time when the daughter is able to engage in it; or simply giving the daughter the treats she planned to enjoy, but by herself. Allowing the daughter to have the treats without her participation will still exert a powerful consequence for the daughter because doing these things *with* the concerned other was an intrinsic part of the reward. As the daughter is still offered a partial reward, it will diminish any extinction burst.

It is imperative in managing the withdrawal of any reward, that the concerned other recognises the signs of intoxication in their loved one. The signs and symptoms of use can vary from person to person. Identifying the specific gestures and signs in the loved one is therefore important in assessing when is it time to withdraw. When this criteria is established, the concerned other can prepare their statement to the loved one and have a planned exit, either to see a member of their support network or to withdraw to an appropriate room in the house. It is important that the withdrawal occurs without conflict and is accepting of the loved one's decision to use. The concerned other should simply state that they find it difficult to be with the loved one when they have used and prefer it when they can be together properly, or that they find it hard to see the loved one intoxicated so will leave them to it and see them later. Care should be taken if there is a history of domestic violence. In these situations the loved one should always be given the reward and the concerned other should withdraw. They should exit the house or avoid any means of being cornered.

Step 1: The practitioner should explain the rationale of the Preparing to Withdraw worksheet. Offering a loved one rewards will only be effective if it is conditional on them not using. Therefore it is important that they can identify the signs and signals that the loved one has used drugs or alcohol as a cue for them to withdraw from the situation. It is important that this occurs without conflict. This sheet will allow the concerned other to identify when and how to withdraw.

Step 2: Signs and Symptoms is an assessment of the indicators of use. The concerned other needs to be confident that the loved one has used and, if necessary, explain what makes them think this to the loved one, who may insist that they have not. The concerned other will have a deep awareness of the signs and symptoms of intoxication, having witnessed this extensively. The practitioner should draw upon this awareness by asking the concerned other what behaviours they have witnessed when they are certain that the loved one has used in the past. Identifying as many of these signs as possible is important. The more signs and symptoms they can observe, the more certain the concerned other will be in withdrawing the planned reward and themselves.

Step 3: Responses considers how the concerned other can withdraw from the situation without conflict. This should begin with an acknowledgement that the loved one has chosen to use drugs or alcohol and an acceptance that they will not argue with them about this. This can be followed with a planned 'I' message that expresses their feelings to the loved one without conflict. The practitioner should explore what the concerned other feels or experiences when they see the loved one intoxicated, or if a reward that they have invested in is interrupted by use. These responses will vary from one concerned other to another. The practitioner should focus on helping the concerned other articulate their feelings first and then formulate them into an 'I' message. Care should be taken to ensure that the concerned other expresses their feelings or hopes rather than passing comment on the loved one's behaviour. This can be extended by the concerned other stating what they had hoped the reward and time spent together would be like. An example of this is:

> *I can see that you want to drink and I know that arguing with you about this is not good for either of us. I was really looking forward to the two of us doing something together. But I just find it really hard to see you like this when we can't be close.*

Step 4: The concerned other should consider their options in terms of withholding the reward. Withholding the reward entirely will be the most powerful response but generate an extinction burst. Delaying the reward can soften the approach and finally just giving the reward to the loved one without participating will generate even less conflict but greater discomfort in the loved one. The concerned other should consider what they feel is most manageable for them, taking into account how the loved one is liable to react. They should choose an option that they are most comfortable with, and one they are confident that they can follow through on. This should be explained simply to the loved one, for example:

- **Withholding the reward:** *I think we should leave it and discuss it another time.*

- **Delaying the reward:** *Let's do this another time when you are more up for it. What about tomorrow night?*

- **Not participating:** *You go ahead and enjoy it. I am going to go up to bed. I will see you in the morning.*

Step 5: The concerned other should have a planned exit statement. The exit statement can bridge the withdrawal with the actions the concerned other will take to remove themselves from the situation. If others are present, the concerned other should discuss this possibility with them and agree on collectively withdrawing from the loved one.

Step 6: The concerned other should plan places to retreat to, ensuring that at the very least they remove themselves from the loved one. If the loved one does not live with the concerned other their own home makes an ideal place to retreat. If the loved one is liable to pester them, then arranging to withdraw to the home of a member of their support network for a short period can be helpful. This will need to be planned for in advance (see 2.29 Building Social Support). If the concerned other lives with the loved one, a similar strategy can be used. Alternatives might be going for a walk, doing something in the garden or going to bed.

Treatment goal:	Treatment Entry: Withdraw Without Conflict
Associated worksheets:	**2.18 Preparing to Withdraw**
Further context:	1.18 Principles of Treatment Entry

2.18 Preparing to Withdraw

	Notes
Signs and signals	
How do they behave differently under the influence? What do they say?	
How does it affect their speech and co-ordination?	
How does it affect their mood?	
What are the tell tale signs that they have used? Smells, disappearances, flushed face etc?	
What could you say to explicitly recognise that the loved one wants to use and you will not stop them?	
Responses	
What can you say to accept the fact that the loved one has decided to use and that you will not argue with them about that?	
What 'I' message can you give them to explain why you find it difficult to see them intoxicated? What did you hope the reward would be like?	
Which option feels best for you: (1) Withholding the reward? (2) Suggesting another time? (3) Giveing the reward without participation? How would you explain this to the loved one?	
How would you announce your withdrawal without conflict? Are others present agreed on this?	
Where could you go for a short period of time? Who could you ask for support in advance with this?	

2.19 Functional Analysis Logs

Aim: Functional Analysis Logs provide a detailed assessment of the loved one's typical use. This will provide a framework within which to orchestrate the four components involved in facilitating treatment entry.

Rationale: Functional analysis is an important behavioural assessment tool that identifies the function of a given behaviour. This is achieved by examining the specific facets of the behaviour including the external and internal triggers that precipitate it, the exact dimensions of the behaviour (time, cost and amount) and the range of rewarding and punishing consequences that follow. The practitioner must work with the concerned other to draw upon their deep understanding of the loved one to map the sequence of use to the best of their knowledge. It is not uncommon for many concerned others to ask their loved one directly about these aspects of their use. This can be a useful means of establishing empathy and rapport between the concerned other and the loved one regarding the drug and alcohol use, which until then has always been an issue of contention. The functional analysis is always based on specific using events and never generalised ones. This is because what may precipitate a loved one to use on one day of the week may be different to another. For example, the loved one using heavily when they receive any welfare benefits differs from why they may use after an argument with another family member.

The analysis should always be as detailed as possible. Each domain is mapped as thoroughly as possible in order to establish a working hypothesis of the drivers of a loved one's drug or alcohol usage in that situation. Therefore, each column can be broken down into further detail. External triggers should include identifying people, places and times of use. Internal triggers of thoughts and feelings should also be described to the best of the concerned other's knowledge. This might be indicated by the loved one's body language, things that they have said about their use or simply based on the intuition of the concerned other. As there are only eight principle determinants of relapse into use, the next column offers insight into the pattern of the loved one's use. Considering the external and internal triggers, the concerned other should identify which of the following determinants best explains their loved one's use at this time, remembering that more than one determinant may contribute to the using experience. This will provide useful information later in the programme should the concerned other support their loved one in treatment.

The concerned others should offer their best guesstimate of the level of intoxication displayed by the loved one at this time. The positive consequences of use include the range of short term positive rewards. These tend to be immediate, such as pleasant feelings, thoughts or pleasure from using with particular people at particular times. The identification of these consequences will give insight into the function of a specific behaviour in a given environment. Long term punishing consequences follow later, usually the next day, and include hangovers, sickness, trouble in relationships, debt, depression and so on. This information will give a clear overview of every facet of the loved one's use and can be used later to plan responses to interrupt this established pattern. The Functional Analysis is laid out in a log form in order to make easy comparisons between different using events, to identify any patterns, to allow the practitioner and concerned other to refine previous assessments and to assess whether consumption is decreasing.

The assessment tool should be used as a framework for the client to tell their story. Each question of the assessment tool should be used to guide this exploration and ensure that all-important aspects are covered. However, specific columns do not have to be completed in order from left to right. The practitioner and concerned other should work to attain mutual understanding of the situation. Once the situation is mapped in detail, a treatment response will be implemented based on the available information.

The Functional Analysis has been arranged in a log format. This has been done because the Functional Analysis is a working hypothesis of the behaviour. This hypothesis will have to be tested by implementing interventions that try to change the behaviour. This means that the log of Functional Analysis allows for easy comparison with previous interventions. Any patterns or differences can be viewed easily and the impacts compared in order to assess the effectiveness of the approaches deployed. The external and internal triggers can also be helpful in treatment planning once the loved one does seek treatment. This will indicate future risk situations for the loved one.

Step 1: Introduce the Functional Analysis Log to the concerned other and explain that it is designed to assess the specific aspects of their loved one's use. This will entail exploring the concerned other's insight into the loved one's behaviour. It does not matter too much if this information is not wholly accurate as these analyses can be refined over time and the concerned other will begin to notice more about their loved one's typical patterns of use. Once this information is gathered, it will provide the framework for planning how to change their loved one's consumption.

Step 2: The concerned other should consider a recent and typical example of their loved one's use. It is important to stress that they will complete the assessment on this specific example and not confuse it with other times the loved one has used drugs or alcohol. Based on this, begin the assessment, explaining the role of each heading as you work through them. As you gain the detail from the concerned other, encourage and praise them for their insight and detail.

Step 3: The External Triggers column asks about the external events that occurred just prior to use. This is important as anything can serve as a trigger for use. Identifying the specific triggers for the loved one is important in planning interventions. Considering this recent using event, the practitioner should ensure they themselves have a very clear picture of these external events. If the practitioner can't 'see' the story in their own mind's eye they are not getting sufficient detail. Useful prompting questions include:

- When did it take place?

- Was it in the week or at the weekend?

- Where was the loved one when they used?

- Were they at home?

- Were they at a friend's house? If so whose?

- Were they on the way home from work?

- Who else was involved?

- Were they drinking and using with other people?

- What people were they using with?

- Do they use with these people often?

Step 4: The Internal Triggers column asks the concerned other to describe the internal prompts that may trigger use. Internal Triggers include the loved one's thoughts, feelings and sensations, which can trigger use. These can be more difficult for the concerned other to identify. They must put themselves in the mindset of their loved one to try and feel what they are going through before they use. Drawing upon their deep understanding of the loved one can be an asset in this. Again, assessing the specific detail becomes very important. For example, asking what they believe their loved one is thinking just before they use needs to be as exact as possible. We want to establish the phrases that the loved one might be thinking, such as 'I deserve it, I work hard.' or 'No-one tells me what to do with my life!' The behaviour and statements of the loved one prior to use may offer clues to their internal state. What do they say prior to use? The loved one's feelings also need to be assessed. Their feelings may be suggested by their emotional appearance, their mood and body language or again through statements. In general, extremes of mood tend to increase risk of use. So when someone is very down or in a very good mood, they are equally likely to use. Finally, what is the loved one feeling prior to use? Do they have any physical sensations? Do they suffer any health problems or any other discomfort that may trigger the need to use? Do they claim that use alleviates any physical pain?

Step 5: The Determinants column lists the eight determinants of relapse. Considering the list of determinants can be helpful in recognising the danger signals for the loved one, which is especially important for supporting them once they are in treatment. The concerned other should be talked through the eight determinants and consider which they think best describes the loved one's use at this time? People may experience more than one determinant at a time. They should underline the determinants that they feel best describes their loved one's motivation to use drugs or alcohol.

Step 6: The Consumption column describes the amount of drugs or alcohol used. Again this may be a best estimate according the information available to the concerned other. It can be hard to establish how much the loved one spent on drugs or alcohol, how long did the use last for and how much they took. If the concerned other is not sure, then ask them to scale the level of intoxication that the loved one experienced from 1–5, with 5 being completely incapacitated. Again, we want these details as exact as possible to serve as a baseline for future reference. Any future use can assessed using a functional analysis and changes in this column will indicate progress made.

Step 7: The Consequences columns describe the reinforcers and punishers of use. The short term positive consequences of use are often more difficult for concerned others to complete. Whilst drug and alcohol use has caused them nothing but pain, they need to gain some insight into the desired experiences of their loved one. For example, what do they feel the loved one enjoys about using at these times, these places and with these people? What does the loved one feel that drugs or alcohol do to alleviate negative thinking, feelings or pain? Is there anything that the loved one says they enjoyed about using? Mapping out these benefits can still remain hard. One way to assist the concerned other in this is to consider the external and internal triggers they have already described. The concerned other may review the benefits of use in contrast to these triggers. How does drug or alcohol use alleviate any stresses or enhance any social relationships? Mapping these benefits can increase the concerned other's empathy with their loved one's destructive behaviour.

The long term negative consequences should chart the impact of use on each area of the loved one's life, particularly where use damages relationships or things that they value highly. This can affect social functioning across all domains including how they feel about themselves, the impact on their partner, their family, their social life and employment. Legal and financial implications may figure heavily for drug users in this section too. Considering this damage, it is important to explicitly identify what the loved one perceives to be important consequences as opposed to what the concerned other believes to be the most damaging consequences, if we are to gain insight into the leverage available to generate change.

Treatment goal:	Treatment Entry: Combining Procedures
Associated worksheets:	**2.19 Functional Analysis Logs** 2.20 Intervention Plan
Further context:	1.15 PACT: A Behavioural Ethos 1.19 Functional Analysis Logs

2.19 Functional Analysis Logs

External triggers: Who, when and where were they just before they used?	Internal triggers: What were they thinking and feeling just before they used?	Determinants: What do you feel are the main determinants of their use?	Consumption: How intoxicated did they get on this occasion?							Short term benefits: What did your loved one enjoy about using?	Long term consequences: What problems did their use cause them?
			No contact	Did not use	Suspected use	Mild signs	Obvious signs	Incapacitated			
			nc	1	2	3	4	5			
1.		Unpleasant mood Conflict Positive mood Positive occasions Social pressure Physical pain Urges Testing control									
2.		Unpleasant mood Conflict Positive mood Positive occasions Social pressure Physical pain Urges Testing control									
3.		Unpleasant mood Conflict Positive mood Positive occasions Social pressure Physical pain Urges Testing control									

	nc	1	2	3	4	5
4.						
Unpleasant mood						
Conflict						
Positive mood						
Positive occasions						
Social pressure						
Physical pain						
Urges						
Testing control						
5.						
Unpleasant mood						
Conflict						
Positive mood						
Positive occasions						
Social pressure						
Physical pain						
Urges						
Testing control						
6.						
Unpleasant mood						
Conflict						
Positive mood						
Positive occasions						
Social pressure						
Physical pain						
Urges						
Testing control						

2.20 Intervention Plan

Aim: The aim of the Intervention Plan is to orchestrate the principles of treatment entry into a single comprehensive intervention to address specific using events in the loved one.

Rationale: The concerned other will have mastered the four principles of facilitating treatment entry for the loved one and even had some experience of implementing them. The concerned other will have also completed a Functional Analysis assessment of the loved one's typical using event. The concerned other can now combine this experience and understanding to develop a systematic approach to addressing the loved one's use into a single and comprehensive intervention. The Intervention Plan provides the framework to organise this response. Each section of the Plan corresponds with the Functional Analysis conducted on the loved one's use. Drawing upon these assessments of typical using events, the Plan identifies where each of the four principles of treatment entry can influence every facet of the loved one's use. This demands that the practitioner and the concerned other work systematically on the information already gathered in the Functional Analysis. Together they can explore how the principles of treatment entry can be applied to the specific using pattern. It is important to remember that the triggers and motivation for the loved one to use may differ at times. For example, heavy drinking at the weekend may be associated with positive mood states whilst drinking mid-week may be associated with boredom. This may mean that more than one plan is necessary depending on the variations in use the concerned other has identified in the functional analysis.

The Intervention Plan then provides guidance on how the four principles can be applied to each of these situations. Inviting the concerned other to reflect upon their experience of the programme so far may help them hone their approaches to the Plan. For example, if certain rewards proved compelling for the loved one or not offers insight into what they might do more of or what strategies they might eliminate. The practitioner and concerned other might also review some of the worksheets already completed, such as the Rewards for the Loved One, Communication Skills, Assessing Enabling and Preparing to Withdraw for further inspiration. How necessary these previous worksheets are will depend upon the progress the concerned other has made in applying the programme already. Whenever the concerned other feels stuck or uncertain, they should review these previous worksheets.

It is important to remember that the Functional Analysis of the loved one's use is always a working hypothesis. The concerned other will apply the intervention and then they will review their progress with the practitioner. In this respect it is important to remind the concerned other that these interventions do not have to be effective first time. Each attempt to implement these plans will offer more insight into their loved one's use and how the interventions can be fine-tuned.

Step 1: The practitioner should explain to the concerned other that the purpose of the Intervention Plan worksheets is to draw together all the skills that they have learned so far in order to target the loved one's use in a seamless approach. The Intervention Plan is a problem-solving worksheet which will help them to identify what skills to use and when, for maximum effect on the loved one's use.

Step 2: The practitioner and concerned other should begin by reviewing a completed Functional Analysis: Logs of Loved One's Use. They should identify a typical example of the loved one's use that they have already assessed and feel confident in addressing. This using event should be one that is fairly frequent.

Step 3: Section A of the Intervention Plan invites the concerned other to consider the typical external triggers of their loved one's use on this using occasion. Considering when the loved one is likely to use offers insight into when any alternative reward should be offered to compromise use. This will also entail consideration of how other external triggers can be avoided or interrupted. For example, if other people are involved in the loved one's use, can they be avoided? Alternatively, if there are certain individuals in whose presence the loved does not drink or takes drugs, can they be invited too? If the loved one's use is entwined in a relationship with someone else, for example a daughter and her boyfriend may drink heavily when together, could this other person be invited to participate in the reward? The Problem Solving worksheet can help here by generating possible ideas and strategies.

Step 4: Section B is based on the internal triggers that drive use. The concerned other may have an opportunity to diminish the need for use by alleviating any particular stresses that drive the loved one to use. This can be done through communication skills that explicitly recognise the pressures on the loved one. Listening sympathetically to their worries can reduce the tension that contributes to using. This may be a current issue, such as a problem at work, or an ongoing problem that the loved one has battled with as identified by the determinants of use such as a depression. Asking the concerned other to consider a time when they were able to soothe a stressed loved one effectively may offer some insight into the kind of approaches that may assist them here. Verbal encouragement is a very profound reinforcer. The concerned other might consider how they reinforce the loved one's engagement in the alternative reward by stating what it means to them to share the experience with their loved one. Again, 'I' messages can be used here to express the concerned other's positive feelings. This should avoid discussing drug or alcohol use and focus on the actual reward that they are engaged in.

Step 5: Section C refers to the amount that the loved one uses if the concerned other's intervention is partially successful or unsuccessful. It will allow for comparison with any future or past episodes of use. This can be important in holding the concerned other's confidence during the programme. Furthermore, whilst use is occurring, it is important that the concerned other retreats from the loved one and allows them to use without contact. Consideration should be given to what the concerned other will say should the loved one use, so that they can remove themselves without conflict. Identifying where they may retreat, whether it be to the home of a member of their support network or even going to bed early, will diminish both conflict and attention-seeking that can reinforce drug and alcohol use.

Step 6: Section D is based on the short term consequences of consumption. These are the immediate effects of intoxication that the loved one desires. These short term benefits reveal the unmet needs in the loved one that they believe drugs and alcohol can fulfil. Whether it is to feel a sense of belonging, relieve stress or escape boredom, they offer important insight into what the loved one is seeking at these times. Needs are important and do not simply diminish. They need to be met in other more positive ways. As such, this element of the Functional Analysis can offer an acid test of the value of the alternative reward. The practitioner and concerned other should consider whether any planned reward will meet these unmet needs. If they do not, then the reward should be revised.

Step 7: Section E is based upon the long-term negative consequences for the loved one. Again, it is important that we identify from these consequences long term positive and negative punishers from the loved one's perspective. Damage to areas of their life which matter to the concerned other but not to the loved one will have little impact. Reviewing the Functional Analysis to explore the typical negative consequences of this type of using event will allow the concerned other to identify any specific components of enabling that they feel safe to disable.

Treatment goal:	Treatment Entry: Combining Procedures
Associated worksheets:	2.19 Functional Analysis Logs **2.20 Intervention Plan**
Further context:	1.15 PACT: A Behavioural Ethos 1.19 Functional Analysis Logs

2.20 Intervention Plan

Section A: External triggers

What alternative rewards could be made available to the loved one at this high-risk time?
(If unsure, use *Rewards for the Loved One* sheet)

What external triggers could be avoided, intercepted or modified?
(If unsure, use *Problem Solving* sheet.)

If others are involved, can they offer support?
(If unsure, use *Others Enabling* sheet).

Section B: Internal triggers

What could you say to acknowledge the loved one's apparent stresses or pressures?
(Use *The 'I' Message* sheet):

What can you say positively about the loved one engaging in the alternative reward?

Considering the determinants of use, what help or support could you offer the loved one?

Section C: Behaviour

	No contact	Certain they did not use	Suspected that they had used	Signs of mild intoxication	Obvious intoxication, affecting mood or behaviour	Intoxicated to incapacitation
Rating	**N/C**	**1**	**2**	**3**	**4**	**5**

What could you say to withdraw without conflict if your loved one uses?

Where could you go if your loved one uses?

Section D: Short term benefits

Will the alterative rewarding activity address the unmet needs of the loved one at this time?
(If unsure, use *Rewards for the Loved One* sheet)

Section E: Long-term consequences

Do you do anything to avert or alleviate these consequences from the loved one?

Does it feel safe to stop doing this?

2.21 Barriers and Hooks to Treatment

Aim: The aim of this worksheet is to identify the barriers and hooks to treatment in order to help the concerned other prepare for treatment entry.

Rationale: Research has identified that there are many reasons why people do not seek help. These can be categorised into five general domains. Firstly there may be psychological barriers derived from the loved one's own perception of their problem and the need for treatment. Social barriers include the fear of shame, embarrassment or judgement from others. Practical obstacles include the ability to physically enter into treatment because of impediments such as transport, childcare or even time of work. Assumptions about treatment, what it involves and the consequences of entering into treatment can generate fears that prevent people seeking any help. And finally, for people who have had treatment, poor past experience can prove a real barrier to seeking help again. It is likely that the suggestion to enter into treatment will elicit objections from the loved one in these key areas. Anticipating any likely objections and being able to respond to them in a constructive way can not only help facilitate treatment entry but can increase the confidence of the concerned other to broach the subject.

These objections can be addressed in one of two ways. This can be through information that challenges any apparent fears or practical solutions that address any physical impediments. Information can be gathered from contacting treatment services and asking specific questions regarding the loved one's fears. For example, a loved one might object to treatment because they are frightened that people will see them going in. Finding treatment providers who do home visits would be useful to counteract the objection. If there are practical concerns, such as transport to the treatment provider, hours of opening or childcare, these can be addressed through problem-solving in advance to overcome logistical problems preventing treatment entry.

At the same time the concerned other will need to identify times when the loved one may be more receptive to the idea of treatment. These 'hooks' which elicit motivation can vary from person to person. Typically, older people tend to be more health conscious and so near misses, fortunate accidents or illness may prompt greater concern. Young people are more sensitive to damage to social status or loss in important relationships with their peers. Motivation will not always appear as a deliberate expression of the need for change in the loved one, but is more likely to appear as dissatisfaction. Reviewing the times in the past when the loved one has demonstrated dissatisfaction with their use, may offer insight into their particular hooks. Likewise, as the concerned other begins to implement the treatment entry procedures and the balance of consequences begins to shift, there will be times when the loved one becomes increasingly dissatisfied with their lives. Identifying these times will create a clear signal of when to bring up the idea of treatment and assist in addressing any objections in advance.

Step 1: Explain the aim and the rationale of the Barriers and Hooks to Treatment worksheet, which is designed to identify any blocks that the loved one may have to enter into treatment. It will also identify the types of experience that prompt concern in the loved one regarding their own use. This will help target the best times to raise the idea of treatment.

Step 2: Work through each of the five barriers one at a time. Beginning with the psychological barriers, review the examples listed and ask the concerned other whether, to the best of their knowledge, they feel that their loved one is likely to object to treatment for any of these or other similar reasons. This might include considering whether their loved one has ever said anything similar, whether a particular objection has been raised in the past or whether they can imagine their loved one making such statements.

Step 3: Record any specific objections in the adjacent column. Again, be as specific as possible in identifying each particular concern that the loved one is likely to raise. The specificity might be captured by asking 'How would your loved one actually say that?' Again, this may provide other clues, such as the loved one might use a pessimistic tone. Work your way through each domain in a systematic way in order to identify as many objections as possible.

Step 4: By reviewing the objections one at a time, we can identify what information may allay the loved one's fears or assumptions about treatment or what strategies may help them overcome physical impediments to change.

Information: Gathering information that can address the loved one's concerns can be done in several ways. Firstly, it may help the concerned other to develop a checklist of questions when contacting agencies to see what help is available to them. Besides any general questions that they have, this will mean that they will be able to focus their enquiries on the specific details that will be important to their loved one. This can also mean that any special needs of their loved one can also be taken into consideration prior to treatment entry. For example, if one fear of the client is that 'treatment does not work' then the concerned other can ask the agency what their success rate is. Every agency should monitor its outcomes and so could give a picture of how other clients have progressed in treatment with their service. Likewise, with the loved one who is too embarrassed to go to the service in case anyone sees them, the concerned other could check to see if any local services in their area do home visits or consultations at neutral venues like GP surgeries.

The practitioner working with the concerned other may also know the treatment landscape in which the concerned other and loved one live. Their knowledge of treatment agencies and services can be extremely helpful in guiding this process. For example, they may know which services offer child care, they will understand confidentiality and referral processes and what the loved one can expect once they enter in treatment. This advice and guidance can be very helpful in pointing the concerned other in the right direction to begin with and allow them to focus on viable service options.

Practicalities: Problem-solving approaches can be used where physical impediments exist to treatment entry such as the loved one's wider commitments to work, childcare or travel.

Anticipating these blocks and preparing possible plans to overcome them can be helpful. So for example, if the loved one is working it will be worth checking services for evening or weekend opening hours. Problem-solving may help generate ideas for how the loved one could overcome these problems. Furthermore, any social support network could be called upon to offer assistance where necessary, for example offering a lift to the appointment. Where social networks are introduced to the scenario it must be handled carefully. The fact that the concerned other has spoken to others regarding the loved one's use may cause a reaction in the loved one as if their trust has been betrayed. It should be made clear that there has been no discussion with others, rather it is just a suggestion at this stage.

Step 5: Any queries that might arise or suggested solutions should be recorded in the respective columns and reviewed once the subject of treatment has been broached. Any new objections should be noted and these can be reviewed in time to address them.

Step 6: Once the objections to treatment have been identified, the concerned other should consider the hooks to treatment. These are the events that appear to increase the loved one's dissatisfaction with their use. Whilst hooks are often the product of negative consequences, individuals vary in their sensitivity to these events. For example, young people are more prone to social judgements and poor self-image amongst peers. Whilst long-term users may be more concerned by health scares. The practitioner should ask the concerned other to consider times in the past when the loved one appeared dissatisfied with their use. Considering these moments, they should try to recall what it was exactly that prompted this concern in the loved one. If the concerned other is not sure, the practitioner can ask them how they think the loved one might respond to different hooks.

Step 7: Considering the times when the loved one did appear dissatisfied with use, the next column invites the concerned other to consider the signs and symptoms of this reaction in the loved one. Signs describes what the concerned other notices in the loved one. For example, they might report that the loved one appears anxious and fretful. Or they withdraw into themselves to ruminate in isolation. The symptoms describe what the loved one reports or hints that they are feeling. For some it may be an explicit statement of concern regarding their use or their health. Others may make statements that are uncharacteristic or disconnected from the present moment, for example asking the concerned other whether they still love them or asking about unrelated but emotive subjects like their childhood. This suggests that they are thinking about deeper issues and reflecting on their life. They may also behave in uncharacteristic ways, such as with an apparent act of kindness or consideration for the concerned other. At other times the loved one may simply exhibit emotional overwhelming and say outright that they cannot cope. The practitioner should explore these moments in order to identify as clear a picture as possible of the loved one at these times. If the practitioner is not clear exactly how the loved one responds in these moments they do not have enough detail. This information is important because it will attune the concerned other to recognise the most appropriate moment to raise the issue of treatment with the loved one, when they would be most receptive to it.

Treatment goal:	Treatment Entry
Associated worksheets:	**2.21 Barriers and Hooks to Treatment** 2.22 What Help is out There? 2.23 Bringing up the Subject of Treatment
Further context:	1.21 Bringing up the Subject of Treatment 1.22 Selecting Treatment Options

2.21 Barriers and Hooks to Treatment

Type	Examples	Loved one's objections	Responses to objections
Barriers **Psychological**	Failure to see use as a problem Think they can handle it on their own Like using too much to give up They believe their problems will go away without any help		
Social	Fear others would find out They feel embarrassed or ashamed Shame the family Someone important disapproves, fear of losing friends		
Practical	They do not know where to get help They have no transport, need child care They do not have the time They could not get time off work		
Assumptions	Afraid it would not help them Believe they are too young/old to get help Thought they will be told what to do Fear of what would happen in treatment Fear of consequences (work/legal/children)		
Experiences	Hate talking about their personal life Afraid they might be put in hospital They do not like to talk in groups Bad experience of treatment before They do not want to go to AA or NA They fear withdrawal		

Type	Examples	Specific hooks for loved one	Signs and symptoms
Hooks **Health**	Near-misses, hospitalisations, long-term health problems, the death or problems of another user close to them, withdrawing, sober		
Relationships	Conflict, after domestic violence, reaction from children, parents, friends, when getting on well.		

Activities	Loss of job, important hobbies or interests, social life breaking down, exclusion from school or college.		
Self-image	Conflicts with faith, self-loathing, other people's comments, social stigma, peer acceptance, social pressures to conform.		
Formal coercion	Courts, social services, drug or alcohol mandated treatment, drink driving offences, work or college.		
Other			

2.22 What Help is out There?

Aim: The aim of the worksheet is to assist the concerned other to identity the most appropriate range of services for their loved one.

Rationale: When encouraging the loved one to enter treatment it is important that they offer the appropriate options. Referral into unsuitable treatment can set the process back considerably. Therefore the concerned other will need to be familiar with the range of treatment options available to the loved one. However, based on an assessment of the degree of social breakdown and the severity of physical dependence of the loved one, it is possible to gauge the least intrusive support options and identify whether detoxification or substitute prescribing is necessary. The scales provided are only indicative and based on the current knowledge of the loved one's problems. They are included as a guide. It is not uncommon for many concerned others to believe that residential rehabilitation is essential. But it is important that the intensity of treatment is relative to the problem and shorter treatment may be more attractive to a loved one who has not yet experienced catastrophic damage to their social relationships. This will offer guidance into the range of treatment necessary for the loved one, which can narrow the concerned other's exploration to the most relevant options.

In some areas there may be a bewildering range of treatment options, whilst in other localities there may be a very limited choice. There can be a wide variety of treatment providers offering a diverse base of services. The practitioner may be familiar with the treatment landscape and provide extensive guidance. Within this, it is important that the practitioner is equitable in their description of other services and providers. What might be meaningful for the practitioner may be different for the loved one. Contact details for each service should be recorded, along with the services they offer. Most agencies will provide further information if requested. It is important that the concerned other recognises that the information provided by agencies will be slanted. It is also important to check whether public services currently have waiting lists for treatment. Concerned others should be cautious of expensive private treatments that they, or another family member, is willing to finance. Most experts advise against rapid detoxification processes. Whilst residential rehabilitation outcomes are good, addiction is a chronic relapse condition and should the loved one fail in treatment it may add additional pressure and conflict. If the loved one has any particular needs, the concerned other should check whether the service provider can account for these requirements. The concerned other may also check any anticipated objections the loved one might have regarding treatment.

Step 1: The practitioner should explain the rationale of What Help is Out There? This worksheet is designed to check what services are available for the loved one experiencing their current range of problems. This is important in ensuring that the most appropriate treatment options are explored and that the concerned other can explain these options to the loved one.

Step 2: The concerned other and the practitioner should consider the severity of the loved one's dependence and the impact of their use on their social functioning. The concerned other should circle the descriptions which best describe the loved one's current use in terms of the loved one's social functioning and the severity of their physical dependence. The bars beneath these scores will give a broad indication of the treatment the loved one might require. These are not validated tools but offer very general indicators. These suggest the least intrusive approaches first, remembering that treatment can always be 'stepped up' if necessary. Brief interventions can range from advice and information, one-off sessions or between one and six sessions. Structured Support is a community based intervention programme which can be up to three months. Intensive treatment may range from comprehensive care planned approaches, intensive day care or even residential rehab. The loved one's dependence will also need to be taken into consideration in terms of prescribing options that may be necessary either for detoxification or stabilisation. Those with additional, complex needs will require more intensively management prescribing options.

Step 3: The practitioner and concerned other should identify services that offer a range of interventions appropriate to the loved one's needs. The practitioner should explain the roles of different types of provider in the area and the services they offer. The practitioner should consider compiling a resource file of up-to-date information on local agencies to discuss with the concerned other. Services contact details should be recorded for more information and reminders to check whether they are operating waiting lists. The cost of private services should be clear from the outset.

Step 4: The concerned other should make a note of any special needs that the concerned other has that might need to be accommodated by any service provider. Whilst some of these are structural, such as child care or disabled access, other are not always clear. If the loved one has a history of enduring mental illness or are on prescribed medication, it may preclude them from some treatment providers. Age may also be a factor. Older people are often neglected within many agencies who are not confident in dealing with their needs. Whilst specific services exist for under 18s, young adults aged between 19–25 face unique challenges. Young people are less likely to experience physical dependence and may not be fully immersed in problematic lifestyles. Selecting services for this age range is a more careful process because, although they are classed as adults, many services are simply not appropriate for them. For example, a residential unit for older long-term users may be difficult for them to manage or even counter-productive. In this eventuality, the concerned other should always check the age range of other service users within the treatment service. Likewise, many agencies may not be confident in dealing with the older drinker who is 70 +.

Step 5: Any possible objections from the loved one regarding treatment itself, identified in the Hooks and Barriers to Treatment worksheet, can be included here. The concerned other can use this as a checklist of questions which will help them address any specific blocks for their loved one. For example, some loved ones fear exploring a painful past, fear groups or fear information about their use being disclosed. All this can be checked with providers to ensure appropriate treament options are available.

Step 6: The concerned other should compile a list of which services appear to be most appropriate for the loved one and why. Having more than one option is not a bad thing as it may increase the loved one's personal sense of control if they can choose. Again, it is important to remember that when treatment works, it does so quickly. The loved one can be encouraged to trial any treatment option to see if it feels right for them before exploring other more intensive options.

Treatment goal:	Treatment Entry
Associated worksheets:	2.21 Barriers and Hooks to Treatment **2.22 What Help is out There?** 2.23 Bringing up the Subject of Treatment
Further context:	1.21 Bringing up the Subject of Treatment 1.22 Selecting Treatment Options

2.22 What Help is out There?

What best describes your loved one's social functioning?				
Holding down meaningful relationships and commitments	Struggling to hold down meaningful relationships and commitments	Meaningful relationships and responsibilities are under threat	Lost important relationships and no longer manages wider commitments	Long term break down of relationships and commitments

Brief intervention   *Structured interventions*   *Comprehensive intervention*

What best describes your loved one's physical dependence?				
No signs of physical withdrawal	Not known	Some mild signs of physical withdrawal	Severe signs of physical withdrawal	Debilitating signs of physical withdrawal

No detox   *Community prescribing/detox*   *Inpatient detox/stabilisation*

This indicates that my loved one needs:

Level of support:
Detoxification:

Local drug or alcohol agency	Service and opening times?	Waiting lists?

NHS drug or alcohol agency	Service and opening times?	Waiting lists?

Local private providers	Service and opening times?	Waiting lists?

Community care assessments	Service and opening times?	Waiting lists

© Phil Harris, *The Concerned Other*, www.russellhouse.co.uk

Private providers	Service and opening times	Costs

Local self-help	Services and opening times	

Loved one's specific needs (gender, age, child care, disability, mental health)

Objections checklist	Notes

Treatment suggestions	Reasons

2.23 Bringing up the Subject of Treatment

Aim: The purpose of this worksheet is to help the concerned other identify the times when the loved one would be most receptive to the idea of seeking help and prepare the suggestion in advance.

Rationale: As the consequences of the loved one's usage begin to shift through rewards, reductions in conflict, withdrawal and disabling enabling, they will become increasing receptive to the idea of treatment. Recognising the optimal time to raise the subject of treatment will maximise chances that the loved one will accept the offer. This may differ from person to person, but it is usually helpful to make the suggestion when the loved one's concerns regarding their use is heightened by circumstances that trouble them. Recognising the loved one's dissatisfaction with their use is a useful barometer of when to raise the subject of change.

The concerned other will have already identified the Barriers and Hooks for the loved one to enter into treatment. This information can now be put to maximum effect in considering raising the subject. The concerned other should use the signs and symptoms of dissatisfaction and external events most likely to trigger concern in their loved one as the indicator of when to raise the subject. This needs to be done sensitively and in the most conducive manner. The concerned other should try to identify the times and place when the loved one appears most open and non-defensive. Whether others should be present may require deeper consideration. If the loved one respects someone's opinion, it might be helpful for this person to be present. However, it must not appear as if the loved one is being ambushed. Considering previous attempts to get the loved one into treatment can help eliminate unhelpful aspects of the request, as well identify any particular nuances that have been helpful in the past. For example, pressuring the loved one or rejecting their preferred treatment options may have caused resistance in the past. Reflecting on these past experiences can offer a great deal of insight into when the loved one is most open to the idea. Even if the loved one refuses subsequent suggestions to seek help, it will reveal more information about the branding of the message for future attempts.

The concerned other should consider how to phrase their treatment request. This needs to be an 'I Message' but should also recognise the struggle for the loved one and recognise the loved one's feelings as much as possible. The concerned other should expect a mixed response from the loved one to the suggestion of treatment. In the first instance they should listen to any mixed feelings that they have regarding entering in treatment. Only then should they call upon their responses to these anticipated objections. Should the loved one refuse any subsequent offer to enter treatment, it is important that the concerned other accepts this decision and does not pressure them into seeking help. This will only polarise the discussion and make it harder for them to enter treatment at a later stage if they have argued extensively that they do not need it. Therefore, having an 'I Message' ready to accept the loved one's position and withdraw without conflict is important. The concerned other should understand that as long as the consequences remained tipped towards change, more opportunities to raise the subject will occur very rapidly. And the loved one's own sense of free choice in entering treatment is an important factor in their compliance with it once they do seek professional help.

Step 1: Explain the rationale of the Bringing Up the Subject of Treatment worksheet. This worksheet will allow the concerned other to identify the most appropriate time to raise the idea of treatment to their loved one and plan their request in advance. This worksheet uses a problem-solving approach that considers the particular hooks and barriers to treatment for the loved one and combines them into a planned approach to raising the subject of entering into treatment. It is important to remember from outset that the loved one may not respond immediately to the suggestion of entering treatment. Whilst this is disappointing, it is important not to pressurise the loved one. There will be increasingly frequent opportunities to broach the subject again, and with every opportunity the probability that the loved one will seek help will increase. Furthermore, whenever the loved one declines the offer to enter treatment, it will reveal how the request can be refined for future attempts.

Step 2: The practitioner and the concerned other should review the completed Barriers and Hooks into Treatment worksheet. In Section A they should note the most powerful hooks for the loved one and the most concrete signs and signals of motivation. These will be the key indicators of when to raise the subject of treatment.

Step 3: The concerned other should consider the setting that the loved one would be most responsive in, when they hear the request to enter treatment. For some this may be in the home with the concerned other alone, or it might be in a different venue with other people present. This should be considered carefully as the setting can have a big impact on the loved one's decision. The concerned other should also consider the time that the issue is raised. Is the loved one more receptive in the evenings or the mornings? The issue of whether someone else should be present is more difficult. Only if there is someone that the loved one respects deeply should someone else be included in this process. If too many people are involved, the loved one may feel overtly defensive and betrayed. This may allow them to focus on the apparent 'underhand' behaviour of those they trusted and this will only distract them from reflecting on the issue of their substance use.

Step 4: The concerned other should reflect on previous attempts to suggest that the loved one enter treatment. Considering these previous occasions: what appeared to work well and what did not work well? The concerned other and practitioner should reflect on these previous experiences and ensure that they eliminate what was unhelpful as well as build on what worked.

Step 5: The concerned other should consider how they would phrase the suggestion. This should overtly incorporate the concerns elicited by the trigger, an 'I Message' of the concerned other feelings and the offer to help them in their treatment. This statement is divided into sections to ensure that the concerned other masters each specific component of this approach.

Again, the practitioner and the concerned other should use this as a template to express their specific feelings. Examples are:

> *You seem really shaken up after the argument with your brother yesterday. I am not sure whether you are most angry with him or yourself but you seem really unhappy. It is hard for me to see you so down all the time. I just want us to be close like we used to be. It would mean so much to me if we could do that. What do you think about getting some help so we can get past this together? I know things are not easy for you now and you are under a lot of pressure, but I will help you get through this in any way I can.*

> *I know that you have been really unwell and that it is worrying you. It really worries me too. I am frightened about what will happen to you if you keep drinking. I don't want you to die. I just want you to be well. I know you said that treatment could not help you but it would mean the world to me if you just gave it a try. How do you feel about getting some help so we can beat this thing together?*

Should the loved one agree to seek help the concerned other should discuss what options are available to the loved one, being careful to allay any fears. This discussion should set out options for the loved one so that they can chose an option themselves. This is where the background research into what treatment is available is most useful. Once the loved one expresses a choice, the concerned other should act promptly in order to arrange an appointment and support the loved one to attend. They can offer to attend with them if the loved one feels this would be helpful. Sometimes a loved one will agree to meet with the concerned other's practitioner in the first instance.

Step 6: The loved one might have mixed feelings about change. The concerned other should explore what the loved one feels would be good and bad about seeking help and show understanding for the loved one's reticence. Accepting what the loved one's position is can then be addressed. Anticipating any objections identified on the Barriers and Hooks to Treatment worksheet can be helpful here. The loved one may reject the offer of treatment for a reason which has been anticipated. The concerned other should accept the loved one's view point and respond to the objection with a strategy that they have already identified. They should be cautious not to suggest that they have been talking about the loved one behind their back as this may antagonise the loved one. They should stress that they have just investigated the options that are available without giving any personal details of either the concerned other or the loved one.

Step 7: Should the loved one refuse to enter treatment, the concerned other should have an 'I message' prepared which tacitly accepts the loved one's decision. This should explicitly accept the loved one's reasons but reiterate their own needs at the same time. For example:

> *Well, it has to be your decision. I am not going to argue with you. But I need to continue to do things for myself. I hope you can understand that I need to do things for myself.*

They should then withdraw from the loved one without conflict.

Treatment goal:	Treatment Entry
Associated worksheets:	2.21 Barriers and Hooks to Treatment 2.22 What Help is out There? **2.23 Bringing up the Subject of Treatment**
Further context:	1.21 Bringing up the Subject of Treatment 1.22 Selecting Treatment Options

2.23 Bringing up the Subject of Treatment

A: Trigger moments:	Signs and signals to raise the subject
Health: Activities: Self-image: Formal coercion:	

B: When would be the best time to bring up the subject?	
Time: Place: With others or alone?	What have you learnt from previous attempts at suggesting treatment?

C. 'I Message' request:

How can you recognise the loved one's current feelings or condition?

What do you find hard about seeing them in this condition?

What would you like them to do?

How can you explain your understanding of why this is hard for your loved one?

What would it mean to you if they did seek help?

How could you support them in treatment?

D. If they object I will suggest . . . Objection	Response

E. If they refuse I will accept their decision by saying . . .

How to Reduce Pressures on the Concerned Other

2.24 Domestic Violence Assessment

Aim: The aim of the Domestic Violence Assessment worksheets is to assist the concerned other to identify what constitutes domestic violence and assess the risks that they currently face.

Rationale: It is important to note that, if during the comprehensive assessment, domestic violence is indicated, then this should always be addressed first. It should be reiterated that the safety of the concerned other will be paramount throughout the programme.

Individuals exposed to domestic violence may not always interpret the aggression that they experience as a form of violence. This may be because they may be exposed to levels of aggression that they do not equate with stereotypical images or assumptions about domestic violence. These are more subtle forms of abuse that are threatening without any overt violence being demonstrated. The concerned other may have lived with these constant levels of abuse for such an extended period of time that they have normalised aggression directed towards them. Finally, aggression may be reciprocated. This means that the perpetrator of the violence is able to minimise their actions by suggesting that they are 'as bad as one another really,' diminishing their responsibility and inculcating guilt in the victim. Therefore expanding the concerned other's awareness of what constitutes domestic violence is important. Simply asking whether they experience domestic violence may not identify the wide range of possible expressions of violence and abuse. Therefore it is important to assess the full spectrum of aggressive behaviour in order to raise the concerned other's awareness and ensure that there is a mutual understanding of the term 'domestic violence'.

The screening process will help the concerned other identify specific experiences of domestic violence. Establishing the detail of these incidents is important, particularly the relationship between drug and alcohol use. Exploring whether the loved one has a history of violence to others may also help determine current and future risk to the concerned other. This relationship can be explored further by considering whether aggression occurs when the loved one is under the influence, withdrawing or sober. Attention also needs to be given to whether incidents of violence and aggression have been increasing or decreasing. The level of threat that the concerned other feels is important in discussing what they feel are the consequences of the behaviour for them. This discussion should allow the concerned other to articulate their own fears and concerns regarding the need for change rather than the practitioner.

It is very difficult for concerned others to break the silence of their experience of domestic violence. Previous experiences of disclosure may have been met with outrage, anger or attempts to impel the concerned other to leave their loved one. The concerned other may feel that they will be judged as foolish for remaining with a loved one who is violent towards them, they may feel guilt for reciprocation or they may feel that they are betraying the confidence of their loved one. As such, the exploration of domestic violence must be conducted with empathy, understanding and sensitivity. Whilst the safety of the concerned other is paramount within the programme, it is important that the practitioner also supports the desires and wishes of the concerned other, even where it causes ethical issues for the practitioner. The practitioner must uphold their duty to protect the concerned other through the confidentiality policy of the agency and work to the wider goals of the concerned other. Any specific difficulties that present within this realm should automatically follow agencies' local policy and procedures. Difficulties for the practitioner should be discussed with their supervisor.

Step 1: The practitioner should explain the rationale of the Domestic Violence Assessment worksheet. It is not uncommon for problem users under the influence or pressures of use to demonstrate high levels of aggression towards those closest to them. This behaviour may constitute domestic violence. However, the family members of the loved one do not always understand the behaviour in these terms. As the concerned other's personal safety is a priority throughout the course of the programme, it is important to examine all incidents which could constitute domestic violence more closely. This exploration is essential to ensure their safety and to plan subsequent responses to escape or reduce the incidents of aggression.

Step 2: The practitioner should ask the concerned other what they believe the term domestic violence means and what it might entail. Concerned others tend to define the term as a direct physical attack. The practitioner should acknowledge that this is a form of domestic violence, but that the term covers a wider range of behaviour. The practitioner should use the worksheet to explain other forms of aggression.

Step 3: Reviewing the Domestic Violence Assessment sheet, the practitioners should explore each form of aggression systematically. Working through each topic one at a time, the concerned other should be invited to consider whether they have ever experienced this form of aggression. The concerned other should briefly describe these incidents. Consideration should be given to the state of the loved one at the time of the incident. For example, were they intoxicated, were they withdrawing from a drug, were they sober but unable to get access to drugs or alcohol. In cases of physical assault, the practitioner should explore whether the loved one has a history of violence to others.

Step 4: The number of incidents of each type that have ever occurred should be identified next and be recorded to the best of the concerned other's knowledge. The concerned other may not always be sure of the exact figure, but a guesstimate can still be useful.

Step 5: The number of similar incidents that have occurred in the last six months can then be established. Again, this can be guesstimated.

Step 6: Alongside this is the concerned other's perception of whether they believe the number of incidents has been increasing or decreasing over the last six months.

Step 7: Finally, for each type of incident, the concerned other should rate how threatening they find the incidents and how serious they feel the risk is to their well-being or to that of another family member. This rating system allows the concerned other to present their actual concerns regarding their own safety without the practitioner having to impress the risk upon them, which tends to be counter-productive by challenging the concerned other's attitude to their situation. If another's safety is involved, this should also be taken into consideration. Special consideration will also need to be given to any children involved in the family and this should be dealt with according to the agency's own policy, which, in turn, should be compatible with Child Protection and Hidden Harm Policies.

Treatment goal:	Reducing the Concerned Other's Stress
Associated worksheets:	**2.24 Domestic Violence Assessment** 2.25 Emergency Plan 2.26 Domestic Violence Functional Analysis 2.27 Domestic Violence Intervention Plan
Further context:	1.27 Reducing Pressure on the Concerned Other

2.24 Domestic Violence Assessment

Example	Details: Was the loved one sober, intoxicated or withdrawing?	Number of incidents ever?	Number of incidents in last six months?	Is it getting better or worse?	How much do you fear for your safety? Low High
Pushing you aggressively					1 2 3 4 5
Threatening					1 2 3 4 5
Name calling					1 2 3 4 5
Threatening family members					1 2 3 4 5
Breaking objects					1 2 3 4 5
Humiliating you in public					1 2 3 4 5
Physical assaults					1 2 3 4 5
Other:					1 2 3 4 5

2.25 Emergency Plan

Aim: To develop and prepare an emergency plan in the light of imminent domestic violence.

Rationale: Even though many concerned others are at risk of domestic violence, they often choose to remain in their relationship with the loved one. If the concerned other expresses this choice it is important to implement as many safety measures as possible in order to minimise the risk. The most basic safety measure is an Emergency Plan, which should be implemented in the light of any physical threat to the concerned other. In this eventuality, the concerned other is always advised to give the loved one what they want (excluding sexual assault), contact the police or escape the situation as quickly as possible.

Escaping the situation demands preparation. This can include practical measures such as identifying escape routes from the home and danger spots to avoid that make escape difficult. But also, escaping the situation can be difficult if it demands readying to leave. Planning in advance can assist in the process by establishing a safe haven which the concerned other can retreat to. Further to this, storing essential and important items in the safe haven or in the boot of the car in advance can facilitate escape.

Step 1: The practitioner should explain the rationale of the Emergency Plan worksheet. Throughout the programme the concerned other's safety will be paramount. This demands that the concerned other and the practitioner plan in advance an Emergency Plan, which can be implemented should physical violence be imminent. In such circumstances, the concerned other should give the loved one whatever they want and escape the situation as quickly as possible. If escape is not possible, they should contact the police immediately.

Step 2: Escaping the situation is not always easy. Preparing for any escape is important. The concerned other and practitioner should discuss the layout of the concerned other's home and identify exit points. This discussion should also include areas of the home which might be difficult to escape from or where they might become trapped. If the home has locks on windows they should be unlocked. Drawing floor plans may assist in this process.

Step 3: Using the Emergency Plan worksheet the practitioner and concerned other should identify a safe place for them to retreat to. A safe place is any environment where the loved one will be refused access. This might be with a friend, family member or neighbour who has agreed to offer the concerned other support in advance. It is important that the concerned other does not write down the safe haven but instead remembers the address of the safe haven.

Step 4: The concerned other may need support or coaching to approach members of their support network for help. They will have to overcome their own feelings of shame or guilt that they experience as a result of the loved one's use and behaviour. They may have hidden the problem for a long period of time or neglected relationships. Formulating how to phrase the approach and role-playing it can help the concerned other to be prepared in advance. Communication Skills and My Social Network can be helpful in formulating these responses.

Step 5: Once a supportive other is identified, it is important to develop a code word which will indicate to the supportive other that the concerned other is in need of support. This code word should be natural and discrete so as to not arouse any suspicion in the loved one. This trigger word should alert the supportive other that the concerned other is on their way.

Step 6: Should the concerned other not have a support network to call upon, then a contact number for refuge centres should be provided. Again, it is important that the concerned other does not write this number down in the pack. It is preferable to memorise this number. Alternatively, a wide range of contact numbers can be provided which may mask which agency the concerned other has sought help from.

Step 7: Escaping can be difficult under the pressure of the situation. This can be compounded by the need for the concerned other to prepare for their exit with packing any necessary belongings. This can be eliminated by having an emergency case packed in advance and stored in a safe haven or in the boot of the car. This emergency case should include everyday domestic items necessary for day-to-day living to cover a period of at least two days. It should also include more strategic items. These might include important documents, passports and copies of keys. Section B offers a comprehensive short list for the concerned other to use to identify items that would be important to them. It is important to remember the needs of children, if they have dependents, or even pets, should they be particularly important to the concerned other.

Step 8: The reminder of the emergency plan can also be given to the concerned other along with a list of helpful telephone numbers. This should be dated and updated regularly.

Treatment goal:	Reducing the Concerned Other's Stress
Associated worksheets:	2.24 Domestic Violence Assessment **2.25 Emergency Plan** 2.26 Domestic Violence Functional Analysis 2.27 Domestic Violence Intervention Plan
Further context:	1.27 Reducing Pressure on the Concerned Other

2.25 Emergency Plan

Section A: Where would be a safe place for you to go, where your loved one would be refused access to you? (Do not write this down here or anywhere else.)

How would you approach friends or family to request help in the situation prior to an incident?

What code word for the telephone can you agree in advance to alert them to your situation without arousing suspicion.

If friends and family are not able to help, get the number of the local women's shelter in your area. Do not write the number or address down. Memorise the address or number.

Section B: Check list for rapid escape

In an emergency you may need to remove yourself from your home for one or two days or even more. Planning in advance for such an emergency can assist a quick exit. These items can be stored in a safe place or in the boot of car in advance of having to leave in a hurry.

Pre-packed toilet bag	
Money for taxi	
Change of clothes	
Extra set of house and car keys	
Birth certificates	
Drivers licence and passport	
Medications and prescriptions	
Cheque book	
Credit cards	

Legal documents	
Address book	
Valuables	
Papers of joint assets	
Other	

In an Emergency

In the likelihood of impending assault, do not allow yourself to be cornered in an area where you cannot escape. Practice escape routes. Escape at the earliest possible opportunity. In the case of extreme violence:

- Give the aggressor what they want.

- Make sure you have an exit route.

- Do not be cornered in a place you cannot escape from.

- Leave the house and go to a safe place.

- If not, call the Police.

Useful numbers in the UK

Domestic Violence Helpline (24 hour freephone): 0808 200 0247
Welsh Women's Aid: 0292 039 0874
BAWSO (For black women in Wales who are the victims of domestic violence): 0292 064 4633
Southall Black Sisters (For black and Asian women in the London Area): 0208 571 9595.
Broken Rainbow (Lesbian, gay, bisexual and transgender domestic violence forum) 0208 539 9507
Victim Support: 0845 303 0900
Shelterline: 080 880 04444
Welsh Domestic Violence Abuse Helpline: 080 880 10800
The Police: 999
Samaritans: 0845 790 9090
National Child Protection Helpline (NSPCC): 0800 800 500
Foreign and Commonwealth Office: 0207 008 0135 / 0207 008 0230
Careline: 0208 514 1177
Legal Aid Advice: www.justask.org.uk/index.jsp
Male enquiry and advice line: 0845 0646 800
Reunite (Advice, information and support for people who have or fear child abduction): 0116 255 6234

This list of contact numbers was last up-dated: _____

2.26 Domestic Violence Functional Analysis

Aim: To identify strategies to reduce the risk of situational domestic violence.

Rationale: Domestic violence can be motivated by a number of different reasons. Some of these reasons are amenable to influence and others are not. Pre-meditated, spontaneous or instrumental violence is very difficult to address. However, where violence is triggered in part by environmental pressures, the incidence of domestic violence can be reduced. This is possible when domestic violence occurs as a result of escalating tension between the loved one and the concerned other. These tensions, stressors and trigger points can be mapped, based on the concerned other's knowledge of their loved one's typical behaviour patterns, using a functional analysis. In the same way the concerned other can analyse drug and alcohol use, the functional analysis of domestic violence will offer insight into the function of the loved one's aggressive behaviour and, more importantly, provide a framework for how it can be defused or intercepted. The more specific the detail gathered on the functional analysis, the more helpful it becomes in planning a response.

The functional analysis should be conducted on an actual incident which is relatively typical of the aggression that the concerned other faces. Again, it should be remembered that the functional analysis does not necessarily need to be conducted in any particular order, left to right. The assessment should provide a comprehensive framework to understand the incident and, as such, provides guidance to an empathetic understanding of the specific details of the incident. Again, the functional analyses are set out as a log of incidents. This is designed so that multiple incidents can be compared easily in order to refine the approach. Patterns or significant differences can then be identified and inform future planning. The functional analysis is used in combination with the Domestic Violence Planning Tool in order to develop a specific plan for addressing the violence that the concerned other faces.

The functional analysis for domestic violence identifies the same key components of behaviour as the functional analysis of the loved one's drug use. The first two columns asks the concerned other to describe the external triggers that occurred prior to the aggression. This should include exact details of when and where it happened, as well whether anyone else was present. This might also include any specific events that may have contributed to the loved one's anger. The internal triggers ask the concerned other to infer what they believe the loved one was feeling or thinking just prior to the aggression. This should also include the using status of the loved one at this time: whether the loved one was under the influence, withdrawing or sober. The concerned other themselves can contribute to these external triggers in ways of which they are not fully aware. Situational violence is often the product of reciprocal antagonism. This is not to suggest that the concerned other is to blame for the incident in any way. It does suggest that if aggression is the final expression of increasing tension, the concerned other can influence the situation before it escalates. The additional Relational Column invites the concerned other to identify this reciprocal antagonism if it was indeed a factor in the aggression. This should include the emotional tone of the concerned other at the time prior to the aggression and specifically what was the last thing they said to the loved one. Conversely the concerned other should describe the signals that the loved one displayed prior to the aggression. The loved one will exhibit typical patterns or telltale signs indicating that they will become aggressive. This might be tone of voice, a certain gesture, such as rubbing the forehead, clenching their fists or wringing their hands. They may begin to use de-humanising language towards the concerned other.

Sometimes the functional analysis may suggest that there was no obvious trigger or escalation towards aggression. For example, the aggression may appear premeditated or spontaneous, it may occur without mutual antagonism, or the loved one's aggressive mood dissipates rapidly in the presence of another. Should this be the case, a second functional analysis can be conducted on a separate incident in order to verify this pattern. Should it be repeated in the second functional analysis, the concerned other should be advised immediately that they are unlikely to influence these types of aggression and should consider the consequences of remaining in this relationship. The neutral stance of the practitioner in allowing the concerned other to recognise this for themselves can be an extraordinarily powerful motivator for the concerned other to terminate their relationship with the loved one after these discussions.

The second element of the functional analysis is the aggressive behaviour exhibited by the loved one. The dimensions of the incident should be established in terms of the actual behaviour and its duration. This can be a base line measure, where future incidences can be reviewed in order to ensure that the frequency and duration of violence is reducing.

The third element of the behaviour is the consequence. Situational violence can be understood as a behavioural response to an intolerable mood state. When the individual experiences pressures and stress that they are unable to process emotionally or articulate, they may resort to violence as the only means available to them to deal with what they feel is either an impossible situation or an overwhelming mood. This means that the situational aggression is functional. There are positive benefits for the loved one in being aggressive. This can include ventilating pent-up stress, forcing another person to do what you want them to do, feeling powerful, escaping an impossible situation or silencing criticism. Understanding the consequences of aggressive behaviour offers a great deal of insight into the motivation of the loved one.

Besides these positive consequences for the loved one, domestic violence also brings long term negative consequences. This can occur on many levels. Negative consequences can be emotional, such as guilt, remorse and shame. They may be relational in terms of the damage caused to their immediate relationships and their wider social network on discovering the violence. Negative consequences may also be legal in terms of the police being called after they have injured someone or damaged property. Identifying the specific negative consequences for the loved one can be important if the diffusing strategy is not effective.

Mapping the specific dimensions of these emotionally charged incidents is difficult for concerned others, even when the violence is not directed at them personally. For example, a loved one who smashes up the house and destroys property creates an impoverished environment, which can make the concerned other so ashamed that they stop anyone from visiting them. Such damage also serves as a constant and immediate reminder of these powerful and painful crises. Sensitivity and a gentle pace is necessary for assisting the concerned other to raise these issues and experiences.

Step 1: Explain to the concerned other that the Domestic Violence Functional Analysis will help assess what triggers their loved one's behaviour and what consequences may sustain it. It is important to recognise the difficulties that the concerned other will experience describing sometimes harrowing moments in their relationship. However, this information will help them plan effective approaches to reduce the aggression they experience. If there are any child protection concerns, the practitioner should remind the client of any policy and confidentiality issues at this stage.

Step 2: The practitioner should invite the concerned other to identify a recent typical incident that they have experienced. This must be an actual example rather than a generalisation or a composite of different incidents. If the concerned other is uncertain, review the incidents listed in the completed Domestic Violence: Assessing Incidents worksheet and ask the concerned other to identify a frequent, common or typical experience that they have experienced in the last month.

Step 3: Considering this event, ask the concerned other to describe, to the best of their knowledge, the external triggers prior to the incident. This should include the time, place, specific whereabouts in the house or other area, and whether others, including children, were present. Do not ask these questions robotically but rather build a picture with the concerned other's story.

Step 4: The internal triggers of the loved one's thoughts and feelings can be explored in a similar way. However, the concerned other may have to infer the loved one's mood based on their body language, statements they make and their knowledge of the loved one's overall demeanour. Establishing the loved one's state of intoxication, withdrawal or sobriety at this time can also be an important dimension.

Step 5: The internal triggers can be further refined by examining the specific interactions between the loved one and the concerned other prior to the aggression. In terms of the loved one, it is important to draw upon the concerned other's deep knowledge of the loved one. They should identify the micro-gestures the loved one made just prior to the assault. This includes body language such as rubbing the forehead, gripping the arms of the chair or abrupt silence. The emotional tone of the loved one may change, their voice may lower, become more of a growl or they may swear more. Their facial expression may change from mocking, dismissive, blank or fixated. Finally the statements that they use may be indicative of imminent aggression: this could be threats, goading the concerned other to keep pushing them or demanding the concerned other to be silent. Capturing the specific nuance of the loved one's behaviour is important for planning responses.

The relational trigger also invites the concerned other to consider whether their behaviour had any inadvertent effect on the loved one. Reviewing these triggers demands sensitivity. The practitioner should emphasise that the concerned other does not deserve their loved one's aggression. However, if their behaviour serves as a trigger to aggression, it is better to identify this in order to amend their future responses. This is not to say that they cannot convey their feelings and emotions to the loved one, but in the light of a history of aggression, timing these moments becomes important if the concerned other is to speak freely and the loved one is able to receive this without anger.

It must be remembered that it can be very easy for the slightest gesture by the concerned other to become an excuse for a reaction in the loved one. Alcohol, cannabis or stimulants are likely to make people paranoid and 'read' hidden messages in the concerned other's statements. Therefore exploring how the concerned other was feeling, acting and what they said just prior to the incident may indicate subtle or direct triggers to the loved one's aggression. Again, specific emotional tones of voice or gestures may all contribute to the situational tension that elicits an aggressive response. Often situational aggression is triggered by verbal cues. Therefore, the last statement the concerned other made prior to the aggression may be a powerful trigger for the loved one. Identifying what these statements were, should be explored empathetically. The concerned other is under huge pressure, may be emotionally exhausted and feel desperate at times and these responses may feel like the only or last resort. At the same time, even the most provocative of statements does not justify violent retaliation in the loved one.

Step 6: It is essential to identify the exact expression of the aggression. Describing the actual event can be incredibly painful for some and a numb and detached experience for others. Any kind of assault will impact on the concerned other's self-worth and may also generate feelings of guilt. However, understanding the incident and its duration can offer a baseline against which to compare any future analysis to assess whether the planned interventions are decreasing or increasing the frequency of aggression that the concerned other is experiencing. Again, should any planned response prove ineffective over time, this can serve as a basis of discussing whether the concerned other can sustain their relationship with the loved one objectively.

Step 7: This area examines the positive consequences for the loved one. This aims to see whether they achieve what they desire in the short term. This can include a feeling of power, controlling the concerned other, securing money for drugs or alcohol or simply ventilating frustration. Considering how their drug and alcohol use may erode other areas of their life and place them under increasing background stress may also make the loved one more reactive. This area may be more speculative but their best guesstimate is still useful and can be refined.

Step 8: This section includes the negative consequences for the loved one in relation to their violence. This should be explored deeply, both in terms of the impact of violence on their own sense of shame and remorse as well as the wider social impact on the relationship with concerned other, wider social network, and legal consequences. Any absence of remorse in the loved one may indicate more complex issues that can be addressed in the functional analysis.

Treatment goal:	Reducing the Concerned Other's Stress
Associated worksheets:	2.24 Domestic Violence Assessment 2.25 Emergency Plan **2.26 Domestic Violence Functional Analysis** 2.27 Domestic Violence Intervention Plan
Further context:	1.19 Functional Analysis Logs 1.27 Reducing Pressure on the Concerned Other

2.26 Domestic Violence Functional Analysis

External triggers	Internal triggers	Relational triggers	Behaviour	Short-term benefits	Long-term consequences
When and where did this occur? Anyone present? Any specific stresses?	What was your loved one thinking and feeling? Had they used drugs or alcohol?	The loved one's body language or tone. The concerned other's tone/last statement made?	What did the loved one do and for how long?	What do you think your loved one wanted at this time?	What were the negative consequences for the loved one in terms of self-image, relationships and legal complications?
When: Where: Who: What else?	Intoxicated Sober Withdrawing	Concerned other: Loved one:	Time: Intensity:		For the loved one: Relationships: Legal:
When: Where: Who: What else?	Intoxicated Sober Withdrawing	Concerned other: Loved one:	Time: Intensity:		For the loved one: Relationships: Legal:

When:	Concerned other:	Time:	For the loved one:
Where:			Relationships:
Who:	Loved one:	Intensity:	
What else?			Legal:
Intoxicated Sober Withdrawing			
When:	Concerned other:	Time:	For the loved one:
Where:			Relationships:
Who:	Loved one:	Intensity:	
What else?			Legal:
Intoxicated Sober Withdrawing			
When:	Concerned other:	Time:	For the loved one:
Where:			Relationships:
Who:	Loved one:	Intensity:	
What else?			Legal:
Intoxicated Sober Withdrawing			

2.27 Domestic Violence Intervention Plan

Aim: The aim of the Domestic Violence Intervention Plan is to develop practical strategies that can reduce or defuse incidents of domestic violence.

Rationale: The Domestic Violence Functional Analysis will have mapped every facet of a typical incident of aggression. Based on this information it is possible to develop an intervention that will prevent, defuse or minimise any future incidence of violence. Again, this plan depends on the quality and detail ascertained in the functional analysis. Whilst this cannot account for all possible types of violence and aggression, it will help reduce established patterns of situational aggression that are a response to environmental pressures. Incidents of aggression that do not relate to environmental pressures in this way are very unlikely to be reduced using this process.

The Domestic Violence Intervention Plan is organised into sections that correspond with the Domestic Violence: Functional Analysis. This is to ensure that an intervention can be brought to bear that addresses every facet of the aggressive behaviour. The practitioner and concerned other should work through each section and examine all possible approaches. It is important that any suggestions are examined and questioned in order to test them thoroughly before implementation. Any approach should be realistic, delivered in a naturalistic manner to reduce reaction in the loved one and the concerned other must be confident that they can implement it. The intervention developed should be able to interrupt the escalation of tension between the loved one and the concerned other, which has previously resulted in violence and aggression. It should be stressed throughout this process, that in the light of impending violence, the concerned other should give the loved one whatever they want and leave immediately. The emergency plan should also be covered as well as the implementation of strategies to reduce the violence.

Step 1: Explain the rationale of the Domestic Violence Intervention Plan worksheet to the concerned other. Based on the Functional Analysis already completed, the practitioner and the concerned other will use this information to develop a series of strategies that will reduce or defuse the incidents of violence. However, the concerned other should be reminded that they will also have an emergency plan should this fail.

Step 2: The concerned other and the practitioner should review a completed Functional Analysis, beginning with the identified External Triggers. Consideration should first be given to the time and place of the incident. Section A of the Intervention Plan offers the opportunity for the practitioner and the concerned other to examine whether there is anything specific about these times that makes aggression in the loved one more likely. For example, does the typical incident occur on payday or when the loved one has no money? Is it more likely to occur after the loved one has associated with certain individuals or when particular issues arise in their life? Does the loved one get more aggressive after use, such as being hyper-tense in the morning after smoking cannabis or taking stimulants the previous night? Where these factors can be identified, the practitioner and the concerned other should examine whether these more routine times can be avoided. If the incidents only occur when the concerned other and loved one are alone, can someone else be invited into the home at these times in the future? There may be another individual involved in the escalation of violence. For example, a younger sibling may antagonise the loved one. A father may be explicitly challenging of a son whilst intoxicated. Consideration should be given to the role other individuals have in escalating the situation. Where they are identified, the concerned other should discuss this with the involved others and identify how they can communicate with the loved one or avoid them at these times to reduce the conflict that may precipitate aggression.

If these options are not available, the Problem Solving worksheet can be used to identify what alternative options are available and evaluate their likelihood of reducing conflict.

Step 3: Section B of the Intervention Plan invites the concerned other to consider how they can influence the underlying emotional states of the loved one. Understanding the internal triggers of the loved one's underlying mood state when they are liable to be aggressive, will have called upon the concerned other's deep insight into the loved one. If there is an underlying pattern or stresses that affect the loved one adversely then the concerned other understands they can draw upon communication skills to recognise the loved one's stresses and pressure. This may allow the loved one to ventilate tension and process intolerable mood states without recourse to violence. The concerned other should acknowledge the mood state of the loved one and invite them to talk about any underlying problems or stresses they are currently experiencing. This may be as simple as saying: 'You seem really stressed. What has happened?'

Recognising that the incidents occur when the loved one is intoxicated, sober or withdrawing can be important markers of imminent aggression and dictate the concerned other's response. If they are intoxicated at a time when violence occurs, it will curtail the concerned other's ability to reason with the loved one. In this eventuality the use of communication skills may be negligible. This should indicate that withdrawing from the situation (see below) is the best option.

Step 4: Section C considers the relational aspects of the aggressive incidents. This begins by developing a checklist for the concerned other's own behaviour. Having recognised their own emotional tone, pitch and body language during the times that conflict is escalating, they need to check that their own responses are not becoming increasingly aggressive. The loved one will automatically associate many of these established patterns of behaviour in the concerned other as a signal of imminent attack and may respond pre-emptively. The Tips to Staying Calm worksheet from the Communication Skills section may be helpful in keeping the emotional intensity of the concerned other lower at this juncture. The issue of what was the last thing that was said prior to the incident offers important insights into the plan. Firstly, it may indicate flashpoints where conflicts repeatedly occur. Avoiding the flashpoint when violence may be imminent is vital. Furthermore, the last thing that the concerned other says needs to be avoided or rephrased using communications skills. Avoidance is the best strategy here if all the conditions are predisposed to abuse.

Step 5: Section D allows the concerned other to recognise and respond to early warning signals in the loved one. Recognising the body language, emotional pitch and statements that the loved one makes immediately prior to the onset of violence, can serve as the early warning system for the concerned other to withdraw. As the loved one's emotional state intensifies, it will be increasingly difficult to reason with them. Therefore responding **immediately** to the first signals of impending aggression is vital. The early warning signs should trigger the concerned other to withdraw from the situation. This should be in the form of a prepared statement which allows the concerned other to step back without being drawn into a confrontation with the loved one. It is important that the concerned other withdraws to a safe place, either within the house or garden, or to the home of a member of their support network. These statements should be short and naturalistic:

> *I can see that you're stressed and this is not a good time for you. We can leave it here. I am going to sort some things out in the garden.*

> *I can see that this is not a good time for you to be discussing this. Let us leave it for another time. I said to Jan that I would drop the catalogue over to her. I will be gone for a while.*

Should these strategies fail to reduce the escalation of violence or threat, the concerned other should escape at the first opportunity. If this is not possible they should give the loved one whatever they want, with the exception of sexual assault, and escape as quickly as possible. If they feel threatened with actual physical violence they should contact the police immediately.

Step 6: Assessing the dimensions of the aggression is important in Section E. The nature of the violence may serve as an indicator of whether the frequency or intensity of the aggression is decreasing. Exploring this pattern may serve as an indicator of whether the intervention is reducing the incidence of violence. In cases where the aggression appears spontaneous or connected to binge patterns of consumption, caution should be taken in interpreting these results.

Step 7: Section F, designed to identify what the desirable consequences of violence are for the loved one, may appear to be odd at first glance. However, it is often the positive reinforcing consequences of situational aggression which sustain it. Considering what the loved one desires from their aggression may allow the concerned other to offer an outlet for these wants without the loved one resorting to violence. For example, the loved one may want to ventilate frustration. The concerned other could invite them to express what was intolerable for them and this may discharge the emotion without resorting to violence. If the loved one wants to escape or avoid tension by silencing the concerned other, then they should be given the space to calm down before any flashpoint for conflict is discussed. If the loved one wants to leave to use drugs and alcohol they should be allowed to do so without conflict. The 'I' message should convey the concerned other's own feelings about this without conflict.

Step 8: Section G allows a planned response to the negative consequences of aggression when it occurs. These consequences range from the individual to the legal. An incident of aggression can have an immense impact on the loved one themselves. The perpetrator may experience guilt, shame and self-loathing, which they may attempt to alleviate with gifts, promises or by avoiding the subject. There are also consequences for the loved one in their wider relationships, including with the concerned other. The concerned other may be tempted to dismiss the incident, accept apologies without discussing their real feelings or even take responsibility for what occurred to alleviate the guilt in the loved one. The shame that concerned others can feel as a result of experiencing domestic violence often means that they want to conceal the consequences or evidence of the incident as much as the perpetrator does. However, this tends to neutralise consequences for the loved one. This balance will need to change in order to prevent further instances of violence. Once the consequences for the loved one have been identified the concerned other should reflect on whether they do anything to diminish these consequences. Disabling this enabling mechanism is important if the loved one is to feel the consequences for themselves. For example, the family paying off the loved one's fines, repairing the damage to property caused by the loved one or concealing injuries from assault from other family members, all reduce the sanctions on the loved one. Again, many concerned others may not want to disable all enabling strategies. And if it feels unsafe for them to do so they are unlikely to follow through with any suggestions from the practitioner. Instead it can be sufficient that there are some consequences for the loved one and that the concerned other become increasingly adept at intercepting the sequence of events that lead to aggression.

Treatment goal:	Reducing the Concerned Other's Stress
Associated worksheets:	2.24 Domestic Violence Assessment 2.25 Emergency Plan 2.26 Domestic Violence Functional Analysis **2.27 Domestic Violence Intervention Plan**
Further context:	1.19 Functional Analysis Logs 1.27 Reducing Pressure on the Concerned Other

2.27 Domestic Violence Intervention Plan

A: External triggers

How can these times or places be avoided (use Problem Solving)?

If others are involved, can they offer support (use Communication Skills)?

B: Internal triggers

What could you say to show understanding for the loved one's stress, tension, worry (if applicable):

How could you offer to help your loved one handle their stresses at this time (if applicable):

C: Relational triggers: the concerned other

What could you do to check your own mood?

What might be useful for you to avoid saying or to rephrase at this time?

What might be useful for you to avoid doing at this time?

D. Relational triggers:

What is the first early warning signal that will trigger your withdrawal?

What could you say to facilitate withdrawal from these situations?

Where is a safe place you can go?
(If unsure, use the Identifying Social Support Sheet)

E. Behaviour		
Event:	Previous episode:	Current episode:
Duration:	Previous episode:	Current episode:

F. Short term benefits

Considering the purpose of aggression for the loved one, could this be achieved in any other way?

G. Long term consequences

Do you do anything inadvertently to reduce or diminish these consequences for your loved one across these areas?

What would happen if you were to stop reducing these consequences for your loved one?

How to Improve the Quality of Life for the Concerned Other

2.28 Identifying Social Support

Aim: To review the current support networks of the client and identify possible sources of support.

Rationale: Building a social network is very important in not only improving the concerned other's life but also in the delivery of support for the loved one. A social support network can offer the concerned other a safe haven if there is an episode of domestic violence. If the loved one uses drugs and alcohol, the members of the social network might provide a space for the concerned other to withdraw to. As importantly, the wider social network can provide informal support as an outlet for stress and greater enrichment through increased social integration. This can be particularly important after long periods of isolation. The practitioner should be mindful not to neglect the role of fun and recreation in the concerned other's own life. This will help to maintain their emotional energy levels in sustaining the programme. The support network can offer moral support when the concerned other's motivation is low. They can assist with practical help where necessary, such as childcare when the concerned other needs to attend appointments. Or they can offer respite care should the concerned other need a break from the pressures that they face. Support needs will vary from individual to individual and this should be recognised in developing a support network.

After long periods of social exclusion a new social network can be difficult to establish at first. This demands reviewing the current social network of the concerned other systematically to review any possible source of support. As wide-ranging and extensive social network as possible is preferable. Reviewing all the concerned other's current relationships, even after a period of long neglect, is important in generating leads.

Where the social network is limited or non-existent, the concerned other should be encouraged to consider entering 'synthetic' social environments. Attendance at a mutual self help group such as Al Anon or a local meeting of concerned others will provide a readymade peer group of accepting others who are both sympathetic to the plight of the concerned other and demonstrate an understanding of their situation. However, whilst this is a very useful forum for ventilating feelings and sharing experiences, it is important to increase social support in every aspect of the concerned other's life. These groups may be seen as an opportunity to develop friendships and associations beyond their experience of the problem loved ones.

Step 1: The practitioner should explain the rationale of the Identifying Social Support worksheet. It is important for the concerned other to recognise that the greater their support network, the more effective the treatment will be. Having a wide range of support means that they will not feel as though they are imposing unduly on one person and offers a wider range of social and recreational options. As such, rebuilding relationships improves the quality of life.

Step 2: The practitioner and concerned other should systematically work their way through each category of relationships one at a time. Within each domain of relationships, they should identify as many named people as possible who may be a source of support or social recreation. In this first evaluation, all the possible names should be included, whether they feel directly appropriate or not. Listing the people that the concerned other has had contact with in the last twelve months can be a useful way of increasing their focus on relationships even if neglected, that may be of assistance.

Step 3: Once the full quota of possible sources of support has been identified, each possible social network member is reviewed in more detail. This covers a wide range of factors. Firstly, is this person aware of the situation with the problem loved one? Remember, such problems are often concealed for long periods of time from close acquaintances and even from other family members. This can be explored in more detail by considering whether the concerned other believes that these individuals would be supportive or not. These individuals can then be assessed on a scale of 1 to 3, with 3 representing a great deal of support has been offered historically. Because network members may be rated lower in terms of the support they have given in the past, or that the concerned other believes they can offer now, does not mean they should not be approached. Rather, the higher the score, the more helpful the network member is likely to be in assisting the concerned other with more difficult, dramatic or significant aspects of their current strategy. Finally the concerned other should assess how they believe the possible network member might respond to a request for support from them. This will help the concerned other to anticipate who would be most approachable or not.

Treatment goal:	Improve the Concerned Other's Quality of Life
Associated worksheets:	**2.28 Identifying Social Support** 2.29 Building Social Support 2.30 Improving Coping 2.31 My Strengths
Further context:	1.26 Improving the Concerned Other's Life

2.28 Identifying Social Support

Domain	Name	Are they aware of your situation?	How supportive are they to you? Not very Very	How do you think they might respond if you asked for their support?
Family: mother, father, brothers, sisters, grandparents, cousins, aunts, uncles or stepfamily			0 1 2 0 1 2 0 1 2	
Friends: boyfriend, girlfriend, friends from the past or present, neighbours			0 1 2 0 1 2 0 1 2	
Work colleagues: boss, co-workers, employees, assistants and supervisors			0 1 2 0 1 2 0 1 2	
Self-help or treatment groups: Al-Anon, local support groups, telephones help-lines, etc.			0 1 2 0 1 2 0 1 2	
Other: anyone else that you have contact with, such as the church, welfare worker, social workers, etc.			0 1 2 0 1 2 0 1 2	

2.29 Building Social Support

Aim: The purpose of the Building Social Support worksheet is to assist the concerned other to prepare approaches to possible network members with requests for assistance.

Rationale: Simply because a concerned other can identify possible sources of support from their social network does not mean that they will act upon and instigate requests for help or recreation with these other people. In general, adults find it difficult to engage in preformed adult groups. Furthermore they may experience psychological barriers to asking for other's help or fear rejection in social settings. The concerned other may have endured the loved one's use for years without telling anyone about the problems they have faced. Asking others for help may feel as if it is an act of disloyalty. And finally, many concerned others are very proud and may interpret seeking help as a weakness. In these situations it is important to normalise these responses. At the same time it is important to reiterate that their loved one's behaviour is not their behaviour. They are not responsible for how the loved one acts and the decisions that they have made. Further to this, most people like being asked to help. This is especially true of people in their existing network. People will be empathetic and will want to help. Reversing this situation can be helpful to illustrate this point. The practitioner can choose a person that the concerned other has identified in their support network. Then explore how the concerned other would respond if that person was in a difficult situation and asked them for help. This can be amplified by exploring how they would feel if they discovered that this person was experiencing a very difficult time but said nothing to them. It can be important to remind the concerned other that the worst outcome in approaching others is that they might not be able to offer support. This occasionally happens and it is important to respect other's reasons for this.

Preparing and rehearsing an approach to others can be very helpful in instigating the request to members of a support network. There are several key aspects to this which can be worked through systematically until the concerned other feels clear regarding who they are going to approach, what they want this person to do and what it will mean to them if they did this. Again, short role-plays can be helpful in this process. The repetition helps the concerned other embed their learning and allows for fine-tuning. Positive feedback to the concerned other on their approach can increase their confidence in following through and approaching others.

Step 1: Explain the rationale of the Building Social Support worksheet. Although the concerned other has identified possible sources of support, approaching others can feel very difficult. Sometimes people feel awkward about doing so. Therefore, this worksheet will offer an opportunity to prepare and practice approaching others.

Step 2: Review the completed Identifying Social Support worksheet and pick the strongest candidates to approach for support. Write their names in the first column. Complete the rest of the sheet on one person at a time.

Step 3: For each individual identified, consider what the concerned other wants this person to help them with. Writing down 'help' is not exact enough. The specific kind of help should be recorded, such as a place to retreat to should the loved one use drugs or alcohol. Remember, these requests do not always have to be about emotional support. Recreation and fun activities are just as valuable for the concerned other. Again, the form of recreational support the concerned other desires should be stated specifically. If it is a social activity it should recorded as specifically as well, such as shopping for clothes on weekend.

Step 4: The concerned other should identify any particular blocks to approaching this person. This should be done in detail in order to acknowledge their fears. These fears can be tested in a number of ways. Firstly, reviewing the Identifying Social Support worksheet would reveal whether this person has been helpful in the past. If they have, the concerned other should consider what will have changed this? Another good question to ask, if the concerned other has a lot of fears about approaching others, is what evidence do they have to suggest that this person would be unwilling to support them? This question will diminish unfounded fears or offer pragmatic reasons why this person might not be appropriate.

Step 5: Strategies to overcome doubt or uncertainties about approaching this other person should be recorded if necessary. Some techniques which can be helpful in this domain include:

- The concerned other can reality check that there is no reason why this person should decline: most people like to help.

- The concerned other can develop counter-arguments to imagined negative responses. If they think that 'No-one has time for me', they develop a response to counter this like 'Lots of people have time for me such as John and Sue at work as well as Sheila my neighbour'.

- The concerned other can remind themselves that the worst outcome is that someone says no. They will not have lost anything by asking and may get a clearer idea of who their real friends are.

Step 6: The concerned other should formulate their approach to the other person. This should use communications skills that we have looked at already such as I Messages. Asking the other specifically what they want them to do is important in the case of seeking support. Others are more likely to agree to support if they know exactly what is expected from them. The concerned other should also state why they would value this help from this particular person and offer them the option to decline with a statement of understanding. For many social activities it may not be necessary to describe these issues in so much detail. It could be enough to simple invite someone out or take people up on an invite that had been declined previously.

Treatment goal:	Improve the Concerned Other's Life
Associated worksheets:	2.28 Identifying Social Support **2.29 Building Social Support** 2.30 Improving Coping 2.31 My Strengths
Further context:	1.26 Improving the Concerned Other's Life

2.29 Building Social Support

Name	I would like them to . . .	What stops me asking is . . .	I will overcome this by . . .	I could approach them by saying . . .
	Help with . . . . Have fun doing	Barriers: Fears: Rejection:		I would really like you to . . . . If you could, it would mean . . . . I understand it might not be possible because . . . .
	Help with . . . . Have fun doing	Barriers: Fears: Rejection:		I would really like you to . . . . If you could, it would mean . . . . I understand it might not be possible because . . . .
	Help with . . . . Have fun doing	Barriers: Fears: Rejection:		I would really like you to . . . . If you could, it would mean . . . . I understand it might not be possible because . . . .
	Help with . . . . Have fun doing	Barriers: Fears: Rejection:		I would really like you to . . . . If you could, it would mean . . . . I understand it might not be possible because . . . .

2.30 Improving Coping

Aim: To identify the strengths, resources and coping skills of the concerned other in order to reduce their stress and improve the quality of their life.

Rationale: Supporting a problem drug and alcohol user places the family members under a huge stress. With these pressures, concerned others develop a wide range of coping strategies. However, as their attention is constantly drawn to addressing the needs of the problem user, they often fail to recognise what resilience, skills and coping strategies they already possess. The following worksheet is based on a core assumption of solution focused therapy: that clients are resourceful in ways they do not appreciate. The Improving Coping worksheet is an assessment of these 'hidden' resources. If it is possible to identify these hidden resources that help the concerned other, they should be encouraged to use these self-developed methods more often in their lives. As they do not have to learn or master new skills, because they already have experience using these approaches, this can be a rapid process of strengthening the concerned other's coping and reducing their stress. This is achieved by asking the concerned other to consider times when they feel more in control, relaxed or able to deal with the loved one's use. It is assumed that in order for these exceptional times to occur the concerned other must be doing something different. And these 'different things' are their natural coping skills.

This approach can be difficult for a number of reasons. There are several typical traps that the practitioner can fall into when applying the procedure. As the process is trying to develop the concerned other's awareness of the coping skills that they do not fully recognise, it can be a difficult process for the concerned other to immediately identify these coping strategies. Instead the concerned other may revert back to talking about problematic times. In this situation the practitioner should acknowledge these stresses empathetically, but then return the concerned other to the question of what it is like when it feels a little easier. Another trap is when the concerned other stresses that the better times occur when the loved is not using. Whilst this is self-evidently true, even within their loved one's use there will be times when they feel a little more in control, less stressed and more focused. By doing this we are asking the concerned other to reflect not on the problem that has been monopolising their thoughts, but on these other experiences, which will be far less vivid for them but occur none the less.

As it is difficult to recognise these times, these experiences are graded from 'what is stopping them feeling even more stressed' to 'what it is like when they feel a lot better'. Asking what makes them stop getting completely overwhelmed invites them to recognise that there is a cut-off point to their stress. We can then build from this with actual examples of when they felt a little less stressed and map what they were doing, thinking or feeling differently at these times. This will begin to draw out their coping strategies and strengths, even when they are under fire.

Some concerned others may misinterpret these questions as suggesting there is no problem. They are not. It is important to acknowledge the stresses and pressures they face, which are profound and ongoing. However, within this, if they can identify times when they feel a little better, more confident or less stressed, it will help them understand the coping strategies they already have at their disposal.

If the concerned other cannot offer any example of these times, they should not be pressured. Instead, the practitioner should ask them to notice when they feel less stressed in the following week. These can then be followed up and explored once the concerned other has had time to notice these different times. Whether the concerned other can recognise these times and what they are doing immediately or at follow-up, they should be invited to consider if doing more of these things would help them reduce their stresses. Even if the concerned other is not fully convinced that this will work, they should be invited to sample them and see whether they have helped. Should these skills not be immediately helpful, they can be explored further in order to refine the concerned other's approach.

Step 1: Explain the rationale of the Improving Coping worksheet to the concerned other. This worksheet is an opportunity to review their existing coping skills and resources. It is important to highlight that because of the daily stresses and crises the concerned other faces, it is easy to lose sight of the skills and resources that we have to take care of ourselves. However, the fact is that the concerned other does manage these stresses and pressures so frequently that they naturally build ways of coping which are not immediately obvious. The worksheet is designed to highlight what they themselves find useful in reducing their stress.

Step 2: Invite the concerned other to consider the first question: what do they feel stops them feeling even more stressed and anxious despite their loved one's use? This is a surprisingly difficult question to answer. The practitioner should take their time and remain vigilant for the concerned other attributing better times just to their loved one not using. Inviting the concerned other to think of an actual time when they have said to themselves that they are not going to let this situation get to them anymore, can be helpful in making the question more concrete. The follow-up questions can also be helpful:

- Even when your loved one is using, what stops this from feeling completely overwhelming for you?

- How do you switch off from all these pressures?

- What is it like when you say to yourself that you cannot think or worry anymore?

- What do you say to yourself when you cannot be bothered worrying about this anymore?

Once the concerned other gains some insight into these times their responses can be expanded. What are they thinking, feeling or doing that is different at these times? The concerned other is often prone to responding to the questions in the negative, for example they might describe being 'less worried,' 'less anxious' or 'not stressed.' In such cases they should be gently brought back to focus on the question of what are they doing differently instead of worrying, being anxious or feeling stressed. Again, taking time to map this in detail is important. The more deliberate the strategies, the easier it is for the concerned other to start to repeat these strategies in their daily life and reduce their stress.

Step 3: This process can be repeated across more intensive levels of change in order to identify as much coping as possible. Again, asking the concerned other to identify a specific time when they were feeling 'a little better' in themselves or an example when they felt 'much better' in themselves despite the loved one's use can be reviewed in similar detail. The practitioner should not force the client to find more coping skills. Having identified a range of coping strategies based on the concerned other's thoughts, they should be encouraged to apply these strategies in the following week as if they are doing them deliberately. These coping skills do not have to be successful. The concerned other should be encouraged instead to try them and see how they progressed. If they were successful, they should be encouraged to apply more of this approach. If the strategies are unsuccessful, the practitioner and concerned other should review how they can be refined further.

Treatment goal:	Improve the Concerned Other's Life
Associated worksheets:	2.28 Identifying Social Support 2.29 Building Social Support **2.30 Improving Coping** 2.31 My Strengths
Further context:	1.26 Improving the Concerned Other's Life

2.30 Improving Coping

Despite the enormous pressure you are under, what do you think stops you feeling even more stressed about this situation?

Example: Can you think of a time when you just switched off from your loved one's behaviour as it felt too much?

What was different about this time? What were you . . .

Thinking differently?	Feeling differently?	Doing differently?	Would doing more of these things be helpful?

Despite these pressures you are under, are there times when you feel a little less stressed?

Example: Can you think of a time when, despite the pressures you were under you felt a little better?

What was different about this time? What were you . . .

Thinking differently?	Feeling differently?	Doing differently?	Would doing more of these things be helpful?

Despite the strain you are under, are the times when you feel a lot better?

Example: Can you think of an example when, despite your loved one's use, you felt much better?

What was different about this time? What were you . . .

Thinking differently?	Feeling differently?	Doing differently?	Would doing more of these things be helpful?

2.31 My Strengths

Aim: The aim of the My Strengths worksheet is to identify possible sources of enrichment and recreation for the concerned other and to implement them in their own life.

Rationale: The concerned other can invest so much time and energy into their loved one for such protracted periods of time that they lose sight of the aspects of their lives which they find enriching. It is common for many concerned others to become socially isolated and neglect their own interests, hobbies or passions. Even partnering relationships can lose intimacy in the joint battle with a loved one's use. However, it is important that the concerned other not only alleviates the stresses in their life but also increases their own fulfilment. This energises the concerned other who is then better equipped to manage the demands of the loved one's use. However, after such protracted periods of self-neglect, the concerned other may have little or no concept of what kinds of rewarding activities might stimulate or engage them. This can make it difficult for them to generate ideas on the positively reinforcing activities that they enjoy.

This worksheet is designed to generate ideas that might provide additional levels of enrichment in the concerned other's own life. It is very useful when the concerned other has no clear insight into what would improve the quality of their life. It is a framework to identify ideas and suggestions that can then be planned into the concerned other's week. These offer the opportunity to trial these ideas to see whether they enjoy them.

What can be striking in this process, is the effect the concerned other's participation in other activities can have on the loved one. The fact that the concerned other is engaging in other activities, and not waiting patiently on the loved one's needs, can have a paradoxical reaction. The loved one no longer has a monopoly on the concerned other's attention, which can provoke power shifting in the relationship. The loved one may have to compete for the concerned other's attention, and in doing so, will tend to start exhibiting more pro-social behaviour.

Step 1: Explain the rationale of the worksheet to the concerned other. The My Strengths sheet is a list of words, activities and qualities which serve as prompts to help them think about their own interests, passions or skills. This is to help the concerned other focus purely on their needs and identify as many sources of enrichment as possible. Whilst this is primarily designed to improve their quality of life, it can have a knock-on effect on the loved one. Engaging in other social activities will give the concerned other more energy and impetus to deal with the loved one's problems. And furthermore it may stimulate broader interest and change in the loved one.

Step 2: Ask the concerned other to read through the My Strengths worksheet. This can be done a column at a time. As they read through the lists of words, they should circle any words that they feel relate to them in some way. For concerned others who are not very confident or are self-conscious, ask for a set number of at least five words.

Step 3: Once the concerned other has read the list and circled each word relating to them, the practitioner and concerned other should review their list. For each word the concerned other has circled, the practitioner should ask the concerned other to offer a concrete example of how that particular quality has expressed itself in their life. For example, if the concerned other circled 'Likes Animals' they may describe how they used to have a dog but miss having one now. Explore the example and make a note of it in the blank space in the item's box. Work through every identified item in this way, recording these examples. It is important that the practitioner uses a great deal of empathy in the identification of these choices. They should look to see the value in the activity for the concerned other and enjoy the passion for the topic with them.

Step 4: Review the items with the concerned other, asking whether they feel that doing more of these things now would enrich their own quality of life? Whilst many of the examples that the concerned other has offered may be implemented quite quickly, others may demand a little trouble shooting. For example, if it is not possible for the concerned other who circled 'Likes animals' to get a new dog, they might offer to walk the neighbour's somewhat neglected one, or go for a walk with a friend who does have a dog.

Step 5: Using the weekly planner, ask the concerned other how they could fit some of these activities or examples into their life in the coming week. Even if the concerned other is reluctant to try this activity, the practitioner should encourage the concerned other to trial it or simply look into the area a little more deeply. For example, if a concerned other enjoys DIY and is only thinking about redecorating their bathroom, they might just buy a home magazine or check out the local DIY store for ideas. The practitioner should ensure that there is a range of activities in the weekly planner in order to stop boredom creeping in.

Step 6: Review the implementation of these activities the following week. Check whether the concerned other initiated the behaviour and what benefits they experienced. If the concerned other initiated the behaviour but felt little benefit, explore whether they made the most of the experience. For example, just because someone goes to a social event, they may still stay withdrawn and not interact with anyone. Discussing how they could have made more of the opportunity or what stopped them engaging fully in it can help them re-initiate with more enthusiasm.

Treatment goal:	Improve the Concerned Other's Life
Associated worksheets:	2.28 Identifying Social Support 2.29 Building Social Support 2.30 Improving Coping **2.31 My Strengths**
Further context:	1.26 Improving the Concerned Other's Life

2.31 My Strengths

Social	Thoughts	Behaviour	Emotions	Motivation	Values	Activities
Team player	Flexible	Creative	Controlled	Adventurous	Religious	Outdoors
Popular	Memory	Lots of energy	Motivated	Competitive	Just	Appearance
Likes children	Reflective	Laugh	Calm	Wilful	Moral	Shopping
Negotiator	Imaginative	Fit	Happy	Go it alone	Giving	Mechanical
Understanding	Rational	Disciplined	Relaxed	Impulsive	Hopeful	DIY
Warm	Practical	Sporty	Expressive	Driven	Self-confident	Sports
Likes animals	Systematic	Limber	Peaceful	Explore	Forgiving	Travel
Good friend	Think on feet	Stamina	Humour	Industrious	Authentic	Food and dining
Honest	Open to ideas	Musical	Patient	Committed	Philosophical	Books/puzzles
Respectful	Clever	Strong	Kind heart	Risk-taker	Honest	Arts and crafts

My Week

	Morning	Afternoon	Evening
Saturday			
Sunday			
Monday			
Tuesday			
Wednesday			
Thursday			
Friday			

How to Support the Loved One in Treatment

2.32 Understanding Slips

Aim: The purpose of the Understanding Slips worksheet is to introduce the concepts of setbacks to the concerned other in order to normalise this experience and prepare the concerned other for probable setbacks in the loved one's progress.

Rationale: Addictions are chronic relapse conditions. Even those individuals who are successful in treatment have setbacks in their battle to achieve sobriety. The concept of relapse is not a well understood or defined concept. Some researchers use the term to describe 'any-use;' others to describe three days or more of continuous use; whilst others again use the term to describe a return to pre-pre-treatment levels of use. At the same time, some treatment models would suggest that any use represents a catastrophic setback that will inevitably lead to the progressive worsening of the user's condition. However, when reviewing the actual pattern of use, even during successful recovery, we see a jagged pattern of use that fades over time. In other words, relapse is part of the recovery process, not the end of it.

The lack of clarity regarding relapse means that the setbacks and slips have a profoundly negative effect on the concerned other's own well-being. On a personal level the concerned other may plunge into despair having made such profound effort to get the loved one into treatment and instigate change. This despair may be compounded by the expectations of the concerned other. They may demonstrate a tendency to interpret any setback as total failure. This can become a self-fulfilling prophecy. It generates highly emotional responses leading to conflict, which will trigger further use in the loved one.

Understanding that setbacks are a common feature of the recovery process can assist the concerned other to maintain perspective despite the disappointment of the slip by their loved one. The graph on the Understanding Slips worksheet is based on multiple treatment studies of smokers, drinkers and heroin users who have undergone treatment. It describes 'any' use in these post-treatment populations as relapse. This strongly suggests that two-thirds of people attempting to change their substance use will use within three months of completing treatment. This is not to say that they failed in their treatment attempt, rather that they had used on at least one occasion. Discussing these findings with the concerned other can be helpful in normalising the incidence of setbacks.

Further to this, it is important that the concerned other recognises the different levels of setback. Describing the possible range of setbacks and how they might manifest themselves for their loved one may give them greater insight into the experience of the loved one and allow the concerned other to plan their responses appropriately.

Step 1: Explain the rationale of the Understanding Slips worksheet to the concerned other. Whilst it is an important landmark that the loved one has entered into treatment, this is not to suggest that the loved one will not experience any setbacks in the change attempt. Furthermore, setbacks are often typical, even in successful changers. This worksheet is designed to explore the idea of setbacks in more detail so the concerned other can have greater insight into how to respond to them and sustain their own focus at the same time.

Step 2: Show the concerned other the slips graph. This graph charts the number of people who experience a set back after treatment completion. It compares alcohol, nicotine and heroin users recovery pattern. This graph is based on over a hundred independent studies. What does the concerned other notice about these relapse curves?

These curves are strikingly similar regardless of the substance used. The concerned other should also notice that the majority of slips occur within the first three months of treatment completion. This is the highest risk period for relapse. It is important to note that these scores are averages of larger treatment populations. They do not represent the probability of risk for a single person. Also, this graph is not suggesting that the individuals who slipped go back into full-blown usage. Even successful changers have slips in their recovery. What is important is not that the loved one slips. It is how the loved one responds to the slip that is critical.

Step 3: Explain to the concerned other that the concept of relapse is not well defined and does not distinguish different types of setback very clearly. Whilst this table does not represent an official categorisation of setbacks, it does describe different kinds of relapse experience that they may encounter. It is important to recognise the severity of the loved one's setback in order to plan a response. Under-reaction and over-reaction can be equally dangerous.

Step 4: Working through each type of setback one at a time. Describe the level of the setback to the concerned other and check their understanding. Once the concerned other is clear on the definition, ask them to imagine what it would be like if their loved one experienced that level of setback. What would be the telltale signs? It is important to remember that re-initiation may be different to relapse. Relapse is understood as a failure to sustain a change in behaviour. Re-initiation describes a conscious choice to return to an old behaviour. This can occur years after the loved one has achieved sobriety and control over their lives.

Treatment goal:	Support the Loved One in Treatment
Associated worksheets:	**2.32 Understanding Slips** 2.33 Risk Factors 2.34 Strengthening Attendance 2.35 Dealing with Setbacks 2.36 Setback Plan
Further context:	1.24 Treatment Outcomes and Relapse

2.32 Understanding Slips

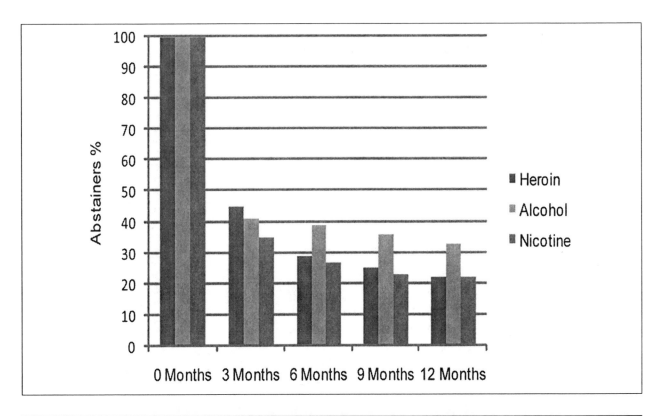

Setback	What would be the tell-tale signs that your loved one had ...
Slip: A failure to maintain a change in behaviour. It is a one-off using event, limited to short episode (less than a day).	
Lapse: A failure to maintain a change in behaviour. It is a bout of continuous use which lasts for less than three days.	
Relapse: A failure to maintain change. It exceeds three days but does not always represent a return to pre-treatment levels.	
Re-initiating: A conscious desire to resume use after long-term abstinence, which may or may not return to pre-treatment levels.	

2.33 Risk Factors

Aim: The aim of the Risk Factors worksheet is to identify the triggers that threaten the early recovery of the loved one and develop responses to diminish them.

Rationale: Slips are an inevitable part of the recovery process. At the same time the loved one may be engaged in a treatment programme the ethos of which is different from the research based ideas that inform the PACT programme. If the concerned other acquires specific skills in relapse prevention work it creates the opportunity for conflict with the loved one who is working with a different programme. There, it can be more helpful for the concerned other to support the loved one by monitoring risk factors and intervening without conflict.

This demands that the concerned other draws upon their deep knowledge of the specific triggers for their loved one. If Functional Analysis Logs have been completed they can prove an invaluable resource in identifying the specific trigger for the loved one, both external and internal. Where determinants have been identified this can serve as a good early warning system to the loved one's vulnerabilities.

Once these vulnerabilities are mapped, the concerned other can use communication skills to address these issues and deflect the loved one from use without conflict. If the loved one is compromised from an expected reward (using drugs or alcohol), it may cause an extinction burst in the loved one. The principle method of defusing this is to offer the loved one an alternative. For example, if a loved one suggests that they go in town because they need to shop for new clothes alone but have a history of using at these times, the concerned other can voice their concerns using the 'I Message' and offer an alternative. For example:

> I know you need some new clothes, but going alone worries me. The last two times you went into town alone you ended up slipping and it's hard for me to see you slip back. Even if you don't use, I am worried all the time you are gone. Why don't we go together instead and get some lunch.

Step 1: The practitioner should explain the rationale of the Risk Factors worksheet. This sheet is designed to assess the specific triggers that may set your loved one back in their progress in treatment. This will entail identifying the specific risks for your loved one and preparing responses that can challenge use without conflict.

Step 2: The practitioner and the concerned other should identify any completed Functional Analysis Logs. Reviewing these assessments, they should identify any recurring triggers for use in the loved one. This might include people, places, times or internal stresses and pressures. These should be recorded in the Triggers column. If the concerned other has not completed Functional Analysis Logs for any reason they should be asked to consider the times when the loved one has slipped or lapsed in the past. Again patterns can be identified in these previous experiences recorded. If they find this difficult, they should be asked to imagine what scenarios may make their loved one vulnerable, based on their knowledge of them.

Step 3: The evidence column offers the chance for the concerned other to consider these events in more detail. This should identify the concrete details on the previous occasions. This should not be based on the opinion of the concerned other but the details surrounding these events. This can include what happened, what the loved one said and any negative consequences for the loved one.

Step 4: The concerned other should consider being faced with this trigger again. Based on these past experiences, what concerns them the most about the loved one who is facing this challenge? This should be formulated into an 'I Message' which expresses their feelings. The evidence for this concern should be summarised from the previous incident.

Step 5: The concerned other should offer an alternative to the risk behaviour that the loved one is contemplating. This should be contingent on the loved one not engaging in the risk-taking behaviour. Should the loved one ignore this offer the concerned other should withdraw without conflict.

Step 6: Any future setbacks should be explored in a similar way to identify other risk factors. This can be done as Functional Analysis Logs.

Treatment goal:	Support the Loved One in Treatment
Associated worksheets:	2.32 Understanding Slips **2.33 Risk Factors** 2.34 Strengthening Attendance 2.35 Dealing with Setbacks 2.36 Setback Plan
Further context:	1.23 Supporting the Loved One in Treatment

2.33 Risk Factors

People, places, times, thoughts, feelings, behaviours, objects, associations, dropping out, treatment, jobs

Triggers that increase risk of a setback?	Evidence that suggests it is a risk?	'I' Message of concern	The alternative I might suggest is . . .
		'I' am concerned that . . . . This is based on the evidence that	Why don't we . . . .
		'I' am concerned that . . . . This is based on the evidence that	Why don't we . . . .
		'I' am concerned that . . . . This is based on the evidence that	Why don't we . . . .

2.34 Strengthening Attendance

Aim: The aim of this worksheet is to ensure that the concerned other understands the treatment programme the loved one has entered and can identify what support can be given to increase attendance.

Rationale: Treatment programmes and requirements are often taken for granted for those that work in the field but are not obvious to those outside of the helping professions. This can cause confusion and uncertainty between the concerned other and the loved one, where treatment may appear counter-intuitive to what the concerned other expected. This can include small details like homework tasks, administration of drugs they are unfamiliar with, to larger issues. For example, some concerned others may not appreciate why the loved one must remain wholly abstinent, others may be confused if their loved one is able to continue to use drugs which are not problematic to the loved one. The greater the understanding the concerned other has of the treatment, including prescribing, the less room for confusion or conflict. It also narrows down the opportunity for 'misrepresentation' of the service by the loved one. Risk behaviours may be justified or diminished in terms of the loved one saying it is part of the programme. Alternatively some loved ones may suggest the treatment agency told them that they no longer needed help. This triangulation can lead to a breakdown in treatment or a breakdown between the concerned other and the service.

Agencies may vary enormously in the degree to which the concerned other is involved in the treatment programme for the loved one. Confidentiality is cited as the major block to this involvement. Confidential protocols are in place in the majority of agencies that the loved one can sign in order for information about their progress to be released. This information may be limited to attendance rather than content of the treatment but may narrow the opportunity for the loved one to present as if they are in treatment when they are not attending.

Consideration can also be given to the timetable of the loved one's treatment and whether the concerned other can offer any assistance in helping them get to their appointment. This might include child care or helping with transport. The concerned other should avoid giving the loved one cash at this vulnerable stage in the loved one's recovery but opt for bus passes instead. Finally, it must be recognised that treatment procedures are difficult, challenging and emotionally hard work. The loved one may have to confront major issues in the past, master new skills or operate in challenging group environments. Change demands wilful effort on the loved one's part. The concerned other has used alternative rewards previously to compete with use. Now they can switch their focus to consider how they can reward treatment attendance. This may not be so appropriate for certain kinds of maintenance treatment, but in order to assist a loved one attempting to change their problematic lifestyle, rewards can be used heavily to incentivise treatment attendance. Using the same Rewards for My Loved One worksheet the concerned other can identify the rewards for the loved one that enrich their lives. This could be the loved one's favourite meal on their return home after their appointment. Rewards can also be verbal in affirming the loved one's commitment to the programme and being interested in their progress. Again, these rewards should be withheld if the loved one does not attend their appointment.

Step 1: The rationale of the worksheet should be explained to the concerned other. The Strengthening Attendance worksheet will help the concerned other understand the treatment programme their loved one has entered and identify where the concerned other can support them in this process.

Step 2: The treatment provider's details and contact number should be recorded and who the loved one's named worker is.

Step 3: The role of confidentiality protocols should be explained to the concerned other. They should check what confidentiality waivers the loved one's treatment provider offers and whether they will release information about their progress. The concerned other should understand the limits to confidentiality waivers in terms of the treatment process.

Step 4: The concerned other should check whether the treatment provider offers a role for the concerned other in the loved one's treatment process. This may include family therapy sessions or inviting the concerned other to be part of the treatment team and attending case management meetings and review sessions. Here they are not seen as a 'client' or contributing to the problem but rather as a resource to increase the support for the loved one.

Step 5: The concerned other should have a clear idea of the treatment philosophy that the loved one is engaged in. The practitioner may offer further guidance here and all this can be researched by the concerned other. The practitioner should remind the concerned other that it is often the relationship the loved one has with their support worker that is critical, regardless of the treatment philosophy. Comments the loved one makes about their worker may be a strong indicator of how much the programme is helping the loved one. A poor working relationship here will not lead to significant treatment gains.

Step 6: There is a wide spectrum of treatment goals that agencies and service providers will offer: from harm reduction to total abstinence. The concerned other should understand the specific treatment goal of the loved one's treatment in order to minimise any confusion. This can be particularly important where the concerned other or wider family are paying for the treatment. The family and the loved one may have very different expectations of what they hope to achieve in the treatment process, which can cause conflict later. In general, young people do better in controlled drinking programmes whilst longer term users do better in abstinence based programmes.

Step 7: The concerned other should have a clear understanding of the treatment structure in terms of length and the weekly timetable. This will help them understand and monitor the commitment that the loved one has made. It also affords the opportunity to identify whether there are any ways in which the concerned other may support attendance. Noticing whether there are any practical demands on the loved one and problem solving these approaches can make attendance easier.

Step 8: Rewarding attendance is an important element of increasing the loved one's motivation and compliance. Treatment can be a gruelling process. This means that the consequences of attending sessions are often negative, making it feel positively punishing to attend. This can be addressed by the addition of rewards that negate these consequences and replace them with positive ones. These rewards should be small but valued by the loved one. They can include favoured meals, going out to cinema, watching favourite TV programmes. Books, as gifts, have also proved to be powerful devices. If the loved one has any particular 'heroes' from sport, music, or the arts who have overcome substance misuse or other problems, these can be very inspiring. Verbal praise is very powerful, telling the loved one how proud the concerned other is of them facing such a challenge, recognising the progress or reminding the loved one how positive it is to have the real them back can be hugely reinforcing of the changes that the loved one has made.

Step 9: The concerned other should be familiar with any medication that the loved one is taking and what its purpose is. Some drugs are prescribed to reduce symptoms of withdrawal discomfort, some to reduce anxiety, other to stabilise the loved one with a substitute drug, others are for detoxification and then there are those anti-craving or blockers for relapse prevention. The concerned other should know the timetable of use, dose and monitor administration in the form of reminders for the loved one to take the drug. This is more important with the use of anti-craving drugs or blockers.

Treatment goal:	Support the Loved One in Treatment
Associated worksheets:	2.32 Understanding Slips 2.33 Risk Factors **2.34 Strengthening Attendance** 2.35 Dealing with Setbacks 2.36 Setback Plan
Further context:	1.23 Supporting the Loved One in Treatment

2.34 Strengthening Attendance

Service provider

Loved one's key worker

Confidentiality disclaimer	**If so, is it signed?**

Do they include CO in treatment?

In what capacity?

What is the service treatment philosophy?

Treatment goals

Harm reduction	Controlled use	Non-problematic use allowed	Maintenance	Abstinence

Treatment programme and length

Loved one's treatment timetable

Mon	Tues	Weds	Thurs	Fri	Sat	Sun

How could you help your loved one to attend?

How could you reward attendance?

Verbal:

_____

Activities:

_____

Treats:

What medications is the loved one on?

How can you support or encourage administration?

_____

2.35 Dealing with Setbacks

Aim: The aim of this worksheet is to assess the typical response of the concerned other to a setback in the loved one's recovery. This information will be used to inform a Setback Plan to help the concerned other preserve their own treatment gains and motivation.

Rationale: One of the biggest setbacks that the concerned other experiences is that their loved one resumes use. This disappointment can be especially frustrating in the light of their continued efforts to assist their loved one to change. No single factor appears to have greater impact on the concerned other's functioning than this return to use. Invariably, the frustration and despair that the concerned other can feel is often expressed as anger. Ironically, the intensity of this emotional response is liable to increase in relation to the duration of success that the loved one has maintained. The better the loved one does in treatment the more profound the reaction is from others to their slips. It is easy for concerned others to equate a slip with total failure of both the loved one and the concerned other's continued efforts. The assumption, that any use will destroy all the gains is a false expectation but can fuel an intense emotional response to the loved one. It should be remembered that conflict is a principle contributory factor in converting slips and lapses in use into full-blown relapses. Therefore, the setback experience must be handled carefully, in a way that respects the emotional responses of the concerned other and provides damage limitation for the loved one.

Normalising setbacks is important. Reminding the concerned other that problem drug and alcohol use is a chronic relapse condition at the start of the programme can help orientate their expectations from the outset of the programme. Whilst everyone hopes for a significant and enduring change to be achieved after one treatment episode that is often further over the therapeutic horizon. The problem is not that the loved one has slipped, it is the magnitude and its reversibility that is most important. Further to this, slips can often be important learning experiences for the loved one and the concerned other in identifying their vulnerabilities, over-confidence or challenging the expectations that drugs and alcohol offer relief.

It is important that the concerned other evaluate their response to setbacks. This may be done hypothetically prior to any actual slip taking place by asking the concerned other to imagine their response to a slip in the loved one after all the effort they have invested in this programme. The concerned other and practitioner should systematically explore each element of this reaction in order to gain clear insight in the concerned other's needs at this time. Where the concerned other has had previous experiences of lapse in the loved one they can of course draw upon this to inform the process. Again, the more specific the detail established here, the more helpful any plan to respond to the setback will be.

Step 1: The practitioner should explain the rationale of the Dealing with Setbacks worksheet. Whilst informing the concerned other that setbacks are common in the recovery process, this form is designed to assess the impact of a setback in them. It will examine different facets of their responses to setbacks in order to help them develop a plan for limiting the impact on them as a person and preserving their motivation at the same time. This is important because even individuals who are successful in overcoming their substance misuse problems have setbacks. It is how we respond to them that is important.

Step 2: The practitioner should invite the concerned other to consider times in the past when the loved one has promised to make, or even implemented some changes, and then suffered a setback. They should consider how this setback affected their loved one. Setbacks are often disappointing for everyone. Signs of defensiveness or aggression in the loved one might indicate their own sense of personal failure to see these changes through alongside the disappointment they see in those around them. Considering the effort the loved one is making now in their attempt to change, how do they think that they would feel if they did have a setback? This should be explored in order for the concerned other to gain insight into the slip from the loved one's perspective.

Step 3: In Section A the concerned other should be asked to consider times in the past when the loved one did slip, or imagine that, despite the loved one's best efforts, they experienced a setback, how might this make them feel? The answers to this should be systematic. The Dealing with Setbacks worksheet describes very specific elements of the concerned other's response. Each section should be completed one at a time with as much concrete detail as possible. Where it asks the concerned other to describe their thoughts, these should be their exact thoughts as best they can recall or imagine and stated as phrases. Likewise, when asked what they might say to the loved one, the exact statements should be recorded as they stand. Each domain should be explored in great depth before moving on.

Step 4: The concerned other and practitioner should explore the responses from Section A and consider, for each one, how helpful these responses would be in terms of the loved one's use and the concerned other other's well being. Some may indeed have proven helpful in the past, whilst others may be more damaging. Rating these responses from 1 to 5 will give a clear indication of what has and what has not helped in the past. Helpful items can be used in the following worksheet on developing a Setback Plan.

Step 5: Section B asks the concerned other to consider any setback traps that they may fall into. These include responses that they feel may increase the loved one's use, ways in which the loved one may provoke them into conflict in order to continue use or behaviours that cause a reaction in them. Again, the specific detail of these events will be helpful. Once identified, the concerned other should consider these behaviours and why the loved one may utilise them. This may be to justify their use, blame the concerned other for it or simply an expression of guilt on their part. Understanding the function of the behaviour can give the concerned other a more dispassionate eye for these behaviours, which often disconnects them from high emotional responses to this apparent antagonism.

Treatment goal:	Support the Loved One in Treatment
Associated worksheets:	2.32 Understanding Slips 2.33 Risk Factors 2.34 Strengthening Attendance **2.35 Dealing with Setbacks** 2.36 Setback Plan
Further context:	1.23 Supporting the Loved One in Treatment 1.24 Treatment Outcomes and Relapse

2.35 Dealing with setbacks

A. When my loved one relapses I find myself	Details	Helpfulness Low High
	The concerned other	
I find myself thinking . . .		1 2 3 4 5
I find myself saying to my loved one . . .		1 2 3 4 5
Seeing my loved one intoxicated is hard because . . .		1 2 3 4 5
I start feeling . . .		1 2 3 4 5
I tend to neglect myself by . . .		1 2 3 4 5
My motivation becomes . . .		1 2 3 4 5

The loved one

B. Traps	Description
What might escalate their use if they have a setback?	
What might they do or say to provoke you when they have had a setback?	
Are there any particular aspects of their behaviour/ times that you find difficult?	

2.36 Setback Plan

Aims: The purpose of the Setback Plan worksheet is to develop the coping strategies of the concerned other to increase their resilience to the loved one's slips.

Rationale: The loved one's setbacks have a profound impact on the concerned other's own well-being. In view of the hope that is fostered through the loved one committing to change, the experience of a setback feels devastating. This can undermine the concerned other's motivation and result in conflicts that increase the loved one's usage. As such, the reaction of the concerned other, whilst wholly understandable, can convert a slip into a lapse or even worse. Normalising setbacks is an important part of this process. Reminding the concerned other that the loved one will not have invested heavily in change for nothing and they may be equally disappointed in themselves too, even though this may be hidden in defensiveness. At the same time, a setback in the loved one's progress is likely to cause a setback in the concerned other's motivation. When setbacks are an inevitable element of the recovery process, it is essential that the concerned other can respond to the situation to preserve their own motivation and maintain their focus.

As setbacks can occur in a range of severity from slips to re-initiation, it is important that the concerned other's responses are proportionate. Recognising the severity of the slip is important. This should allow them to monitor the loved one's use and intervene appropriately. Based on this, the concerned other can implement a plan that will address their needs in the first instance and then consider their responses to the loved one secondly. This means that should the loved one experience a slip in use, the concerned other's motivation is preserved, whilst any greater duration of use can be met with skills to interrupt it. Lapse should be addressed through the rapid implementation of the Treatment Entry procedures. If use develops into a relapse, then the concerned other should seek additional support from the social network to help them at these times or even emergency appointments with their practitioner. If the loved one reinitiates use, consciously decides to resume use, the concerned other may need to make more profound decisions about their continued relationship with the loved one and this may signal a carefrontation approach. The escalating response to the loved one's use is an ideal laddering of interventions. Not all steps need to be followed. Some concerned others may wish to implement more intensive options sooner. This can be useful for more profound setbacks but may not be appropriate for slips.

Step 1: Explain the purpose of the Setback Plan worksheet to the concerned other. As setbacks have a profound effect on the concerned other's well-being, it is important that a clear plan of action is developed in advance in order to support them through what is a difficult event. In the event of a setback, it is important that the concerned other maintains their own motivation and well being whilst increasing the likelihood that the loved one will cease using drugs or alcohol again. Within this, as many setbacks are short lived, it is important that the responses to them are proportionate. The priority in the first instance is to support the concerned other and limit the impact on them. Should the setback escalate, then increasingly intensive responses can be applied to address the loved one's use.

Step 2: The Setback Plan worksheet is completed in reverse, starting with slips at the bottom of the table and working upwards. The first part of this, Section A, examines traps the concerned other may fall into when the loved one experiences a setback The practitioner and concerned other should review the information from Section B of the Dealing with Setbacks worksheet. Considering the traps that the loved one may set for the concerned other when they use, are there any typical responses that the concerned other should not engage in? This might include taking the bait in an argument, responding to particular criticisms or being drawn into conflicts. It might also include eliminating any responses which have or may escalate use further.

Step 3: Consider the responses described by the concerned other. In the eventuality of the loved one experiencing a slip, we need to consider how we can assist the concerned other manage this without conflict. Practicing the 'I Message' that voices the concerned other's feelings prior to withdrawing is important. This should show understanding but emphasise that they have found their drug/alcohol free time together really wonderful. If the loved one wishes to use they can, but that the concerned other finds this hard so will retire to a safe place. Once they retire they must implement their own emergency plan. This should counter their emotional response.

Step 4: The first response that the concerned other must implement is challenging any immediate negative thoughts concerning the loved one's setbacks. In this situation it is easy for the concerned other to catastrophise the situation and convince themselves that the situation is impossible to overcome. This in turn will generate powerful emotional responses. Again, there is a paradox here in that the more successful the loved one has been in changing, then the more profoundly the concerned other interprets the setback.

Based on the thoughts identified in the Dealing with Setbacks sheets, the concerned other should consider how they can respond to this negative thinking. One way to respond to this is reminding themselves that a slip is not a relapse. This information can help them adopt a 'wait-and-see' approach before responding to them with counter-arguments. Another way of dealing with negative thoughts is through thought modification. This is when the concerned other formulates counter-arguments to their established pattern of negative thinking. For example, if a setback typically makes the concerned other think 'This is hopeless, they are never going to change,' they could develop a counter-argument which challenges this, 'But even people who are successful in change have slips.' This can comprise the power of negative thinking.

In terms of talking to the loved one, they should express an 'I Message' regarding their use. This should emphasis the gains that the loved one has made and how their life has improved. Again, the Dealing with Setbacks sheet section on why it is difficult for the concerned other to see the loved one use can inform this statement. It is important that the concerned other delivers this message without conflict. For example:

You have worked so hard to make these changes and you have done so well. Our life feels so much better now. I just find it hard to see you go back to how you were. You seemed so unhappy back then and I really don't want to see that in you again.

The concerned other should withdraw at this point without conflict. Having a clear place to go, be it a quiet room in the house or to a member of their social networks is essential in separating from the loved one at this time and leaving them to their own decision. Despite this separation and the other approaches, the concerned other often experiences profound doubt at this stage. It is important to express these emotions and feelings. Ironically it is usually after a setback that has been responded to without conflict which often increases the motivation of the loved one to change. Many concerned others on the PACT programme report that withdrawing from the loved one at this time leaves them dwelling on the possibility that the programme is not working for them and consider giving up only to find the loved one more focused on change the next day. Having someone to vent their emotions to this at this time can help the concerned other discharge their stress and regain a focus quickly in what can feel a desolate and lonely time.

During this time it is important the concerned other does not neglect the activities and pursuits that nourish and enrich them. The fact that they continue to prioritise their own needs is often a shock to the loved one who has acclimatised to the fact that the concerned other has dropped everything for them before. Crisis is easily rewarded by attention-giving and thereby strengthening this behaviour. The concerned other who remains in contact with a rich variety of activities is less likely to suffer from depression and low mood than those who isolate themselves. The concerned other should identify specific activities and recreations that they will maintain at all costs.

Finally the concerned other must consider how they can maintain their motivation for the programme. This can be done in a number of ways. Firstly, recalling the stated desire that they made in the comprehensive assessment can remind them of why they are doing the programme. If this was to regain the partner they once had, to rescue the child they have lost or fulfil life ambitions with the loved one, all these can reinvigorate compromised motivation. A second way of keeping their motivation intact is to review the progress that they have made so far. After all, a setback can only occur against a context of progress. Reviewing the gains that they have made systematically can help them keep this focus. Repeating the base line measures taken at intake is a methodical and more convincing way of doing this. Alternatively, they might consider three things that have significantly improved in their life since entering the programme. If they cannot think of three things, then they should review this with the practitioner and a more systematic assessment of progress can be conducted.

Step 5: If the setback continues to a lapse the concerned other should prioritise what parts of the programme that they need to deploy. This is important as in the light of the lapse many concerned others do not generally apply their skills to this new situation. Review what skills they have learned from the programme that can assist them in this eventuality. The most obvious skills are the four principles of treatment entry (alternative rewards, reduce conflict, disable enabling, withdraw). The concerned other may feel that they need to use other skills at this time and these should be included in the plan.

Step 6: Should the usage progress into relapse the concerned other should call upon any wider support that they will feel is most helpful. This may include drawing on support from their practitioner, wider social network, mutual support or other family members. Taking a respite from the situation if possible may offer the concerned other more clarity on their situation.

Step 7: When the loved one re-initiates after a sustained period of abstinence the concerned other might consider a final ultimatum. This needs to be discussed and planned carefully with the practitioner. The concerned other should consider a carefrontation approach as outlined in the Carefrontation Worksheet should all efforts fail. Any ultimatum made to the loved one must be final and the concerned other must follow through lest all their efforts to change their loved one will come to nothing. The concerned other must recognise that it is a high risk strategy and as such, should be their last resort when they feel they have nothing else to lose by going for such a strategy.

Treatment goal:	Support the Loved One in Treatment
Associated worksheets:	2.32 Understanding Slips 2.33 Risk Factors 2.34 Strengthening Attendance 2.35 Dealing with Setbacks **2.36 Setback Plan**
Further context:	1.23 Supporting the Loved One in Treatment 1.24 Treatment Outcomes and Relapse

2.36 Setback Plan

Reinitiate

The decisions that I have to make are ...?

Relapse

I will need extra support from ...	They can help by ...

Lapse

The parts of the programme I will need to focus on are ...

1.

2.

3.

4.

Slips

I will stay focussed by . . .	Setback plan
I will keep motivated by reminding myself . . .	
I will not neglect myself by continuing to . . .	
I will express my feelings by talking to . . .	
I will withdraw from my loved one by going . . .	
I will say to my loved one . . .	
I will counter negative thinking by saying . . .	
Things I must resist doing are . . .	

Ending

2.37 The Carefrontation

Aim: The aim of The Carefrontation is to devise a letter to the loved one which describes the final ultimatum that the concerned other will make in the light of all other options failing to change the loved one's drug or alcohol use.

Rationale: Research demonstrates that whilst skills based programmes are very effective in enabling the concerned others to influence their loved one to enter treatment, they are not effective in all cases. Should this prove to be the case the concerned other can be offered a final option. This is the application of a carefrontation with the loved one. Unlike confrontational approaches, the carefrontation is delivered in the form of a letter, which is given to the loved one when they are able to assimilate the contents. The loved one should be given a period of time of at least two hours to consider the contents of the letter before the concerned other follows up the loved one's response. Again, this follow-up should only be conducted when the loved one is in a condition to reason clearly. Highly intoxicated states in the loved one will rule out any opportunity for discussion. The concerned other should delay any discussions until the loved one is able to engage with them.

The Carefrontation letter spells out the importance of the relationship with the loved one before stating an ultimatum. This is always expressed in terms of love and affection where the loved one's interests are always explicit. However the ultimate is a final plea to seek treatment or the concerned other will terminate the relationship with them. The loved one will have to make a choice between continued use and remaining in the relationship. It is important the concerned other understands the magnitude of this ultimatum. And that should the loved one choose substances, they will have to follow through and carry this sanction out. If they do not, it will signal to the loved one that there will be no actual sanctions to their behaviour and any responses from the concerned other will be understood as hollow threats that need not be taken seriously. The concerned other can offer future contact with the loved one on the single proviso that the loved one is not using.

The Carefrontation letter is an extremely powerful device. This approach can be effective if delivered in low stress environments but the magnitude of this approach means that it is best reserved for a final option when all other measures have failed and the concerned other feels that they have nothing else to lose having exhausted all other options.

Step 1: Explain the rationale of the Carefrontation worksheet. This worksheet is a proforma letter to the loved one. This letter will offer your loved one a final ultimatum: they must enter treatment or the concerned other will terminate the relationship. This is a powerful intervention and represents the last option to change the loved one. If this ultimatum is delivered, the concerned other must be prepared to stand by this statement.

Step 2: The concerned other needs to consider this very carefully. The practitioner should ask the concerned other whether they feel ready to commit to this process or whether they wish to continue to apply the principles of treatment entry. If the concerned other believes they simply cannot continue in their current situation, then the Carefrontation should be applied.

Step 3: The practitioner should explain that the construction of this letter is a powerful experience in itself. They will work through each section thoroughly in order to construct the letter. This will demand exploring the most emotionally charged aspects of their relationship with the loved one and this can feel even more powerful in the context of an imminent ultimatum. Not all sections are necessarily relevant, but should be seen as guiding principles offering direction to the format of the letter.

Step 4: Section A of the pro forma sets the context for the letter. The concerned other should introduce the letter by stating as simply as possible why they are writing this letter to the loved one. This should be placed in relation to any recent critical events that have lead the concerned other to this point.

Step 5: Section B needs to make a clear statement of the concerned other and the loved one's life and experience prior to the problem. Any intimacies that they shared that will be emotionally vivid for the loved one, and should be called upon in order to remind the loved one of the better times they shared. These past experiences, promises or plans should be stated as explicitly as possible in the context of their previous life.

Step 6: Section C provides a contrast to the previous life. If should express the concerned other's perception of what has changed with the advent of the loved one's drug or alcohol use. This should detail how the concerned other believes that the use has impacted on their relationship and how it has changed. This might include the concerned other's perception of how the loved one themselves have changed, comparing their non-using self with the problem, using self. This can be especially powerful where this comparison contrasts important goals, values or qualities the loved one once held dear with their current behaviour. Where use has eroded cherished or important beliefs in the loved one it can generate a deep internal inconsistency that prompts change. This section may also include any substantive fears the concerned other has for the loved one. This should be grounded in evidence of intensifying health or legal problems. Again this should be stated in terms of care and concern rather than judgement. The concerned other should explain why this is hard for them to witness.

Step 7: Section D should state why the concerned other can no longer continue and as a result they are asking them to make a decision: whether they wish to continue to use or make changes. The concerned other should state clearly why they are making this ultimatum. They can explain that they do not want to do this, and which option they would prefer the loved one to make, but why they must stick to this ultimatum if the loved one chooses to continue their use. They should reinforce this message by summarising the decision they are asking the loved one to make. They should state the decisions available to the loved one as simply as possible. Any other closing comments can be included.

Step 8: Once the notes are taken it should be possible to begin to construct a Carefrontation letter from these elements. This should be in the concerned other's own words as much as possible so that the loved one cannot dismiss the content easily.

Step 9: The concerned other and the practitioner should consider when best to give the love one the letter. The concerned other should plan their intervention and seek out support from their support network for at least two hours whilst they allow the loved one to digest the contents. Again they should make contact with the loved one only when they are sober enough to discuss the letter. The concerned other should ask the loved one outright what their choice is. Any other information the loved one offers is deemed irrelevant to their decision regarding the ultimatum.

Step 10: Should the loved one decide to continue use, the concerned other should be supported in developing their new life. Should the loved one agree to treatment then appointments should be made immediately.

Treatment goal:	Carefrontation
Associated worksheets:	**2.37 The Carefrontation**
Further context:	1.9 The Intervention 1.25 Carefrontation and Termination

2.37 The Carefrontation

A. Why are you writing this letter to the loved one?

What recent circumstances have compelled you to do this?

B. What memories did you and your loved one cherish before these problems occurred?

What promises did you both make or what hopes did you once share?

What things did your loved one say about how important you are to them?

What hopes did you share for your future together?

What do you miss about these times?

© Phil Harris, *The Concerned Other*, www.russellhouse.co.uk

C. How have drugs or alcohol diminished your relationship? (Give concrete examples)

What are your fears for your loved one's continued use? (Give evidence)

How can you show understanding of the loved one's use?

How can you share responsibility for what has unfolded?

What would it mean to you if they entered into treatment?

How would you support them if they were to make this decision?

What do you fear will happen if they do not?

D. Why the concerned other can no longer continue and what their ultimatum is?

Why do you need to do this if your loved one will not change?

How can you reiterate what you want to happen instead?

What is the explicit choice you are asking the loved one to make?

Any other comment you would like to make?

2.38 Crisis Termination: When is it Time to Quit?

Aim: The aim of the When is it Time to Quit? worksheet is to offer the concerned other who is considering terminating a relationship with the loved one the opportunity to explore this option in detail before making the decision to end their relationship.

Rationale: Living with a problem user takes a huge toll on the concerned other. The concerned other may realise that the effort it takes to change the loved one is too demanding. They may see that, despite their best efforts, the loved one does not appear to respond to the changes that they are making. Alternatively, a relapse in the loved one or some other crystallising event, may trigger the desire to terminate their relationship. The programme does not view terminating the relationship with a loved one as a bad outcome. The programme collaborates with the wishes of the concerned other. Sometimes termination can be the best option, particularly where the loved one is violent or aggressive. What is important in addressing the issue of termination is that the concerned other feels certain that this is the best option for them. Separation is a profound change for both parties and it is essential the concerned other does this with good heart and without regret. This worksheet is designed to allow the concerned other to review their decision first before implementing a plan of action to initiate the termination. It is important that the concerned other is still supported, even after separation. The skills to improve their 'new' life will still apply outside of the relationship with the loved one. This worksheet should be referred to at any point in the programme when the concerned other is considering termination.

Step 1: When the concerned other raises the issue of terminating the relationship with the loved one, the practitioner should explain the rationale of the When is it Time to Quit? This worksheet will allow the concerned other to think through whether they feel that they have done all they can to change the loved one, whether their efforts have or have not made sufficient impact on the loved one's use and whether the concerned other can see a better future without the loved one. This will enable the concerned other to make a clear decision regarding termination.

Step 2: The concerned other will need to repeat the baseline measures that were taken as part of the initial comprehensive assessment. The first of these is the Mood Screener and the CES Depression Scale. The concerned other should complete blank screening tools before they review their original score. Discuss any difference in these scores.

Step 3: The concerned other should complete the loved one's use table for the last week, rating how intoxicated their loved one appeared to them in the last seven days. Once this table is completed, it can be compared to the intake score. Discuss any difference in these scores.

Step 4: The concerned other should complete the life audit section on the current satisfaction with life. Once this is completed it can be compared to the intake score. Any differences should be discussed.

Step 5: The concerned other should consider the application of the programme. Each core component should be reviewed with regard to the consistency with which the concerned other applied the technique, whether they did it fully, partially or not at all. Any areas of weakness should be reviewed more deeply, especially with regard to whether the concerned other believes any renewed efforts might make a difference to the loved one or their life.

Step 6: The final section of the worksheet asks the concerned other to consider the consequences of terminating the relationship. This checklist is a more pre-emptive area and can represent powerful questions. The concerned other should be allowed to explore each question as deeply as possible.

Step 7: Once they have considered these questions, the practitioner should review this feedback and ask, considering all this, whether termination is the best option for the concerned other. If they feel that termination is their best option, the practitioner and concerned other should explore how they will end the relationship. The Problem Solving worksheet may be helpful in this process. Where a history of domestic violence has occurred, the safety of the concerned other may also need to be considered. The concerned other may have to move to temporary accommodation or have members of their social network present when implementing termination. The practitioner should make it clear to the concerned other that they will continue to work together to support them in the establishment of a new life.

Treatment goal:	Crisis Termination
Associated worksheets:	**2.38 When is it Time to Quit?**
Further context:	1.25 Carefrontation and Termination

2.38 When is it Time to Quit?

Measure	Scores at intake	Current scores

Mood screener

CES depression scale

Day	No contact	Certain no use	Suspect use	Mild signs	Obvious signs	Incapacitated	Intake ratings
Monday	N/C	1	2	3	4	5	
Tuesday	N/C	1	2	3	4	5	
Wednesday	N/C	1	2	3	4	5	
Thursday	N/C	1	2	3	4	5	
Friday	N/C	1	2	3	4	5	
Saturday	N/C	1	2	3	4	5	
Sunday	N/C	1	2	3	4	5	

Domain	Current score	Intake scores
Partnering	1 2 3 4 5 6 7 8 9 10	1 2 3 4 5 6 7 8 9 10
Family	1 2 3 4 5 6 7 8 9 10	1 2 3 4 5 6 7 8 9 10
Finances	1 2 3 4 5 6 7 8 9 10	1 2 3 4 5 6 7 8 9 10
Social life	1 2 3 4 5 6 7 8 9 10	1 2 3 4 5 6 7 8 9 10
Housing	1 2 3 4 5 6 7 8 9 10	1 2 3 4 5 6 7 8 9 10
Employment and training	1 2 3 4 5 6 7 8 9 10	1 2 3 4 5 6 7 8 9 10
Physical health	1 2 3 4 5 6 7 8 9 10	1 2 3 4 5 6 7 8 9 10
Mental health	1 2 3 4 5 6 7 8 9 10	1 2 3 4 5 6 7 8 9 10
Your substance use	1 2 3 4 5 6 7 8 9 10	1 2 3 4 5 6 7 8 9 10
Hopes and aspirations	1 2 3 4 5 6 7 8 9 10	1 2 3 4 5 6 7 8 9 10
Other: Please state	1 2 3 4 5 6 7 8 9 10	1 2 3 4 5 6 7 8 9 10

Did I . . .	
Offer rewards	
Apply communication skills	
Disable enabling	
Withdraw	
Time raising the subject	
Find a suitable treatment	
Reduce my stress	
Improve my life	
Do I . . .	
Feel that I have done all I can?	
See a better future for myself without my loved one?	
Feel in my heart of hearts that ending the relationship is my best option?	

2.39 Closure and Review

Aim: The purpose of this worksheet is to review the outcomes of the programme and offer the opportunity to end with positive closure for the concerned other and the practitioner.

Rationale: The PACT programme is a powerful experience for the concerned other. The concerned other often presents for help because the despair of their situation has reached a crisis point. At the outset of the programme many concerned others do not believe that anything can actually help them. Not only are they exhausted by their own efforts, their situation is often further confused by the advice of others, the response of other professionals as well as misguided internet advice. The impact of the programme on changing their situation in a way that they once felt impossible, strikes a profound emotional response. In return, the courage and the tenacity demonstrated by concerned others is a powerful experience for the practitioner. Therefore, having the opportunity to reflect on the programme, their experience and the degree of change that has occurred can provide a ceremony of closure for both.

Further to this, it is important that the impact of the programme is quantified in terms of outcomes that demonstrate its efficacy. This will be required by current or potential funders. It can also be important to collate this data on the effectiveness of the programme to share with concerned others who are considering whether to enter into the programme. Often they are dispirited and pessimistic regarding their situation. Providing them with objective feedback regarding how the programme has assisted others can be very powerful.

The simplest way to establish the treatment outcomes is to contrast the measures taken at intake with the concerned other's current scores. This should repeat the measures taken in the comprehensive assessment. The concerned other should also offer their personal feedback about the programme. The feedback they can offer regarding their experience of the programme can be helpful in refining it, particular when the feedback follows a pattern. Conversely, every client experience enriches the practitioner's understanding. The practitioner should consider what they have learned from this unique experience and offer this feedback to the concerned other. This can be a powerful way of ending the programme.

Sometimes it is not possible for the concerned other to attend a review. This may be due to a sudden change in circumstances or other unforeseen pressures. Wherever possible concerned others should be encouraged to attend a final session. The practitioner should emphasise that this is important to the programme as a whole and represents a chance for the concerned other to offer something back to the programme. Should they still not be able to attend, they should be asked for permission to send them the assessment tools and ask them to complete these and return them in a stamped addressed envelope.

Step 1: Explain the rationale of the Closure and Review worksheet. This worksheet will allow the concerned other to measure their progress through the programme and how it has helped them. This will involve re-taking some of the screening tools and measurements that were taken at the outset of the programme. The concerned other will also have a chance to offer feedback on their experience of the programme. This information will be used to demonstrate how effective the programme is to the funder of this service. It will also be used with other concerned others who are considering whether to undertake the programme.

Step 2: Ask the concerned other to complete the Mood Screener and the CES Depression Scale. Once they have completed these screening tools compare them to the intake score. The concerned other and the practitioner should discuss any differences in these scores and how they have been experienced by the concerned other in their daily life.

Step 3: The practitioner should ask whether the loved one has entered treatment. If they have, and are currently abstinent, they should record for how long. The concerned other should then complete the loved one's intoxication table for the last seven days. Once completed, these should be compared to the intake score taken at assessment.

Step 4: The concerned other should complete the blank Life Audit on how satisfied they are in their current life. Once completed, these results should be compared to their intake score. The concerned other and the practitioner should discuss any differences in these scores and how they have been experience by the concerned other in their daily life.

Step 5: The practitioner should invite the concerned other to consider the difference that the programme has made on their life. Reviewing these changes in scores, the concerned other should consider what aspects of the programme they found most helpful.

Step 6: In view of the changes in their life, the concerned other should be invited to consider what aspects of the programme were not as helpful. The practitioner should encourage them to be as honest as possible and be non-defensive in receipt of this feedback. The practitioner should note this and consider whether this forms a pattern in the feedback from a number of individuals.

Step 7: The concerned other should be asked whether they would recommend the programme to others in their life situation. What would they say to encourage others to enter into this programme? These comments can be used anonymously in literature promoting the programme.

Step 8: The practitioner should reflect on their experience of working with this concerned other. Every client-practitioner relationship offers new insight into the programme and the practitioner's own practice. This should be offered as clear feedback to the concerned other and their contribution to the continued development of the programme explicitly acknowledged.

Treatment goal:	Treatment Closure
Associated worksheets:	**2.39 Closure and Review** Baseline measures taken at assessment
Further context:	1.28 Closing Treatment

2.39 Closure and Review

Mood screener		CED	
Intake:	Current:	Intake:	Current:

Has your loved one entered treatment?

Yes/No   If yes, how long have they been in treatment?

Is your loved one currently abstinent?

Yes/No   If yes, how long?

Has your loved one reduced their use? Consider the last week and what best describes their levels of intoxication.

Day	No contact	Certain not use	Suspected use	Mild intoxication	Obvious intoxication	Incapacitated	Intake rating
Monday	N/C	1	2	3	4	5	
Tuesday	N/C	1	2	3	4	5	
Wednesday	N/C	1	2	3	4	5	
Thursday	N/C	1	2	3	4	5	
Friday	N/C	1	2	3	4	5	
Saturday	N/C	1	2	3	4	5	
Sunday	N/C	1	2	3	4	5	

Life audit

Domain	Current score	Intake score
Partnering	1 2 3 4 5 6 7 8 9 10	
Family	1 2 3 4 5 6 7 8 9 10	
Finances	1 2 3 4 5 6 7 8 9 10	

Social life	1 2 3 4 5 6 7 8 9 10
Housing	1 2 3 4 5 6 7 8 9 10
Employment and training	1 2 3 4 5 6 7 8 9 10
Physical health	1 2 3 4 5 6 7 8 9 10
Mental health	1 2 3 4 5 6 7 8 9 10
Your own drug or alcohol use	1 2 3 4 5 6 7 8 9 10
Hopes, future plans or aspirations	1 2 3 4 5 6 7 8 9 10
Other: Please state	1 2 3 4 5 6 7 8 9 10

What did you find most helpful about the programme?

What did you find least helpful about the programme?

Would you recommend the programme to others in your situation?

What I learned from working with you is . . .

References

ACMD (2003) *Hidden Harm: Responding to the Needs of Children of Problem Drug Users.* The report of an Inquiry by the Advisory Council on the Misuse of Drugs.

Adfam Report (2006) *Forgotten Families.* www.grandparentsplus.org.uk

Azrin, N. et al. (1982) Alcoholism Treatment by Disulfiram and Community Reinforcement Therapy. *Journal of Behaviour Therapy and Experimental Psychiatry,* 13, 105–12.

Balaban, B.J. and Melchionda, R. (1979) Outreach Redefined: The Impact on Staff Attitudes of a Family Education Project. *International Journal of Addiction,* 14: 6, 833–46.

Barber, J. G. and Gilbertson, R. (1996) An Experimental Study of Brief Unilateral Intervention for the Partners of Heavy Drinkers. *Research on Social Work Practice,* 6: 3, 325–36.

Barber, J.G. and Crisp, B.R. (1995) The Pressures to Change Approach to Working with the Partners of Heavy Drinkers. *Addiction,* 90, 269–76.

Barber, J.G. and Gilbertson, R. (1998) Evaluation of a Self-Help Manual for the Female Partners of Heavy Drinkers. *Research on Social Work Practice,* 8: 2, 141–51.

Barbor, T.F and Del Boca, F.K. (Eds.) (2003) *Treatment Matching in Alcoholism.* Cambridge: Cambridge University Press.

Barnard, M. (2007) *Drug Addiction and Families.* Jessica Kinglsey.

Berg, I. K. and Miller, S.D. (1992) *Working with the Problem Drinker: A Solution-Focused Approach.* W.W. Norton.

Berg, I.K. and Ruess, N.H. (1998) *Solutions Step by Step: A Substance Abuse Treatment Manual.* W.W. Norton.

Boyd, C. and Guthrie, B. (1996) Women, Their Significant Others and Crack Cocaine. *The American Journal of Addiction Psychiatry,* 5: 2, 156–66.

Bradshaw, J. (1988) *Bradshaw on: The Family.* Health Communication.

Bratfos, O. (1974) *The Course of Alcoholism, Drinking, Social Adjustment and Health.* Universtiy Forlaget.

Brisby, T., Baker, S. and Hedderwick, T. (1997) *Under the Influence: Coping with Parents who Drink Too Much.* Alcohol Concern.

Brook, J. et al. (1989) The Role of Older Brothers in Younger Brothers' Drug Use Viewed in Context of Parent and Peer Influences. *The Journal of Genetic Psychology,* 151: 1, 59–75.

Brown, J., Dries, S. and Nace, D.K. (1999) What Really Makes a Difference in Psychotherapy Outcome? Why Does Managed Care Want to Know? In Hubble, M.A. et al. (Eds.) *The Heart and Soul of Change: What Works in Therapy?* American Psychological Association.

Campbell, T.W. (1992) Therapeutic Relationships and Iatrogenic Outcomes: The Blame-and-change Manoeuvre in Psychotherapy. *Psychotherapy,* 29: 3, 474–80.

Cavell T.A. et al. (2002) The Natural Mentors of Adolescent Children of Alcoholics (COAs): Implications for Preventive Practices. *Journal of Primary Prevention.* 23: 1, 23–42.

Chan, J.G. (2003) An Examination of Family Involved Approaches to Alcoholism Treatment. *The Family Journal,* 11, 129–38.

Chick, J. (1980) Alcohol Dependence: Methodological Issues in its Treatment: Reliability of the Criteria. *British Journal of Addictions,* 75, 175–86.

Clark, W.B. and Hilton, M.F. (Eds.) (1991) *Alcohol in America: Drinking Practices and Problems.* State University of New York Press.

Cohen, M. et al. (1971) Moderate Drinking by Chronic Alcoholics. *Journal of Nervous and Mental Disease*, 53, 434–44.

Cottler L.B., Phelps, D.L. and Compton, W.M. (1995) Narrowing of the Drinking Repertoire Criterion: Should it be Dropped From ICD 10? *Journal of Studies on Alcohol*, 56, 173–6.

Cottler, L.B. (1993) Comparing the DSM-IIIR and ICD10 Substance Abuse Disorders. *Addictions*, 88, 689–96.

Curran, P.J. and Chassin, L. (1996) A Longitudinal Study of Parenting as a Protective Factor for Children of Alcoholics. *Journal of Studies on Alcohol*, 57: 3, 305–13.

DeLeon, G. (1996) Integrative Recovery: A Stage Paradigm. *Substance Abuse*, 175: 1–63.

DoH (2004) *National Service Framework for Children, Young People and Maternity Services.*

DoH (2005) *Independence, Wellbeing and Choice.*

DoH (2005) *The Carers (Equal Opportunities) Act (2004) (England) Order 2005.* The Stationary Office.

DiClemente, C.C. (1991) Motivational Interviewing and the Stages of Change. In Miller, W.R. and Rollnick, S. (Eds.) *Motivational Interviewing: Preparing People to Change Addictive Behaviour.* Guildford Press.

Donahue, B. et al. (1998) Improving Initial Session Attendance of Substance Abusing and Conduct Disordered Adolescents: A Control Study. *Journal of Child and Adolescent Substance Abuse*, 8, 1013.

Dore, M.M. and Alexander, L.B. (1996) Preserving Families at Risk of Abuse and Neglect: The Role of The Helping Alliance. *Child Abuse and Neglect: The International Journal*, 20: 4, 350–64.

Douglas, L.J. (1987) *Perceived Family Dynamics of Cocaine Abusers, as Compared to Opiate Abusers and Non-Drug Users.* PhD. Diss. University of Florida.

Draycott, S. and Dabbs, A. (1998) Cognitive Dissonance 1: An Overview of the Literature and its Integration into Theory and Practice in Clinical Psychology. *British Journal of Psychology.* 37: 341–53.

Duncan, T. et al. (1996) Multilevel Covariance Structure Analysis of Sibling Substance Use and Interfamily Conflict. *Journal of Psychotherapy and Behavioural Assessment*, 18: 4, 347–69.

Edwards G. et al. (1977) Alcoholism: A Controlled Trial of 'Treatment' and Advice. *Journal of Studies on Alcohol*, 38,1813–16.

Edwards, G. and Gross, M. (1976) Alcohol Dependence: Provisional Description of a Clinical Syndrome. *British Medical Journal*, 1: 1058–61.

Edwards, G. et al. (1994) *Alcohol Policy and the Public Good.* Oxford University Press.

Edwards, G. et al. (1977) *Alcohol Related Disabilities.* WHO Offset Publication No. 32. World Health Organisation.

Edwards, G., Marshall, E.J. and Cook, C.C. (2003) *The Treatment of Drinking Problems.* Cambridge: Cambridge University Press.

Edwards, P., Harvey, C. and Whitehead, P.C. (1973) Wives of Alcoholics: A Critical Review and Analysis. *Quarterly Journal of Studies on Alcohol*, 34, 112–32.

Emrick, C.D. and Hanson, J. (1983) Assertions Regarding Effectiveness of Treatment for Alcoholism: Fact or Fantasy? *American Psychologist*, 38, 1078–88.

Emrick, C.D. (1975) A Review of Psychologically Orientated Treatment of Alcoholism II: The Relative Effectiveness of Different Treatment Approaches and the Effectiveness of Treatment versus No Treatment. *Journal of Studies on Alcohol*, 36, 88–109.

Endicott, J. et al. (1976) The Global Assessment Scale: A Procedure for Measuring the Overall Severity of Psychiatric Disturbance. *Archives of General Psychiatry*, 33, 766–71.

Fearing, J. (1996) The Changing Face of Intervention. *Behavioural Health Management*, 16: 5, 35–7.

Fearing, J. (2000) *Workplace Intervention: The Bottom Line on Helping Addicted Employees Become Productive Again*. Hazelden.

Feingold, A. and Rounsaville, B. (1995) Construct Validity of The Dependence Syndrome as Measured by DSM-IV for Different Psycho-Active Substances. *Addiction 90*, 1661–9.

Feinstein, C. and Tamerin, J.S. (1972) Induced Intoxication and Video Feedback in Alcoholism Treatment. *Quarterly Journal of Studies on Alcohol*, 33, 408–16.

Futterman, S. (1953) Personality Trends in Wives of Alcoholics. *Journal of Psychiatric Social Work*, 23, 37–41.

Godsall, R.E. (1995) *Why Some Kids do Well in Bad Situations: The Effects of Parentification and Parental Impairment on Childhood Self-esteem*. Dissertation Abstracts International: Section B: The Sciences and Engineering 56(6-B).

Gogineni, A. (1995) *Predictors of Psychiatric Problems among Adult Offspring of Alcoholic and Non-Alcoholic Mothers*. Dissertation Abstracts International A: Humanities and Social Sciences 56(6-A).

Gordon, J.E. (1995) *The Psychological and Social Functioning of Adult Children of Alcoholics: An Attachment Perspective*. Dissertation Abstracts International B: The Sciences and Engineering 55(11-B).

Gossop, M. (2000) *Living with Drugs*. Ashgate.

Gossop, M. (2003) *Drug Addiction and its Treatment*. Oxford University Press.

Grant, B.F. et al. (1992) DSM-IIIR and Proposed DSM-IV Alcohol Use Disorders, United States 1988. A Methodological Comparison. *Alcoholism: Clinical and Experimental Research*, 16, 215–21.

Harris, P. (2007) *Empathy for the Devil: How to Help People Overcome Drug and Alcohol Problems*. Lyme Regis: Russell House Publishing.

Hartjen, C.A., Mitchell, S.M. and Wahburne, N.F. (1976) *Dynamics of Treatment in Therapeutic Communities*. Technical Report No. 13. Rutgers University.

Hasin, D. et al. (2000) Withdrawal and Tolerance: Prognostic Significance in the DSM-IV Alcohol Dependence. *Journal of Studies on Alcohol*, 61, 431–8.

Heather, N. et al. (1983) A Comparison of Objective and Subjective Measures of Alcohol Dependence as Predictors of Relapse Following Treatment. *British Journal of Clinical Psychiatry*, 22, 11–7.

Hill, E.M., Nord, J.L. and Blow, F.C. (1992) Young-Adult Children of Alcoholic Parents: Protective Effects of Positive Family Functioning. *British Journal of Addiction*, 87: 12, 1677–90.

Hoggans, J. (2008) *A Comprehensive Care Planning Assessment Tool*. Unpublished.

Holder, H. et al. (1991)The Cost-Effectiveness of Treatment for Alcoholism: A First Approximation. *Journal of Studies on Alcohol*, 52, 517–20.

Home Office (2002) *Updated Drug Strategy 2002.* Home Office.

Homme, L. (1971) *How to Use Contingency Contracting in the Classroom.* Research Press.

Hunt, W.A., Barnett, L.W. and Branch, L.G. (1971) Relapse Rates in Addiction Programmes. *Journal of Clinical Psychology,* 27, 355.

Hurcom, C., Copello, A. and Orford, J. (2000) The Family and Alcohol: Effects of Excessive Drinking and Conceptualizations of Spouses over Recent Decades. *Substance Use and Misuse,* 35, 473–502.

Johnson, V.E. (1998) *Intervention: A Step-by-Step Guide for Families and Friends of Chemically Dependent Persons.* Hazelden.

Kalashian, M.M. (1959) Working with the Wives of Alcoholics in an Outpatient Clinic Setting. *Marriage and Family,* 21: 130–3.

Kannar, A.D. et al. (1981) Comparison of Two Models versus Stress Measurement: Daily Hassles and Uplift versus Major Life Events. *Behavioural Medicine,* 4, 1–39.

Kaskutas, L., Weisner, C. and Caetano, R. (1997) Predictors of Help Seeking Among a Longitudinal Sample of the General Population, 1984–1992. *Journal of Studies on Alcoholism,* 58, 155–61.

Kelleher, K. et al. (1994) Alcohol and Drug Disorders Among Physically Abusive and Neglectful Parents in a Community Based Sample. *American Journal of Public Health,* 84, 1586–90.

Kessler, R.C. et al. (1994) Lifetime and Twelve-month Prevalence of DSM-III-R Psychiatric Disorders in the United States: Results from the National Co-morbidity Survey. *Archives of General Psychiatry,* 51, 8–19.

Kidorf, M., Brooner, R.K. and King, V.L. (1997) Motivating Methadone Patients to Include Drug-Free Significant Others in Treatment: A Behavioural Intervention. *Journal of Substance Abuse Treatment,* 14: 23–8.

Kirby, K.C. et al. (1999) Community Reinforcement Training for Family and Significant Others of Drug Abusers: A Unilateral Intervention to Increase Treatment Entry of Drug Users. *Drug and Alcohol Dependence,* 56, 85–96.

Klingemann, H.K. (1991) The Motivation for Change from Problem Alcohol and Heroin Use. *British Journal of Addiction,* 86, 727–44.

Kroll, B. and Taylor, A. (2003) *Parental Substance Misuse and Child Welfare.* Jessica Kingsley.

Landau, J. et al. (2001) *A Relational Intervention Sequence (ARISE) For Engaging Resistant Substance Abusers in Treatment.* Poster session at the Fourth European Family Therapy Association Conference and the Fifteenth Hungarian National Conference on Family Therapy, Budapest, Hungary.

Landau, J. et al. (2004) Outcomes with ARISE Approach to Engaging Reluctant Drug and Alcohol Dependent Individuals in Treatment. *The American Journal of Drug and Alcohol Abuse.* 30: 4, 711–48.

Lawental, E. et al. (1996) Coerced Treatment For Substance Abuse Problems Detected Through Workplace Urine Surveillance: Is it Effective? *Journal of Substance Abuse,* 8: 1, 115–28.

Laybourn, A., Brown, J. and Hill, M. (1996) *Hurting on the Inside.* Avebury.

Lewinsohn, P.M. et al. (1992) *Control your Depression.* Fireside.

Liepman, M.R., Nirenberg, T.D. and Begin, A.M. (1989) Evaluation of a Program Designed to Help Family and Significant Others to Motivate Resistant Alcoholics into Recovery. *American Journal of Drug and Alcohol Abuse,* 15, 209–21.

Logan, D.G. (1983) Getting Alcoholics to Treatment by Social Network Intervention. *Hospital and Community Psychiatry*, 34: 4, 360–1.

Maisto, S.A. et al. (1988) Alcoholics Attributions of Factors Affecting their Relapse to Drink and Reasons Terminating their Relapse Events. *Addictive Behaviours*, 13, 79–82.

Marlatt, G.A. (1985) Situational Determinants of Relapse and Skill Training Interventions. In Marlatt, G.A. and Gordon, J.R. (Eds.) *Relapse Prevention*. Guildford Press.

Marlatt, G.A. and Gordon, J.R. (1980) Determinants of relapse. Implications for the maintenance of behaviour change. In Davidson, P.O. and Davidson, S.M. (Eds.) *Behaviour Medicine: Changing Health Lifestyles*. Brunner Mazel.

Marlowe, D.B. et al. (2001) Multidimensional Assessment of Perceived Treatment-Entry Pressures Among Substance Abusers. *Psychology of Addictive Behaviours*, 15: 2, 97–108.

Marshal, E.J. (2001) Drinking Problems. In Ramsey, R. et al. (Eds.) *Mental Illness: A Handbook for Carers*. Jessica Kingsley.

Mattrick, R.P. et al. (1998) The Role of Counselling and Psychological Therapy. In Ward, J., Matterick, R.P. and Hall, W. (Eds.) *Methadone Maintenance Treatment and Other Opioid Replacement Therapies*. Harwood Academic Publishers.

Meehan, J.P. et al. (1985) The Severity of Alcohol Dependence Questionnaire (SADQ) in a Sample of Irish Drinkers. *British Journal of Addictions*, 80, 57–63.

Mertins, G.C. and Fuller, G.B. (1964) *The Therapist Manual*. Mimeograph.

Meyers, J. and Smith, J.E. (1995) *Clinical Guide to Alcohol Treatment: The Community Reinforcement Approach*. Guildford Press.

Meyers, R.J. et al. (1999) Community Reinforcement and Family Training (CRAFT): Engaging Unmotivated Drug Users in Treatment. *Journal of Substance Abuse*, 10, 291–308.

Meyers, R.J. et al. (2002) A Randomised Control Trial of Two Methods for Engaging Treatment-Refusing Drug Users through Concerned Significant Others. *Journal of Consulting and Clinical Psychology*, 70, 1182–85.

Meyers, R.J., Miller, W.R. and Smith, J.E. (2001) Community Reinforcement and Family Training. In Meyers, R.J. and Miller, W.R. (Eds.) *A Community Reinforcement Approach to Addiction Treatment*. Cambridge: Cambridge University Press.

Miller, S.D. et al. (2004) Using Outcome to Inform and Improve Treatment Outcomes. *Journal of Brief Therapy*. In Press.

Miller, S.D. et al. (2005) Making Treatment Count: Client Directed, Outcome Informed Clinical Work With Problem Drinkers. *Psychotherapy in Australia*, 11: 4, 42–56.

Miller, W.R et al. (2003) What Works? A Summary of Treatment Outcome Research. In Hester, R.K. and Miller, W.R. (Eds.) *Handbook of Alcohol Treatment Approaches: Effective Alternatives*. Allyn and Bacon.

Miller, W.R. (1983) Controlled Drinking: A History and Critical Review. *Journal of Studies on Alcohol*, 44, 68–83.

Miller, W.R. (2003) Commentary: A Collaborative Approach to Working With Families. *Addiction*, 98, 5–6.

Miller, W.R. and Rollnick, S. (2002) *Motivational Interviewing: Preparing People for Change*. Guildford Press.

Miller, W.R., Meyers, R.J. and Tonigan, J.S. (1999) Engaging the Unmotivated in Treatment for Alcohol Problems: Comparisons of Three Strategies for Intervention Through Family Members. *Journal of Consulting and Clinical Psychology*, 67, 688–97.

Mohr, A.F. (2000) *Adolescent Substance Abuse: Vulnerability and Protective Factors from a Developmental Perspective.* Dissertation Abstracts International A: Humanities and Social Sciences 60(7-A).

Moos, R., Finney, J. and Cronkite, R. (1990) *Alcoholism Treatment: Process and Outcome.* Oxford University Press.

National Treatment Agency (2006) *Supporting and Involving Carers.* NTA.

O'Farrell, T.J. (1995) Marital and Family Therapy. In Hester, R.K. and Miller, W.R. (Eds.) *Handbook of Alcoholism Treatment Approaches. Effective Alternatives.* Allyn and Bacon.

Orford, J. (2001) *Excessive Appetites: A Psychological View of Addictions.* John Wiley.

Orford, J. et al. (2005) *Coping with Alcohol and Drug Problems: The Experiences of Family Members in Three Contrasting Cultures.* Taylor and Francis.

Orford, J. et al. (1998) Tolerate, Engage or Withdrawal: A Study of the Structure of Families Coping with Alcohol and Drug Problems in South West England and Mexico City. *Addiction*, 95, 1799–813.

Paolino, T.J. and McCrady, B.S. (1977) *The Alcoholic Marriage: Alternative Perspectives.* Grune and Statton.

Pattison, E.M. (1976) A Conceptual Approach to Alcoholism Treatment. *Addictive Behaviours*, 1, 177–92.

Perzel, J.F. and Lamon, S. (1979) *Enmeshment within Families of Polydrug Abusers.* Paper presented at the National Drug Abuse conference, New Orleans.

Polcin, D.L and Weisner, C. (1999) Factors Associated with Coercion in Entering Treatment for Alcohol Problems. *Drug and Alcohol Dependence*, 54, 63–8.

Polich, M., Armour, D.J. and Braiker, H.B. (1981) *The Course of Alcoholism: Four Years After Treatment.* Wiley.

Premack, D. (1965) Reinforcement Theory. In Levine, D. (Ed.) *Nebraska Symposium on Motivation.* University of Nebraska Press.

Price, R.K., Cottier, L.B. and Robins, L.N. (1991) Patterns of Drug Abuse Treatment Utilization in a General Population. In Harris, L. (Ed.) *Problems of Drug Dependence.* (1990) US Government Printing Office.

Prime Minister's Strategy Unit (2004) *Alcohol Harm Reduction Strategy for England.* Cabinet Office.

Prochaska, J.O., Norcross, J.C. and DiClemente, C.C. (1994) *Changing for Good.* William Morrow.

Prochaska, J.O. and DiClemente, C.C. (1986) Toward a Comprehensive Model of Change. In Miller, W.E. and Heather, N. (Eds.) *Teating Addictive Behaviours: Processes of Change.* Plenum Press.

Radloff, L.S. (1977) The CES-D Scale: A Self Report Depression Scale for Research in the General Population. *Applied Psychological Measurement*, 1, 385–401.

Rankin, H. et al. (1982) Cues for Drinking and Degrees of Alcohol Dependence. *British Journal of Addiction*, 77, 287–96

Reiger, D.A. et al. (1993) The de Facto US Mental and Addictive Disorders Service System. *Archives of General Psychiatry*, 50, 84–94.

Repp, A.C. et al. (1997) Hypothesis Based Interventions: A Theory of Clinical Decision Making. In O'Donohue, W. and Krasner, L. (Eds.) *Theories of Behaviour Therapy: Exploring Behaviour Change.* American Psychological Association.

Rounsaville, B.J. and Kleber, M.D. (1985) Untreated Opiate Addicts: How do They Differ from Those Seeking Treatment? *Archives of General Psychiatry*, 42, 1072–7.

Safran, J.D. and Muran, J.C. (2000) *Negotiating the Therapeutic Alliance.* Guildford Press.

Schaef, A.W. (1986) *Codependency: Misunderstood, Mistreated.* Harper.

Schuckit, M.A. et al. (1998) Clinical Relevance of the Distinction Between Alcohol Dependence With and Without a Physiological Component. *American Journal of Psychiatry.* 41, 1043–9.

Schwartzman, J. and Bokos, P. (1979) Methadone Maintenance: The Addict's Family Recreated. *The International Journal of Family Therapy*, 4: 338–55.

Sher, K.J. (1991) Children of Alcoholics: A Critical Appraisal of Theory and Research. *Clinical Psychology Reviews*, 14, 87–90.

Shulman, L., Shapira, S. and Hirshfield, S. (2000) Outreach Development Services to Children of Patients in Treatment For Substance Abuse. *American Journal of Public Health*, 90: 12, 1930–3.

Simpson, D.D. and Sells, S.B. (Eds.) (1990) *Opioid Addiction and Treatment: A 12-Year Follow-Up.* Krieger Publishing.

Sisson, R.W. and Azrin, N. (1986) Family-member Involvement to Initiate and Promote Treatment of Problem Drinkers. *Journal of Behavioural Therapy and Experimental Psychiatry*, 17, 15–21.

Skinner, B.F. (1938) *The Behaviour of the Organism.* Appleton-Century-Crofts.

Smith, J.E. and Meyers, R.J. (2004) *Motivating Substance Abusers to Enter Treatment: Working with Family Members.* Guildford Press.

Sobell, L.C., Cunningham, J.A. and Sobell, M.B. (1996) Recovery From Alcohol Problems With and Without Treatment: Prevalence in Two Population Surveys. *American Journal of Public Heath*, 86, 966–72.

Sobell, M.B. and Sobell, L.C. (1993) *Problem Drinkers: Guided Self-Change Treatment.* Guildford Press.

Soyez, V. and Broekaert, E. (Undated) *Are We Expecting Too Much From Social Network Members?: Impact of a Social Network Intervention on Retention in and Success After Therapeutic Community Treatment.*

Spivack, G. Platt, J.J. and Shure, M. (1976) *The Problem-Solving Approach to Adjustment.* Jossey-Bass.

Stanton, M.D. (1982) Review of Reports on Drug Abusers' Family Living Arrangements and Frequency of Family Contact. In Stanton, M.D. and Todd, T.C. (Eds.) *The Family Therapy of Drug Abuse and Addiction.* Guildford Press.

Stanton, M.D. (1997) The Role of Significant Others in The Engagement and Retention of Drug-Dependent Individuals. In Onken, S., Blaine, J.D. and Boren, J.J. (Eds.) *Beyond the Therapeutic Alliance: Keeping Drug Dependent Individuals In Treatment.* National Institute on Drug Abuse.

Stanton, M.D. (2004) Getting Reluctant Substance Abusers to Engage in Treatment Self Help: A Review of Outcomes and Clinical Options. *Journal of Marital and Family Therapy*, April.

Stockwell, T. et al. (1979) The Development of a Questionnaire to Measure Alcohol Dependence. *British Journal of Addiction*, 74, 145–55.

Stockwell, T. et al. (1983) The Severity of Alcohol Dependence Questionnaire: Its Use, Reliability and Validity. *British Journal of Addictions*, 78, 145–55.

Sundby, P. (1967) *Alcoholism and Mortality.* University Forlaget.

Szapocznik, J. et al. (1988) Engaging Adolescent Drug Abusers and Their Families in Treatment: A Strategic Structural-Systems Approach. *Journal of Consulting and Clinical Psychology*, 56, 552–7.

Taylor, C. (1994) What Happens Over The Long Term? In Edwards, G. and Peters, T.J. (Eds.) *Alcohol and Alcohol Problems.* Churchill Livingstone.

Thomas, E.J. et al. (1987) Unilateral Family Therapy with Spouses of Alcoholics. *Journal of Social Science Research*, 10, 145–62.

Tyrer, P. and Casey, P. (1998) *Social Functioning in Psychiatry.* Wrightson Biomedical Publishing.

Vaillant, G. E. (1995) *The Natural History of Alcoholism – Revisited.* Harvard Academic Press.

Vakalia, H. (2001) Adolescent Substance Abuse and Family Based Risk and Protective Factors: A Literature Review. *Journal of Drug Education*, 31: 1, 29–46.

Velleman, R. and Orford, J. (2000) *Risk and Resilience: Adults Who Were the Children of Problem Drinkers.* Harwood Academic Publishers.

Velleman, R. et al. (1993) The Families of Problem Drug Users: The Accounts of Fifty Close Relatives. *Addiction*, 88, 1275–83.

Wegscheider-Cruse, S. and Cruse, J. (1990) *Understanding Co-dependency.* Health Communications.

Weisner, C. (1992) A Comparison of Alcohol and Drug Treatment Clients: Are They the Same Population? *American Journal of Drug and Alcohol Abuse*, 18: 4, 429–44.

Weisner, C., Greenfield, T. and Room, R. (1995) Trends in the Treatment of Alcohol Problems in the US General Population, 1979 through 1990. *American Journal of Public Health*, 85: 1 55–60.

Whalen, T. (1953) Wives of Alcoholics: Four Types Observed in a Family Service Agency. *Quarterly Journal of Studies on Alcohol*, 14, 632–41.

Yates, F.E. (1988) The Evaluation of a 'Co-Operative Counselling' Alcohol Service Which Uses Family and Affected Others to Reach and Influence Problem Drinkers. *British Journal of Addiction*, 83, 1309–19.

Empathy for the devil
How to help people overcome drugs and alcohol problems

By Phil Harris

Examining the core skills necessary for effecting change in problematic substance users, this important book explores practical ways of establishing or improving your practice. It steps beyond clinical, theoretical and moral undertones to the reality of working with substance misuse. Where society, the media and our imaginations are full of the modern day social demons of drug users, it provides positive and reflective support for both experienced and novice workers – or those affected by others' use. It suggests ways ahead to workers stuck in seemingly perennial impasses, as they strive with their colleagues to address multi-faceted and entrenched problems.

Increasingly, social policy now demands evidence-based practice, putting ever greater pressure on professionals from all disciplines to grasp the core ideas and skills drawn from research findings. But this research is often too arid and abstract to overlay upon the life of the individual sat before us, and can make the lay person feel even more under skilled. This book bridges this chasm, **bringing together a wide range of proven skills in supporting people through change in an open and accessible way**. It:

- invites you to re-consider your own experiences so as to illuminate the key ideas, skills and techniques in addiction work
- lucidly explains the latest findings in effective practice
- illustrates them with case examples
- provides optional **self-reflective exercises and activities to aid learning and training**.

Empathy for the Devil will give anyone working with people whose lives are affected by drugs or alcohol new ideas and perspectives to address old and intractable problems.

'Discusses the complexity of drug and alcohol problems with more references to cultural and social aspects than previous work that I have read in this area . . . The focus is explicitly and empathically on helping clients to establish and achieve their own goals to overcome their addiction. However Harris does not treat people as living in a vacuum, but as living within and being part of an extremely influential cultural context. I particularly enjoyed Harris's astute reflections upon the therapeutic relationship, something not always talked about, and found the chapter on solution-focused therapy so inspiring that I wanted to rush out and try it . . . I thoroughly enjoyed this book, it is a great read.'' *The Psychologist*

'Book of the month . . . his bibliography makes for extensive further reading.' *Drugscope Members Briefing*

978-1-903855-54-6

Drug Induced
Addiction and treatment in perspective

By Phil Harris

'It would be difficult for anyone involved in working with addiction whether as a practitioner, or manager, or policy maker to come away from reading this informative and interesting book without some spur to reflecting on and changing their own thinking and practice.' *VISTA*

'Should be essential reading . . . his critique of peer pressure, the importance of relationships throughout adolescence and why some young people are more prone to drug dependency than others are brilliant . . . **an excellent book** . . . Much to my own surprise I thoroughly enjoyed *Drug Induced* and found myself repeating to colleagues much of what I read. I found it to be a refreshing, courageous book that radically challenges many of our widely held beliefs about addiction and treatment: it is just up to you now to read it.' *Youth & Policy*

'This **thought-provoking** book challenges many aspects of the theoretical base and clinical practices prevalent in the addictions field today . . . The disease concept, motivational interviewing, stages of change and dual diagnosis are all examined in a way which will, hopefully, **encourage alcohol and drug workers to re-evaluate their 'sacred cows'**. The authors' clinical experience shines through what I largely experienced as a social-science perspective with a developmental and environmental focus.' *Addiction Today*

'He supports his arguments with a comprehensive array of references from both friend and foe of his stance . . . it hangs together well . . .' *Journal of Mental Health*

978-1-903855-53-9

Secret lives: growing with substance
Working with children and young people affected by familial substance misuse

Edited by Fiona Harbin & Michael Murphy

Includes the chapter *Where it all begins: growing up and the helping relationship* by Phil Harris.

Secret Lives offers new and challenging insights into the task of working with children and young people who are affected by substance misuse. This includes the needs of children brought up in substance misusing households, and young people who are beginning to misuse substances themselves.

'The authors aim to help practitioners and managers in the identification, assessment, treatment and support of the children and siblings of substance misusers. Buy this book as a reference and investment.' *Addiction Today*

'All the contributions are interesting, and informed my knowledge of what services should be available to assist children . . . the book succeeds in allowing the views of children and young people caught in this sad situation poignantly to come through.' *Seen & Heard*

'Founded on current research . . . informed, accessible and relevant.' *Rostrum*

'Most books of this genre discuss either how to assess the issue or how to work with it: this book does both . . . I recommend this book.' *Community Care*

'Impressive . . . for anyone working with children, young people, parents and families.' *Community Safety Journal*

978-1-903855-66-9

The carrot or the stick?
Towards effective practice with involuntary clients in safeguarding children work

Edited by Martin C Calder

Includes the chapter *Engaging Substance Misusers Through Coercion* by Phil Harris.

In child protection, family support, domestic violence, youth justice . . . many practitioners and managers struggle to engage clients who resist involvement with services that are needed or offered, often with wearying and dispiriting effect on everyone.

This book offers systematic, evidence-based approaches to work with children and young people, men and women, fathers and mothers in all relevant circumstances. They are 'no-nonsense' approaches that will fit with practice wisdom and practice realities of work with clients who: actively seek help; only accept services when legally mandated or institutionalized; show varying degrees of motivation at different times, towards different services, or within their family or group.

'Excellent material . . . **how do we work with service users who don't want to work with us?** The book ranges from the theoretical to the practical in responding to this question . . . a very useable framework for working with involuntary clients . . . would offer busy practitioners some useful tools.' *Community Care*

'Extensive, yet concise and widely referenced, yet practical, this book is relevant to practitioners, managers and planners. Accessible for students and teachers, the text is like effective practice – engaging, well structured, disciplined and encouraging . . . A motif emerging repeatedly in this richly layered text is that "coercion should not replace engagement as the central force in change".' *Rostrum*

978-1-905541-22-5

Electronic supply of the copiable materials from *The Concerned Other*

If you would like to receive a PDF of the 67 pages of copiable materials from this book, please complete the form below, tear out this page, and return it to us. Please note that photocopies are not acceptable, nor are applications made through e-mail, phone or fax.

Please keep a copy of the completed form for your own records.

This PDF is free.

Please note

RHP reserves the right to withdraw this offer at any time without prior notice.

RHP reserves the right to qualify or reject any application which it is not completely satisfied is on an original torn-out page from the back of a purchased book.

Terms and conditions for use of the copiable materials from *The Concerned Other*

1. Buying a copy of *The Concerned Other* and completing this form gives the individual who signs the form permission to use the materials in the PDF that will be sent from RHP for their own use only.

2. The hard copies that they then print from the PDF are subject to the same permissions and restrictions that are set out in the 'Copying permissions' section on page xix of this book.

3. Under no circumstances should they forward or copy the electronic materials to anyone else.

4. If the person who signs this form wants a licence to be granted for wider use of the electronic materials within their organisation, network or client base, they must make a request directly to RHP fully detailing the proposed use. All requests will be reviewed on their own merits.

   - If the request is made when submitting this form to RHP, the request should be made in writing and should accompany this form.

   - If the request is made later, it should be made in an email sent to help . . . russellhouse.co.uk, and should not only fully detail the proposed use, but also give the details of the person whose name and contact details were on the original application form.

RHP and the author expect this honour system to be followed respectfully, by individuals and organisations whom we in turn respect. RHP will act to protect authors' copyright if they become aware of it being infringed.

I would like to receive a free PDF of the copiable materials from *The Concerned Other*.

*Name _____

*Address _____

_____

_____ *Post code _____

*Contact phone number _____

*e-mail addr _____ (to which the PDF will be e-mailed).

I have read, and accept, the terms and conditions. I understand that RHP may use this information to contact me about other matters and publications, but that RHP will not make my details available to other organisations.

*Signed: _____ *Date _____

All sections marked with an asterisk **must be completed**, or the form will be returned to the postal address given here.

Please return to: Russell House Publishing Ltd, 4 St Georges House, Uplyme Road, Lyme Regis, Dorset DT7 3LS.